Praise for *Inspired & Unstoppable*

"A revelatory book that brilliantly applies inspiration, practicality, and humor to identifying and living your highest potential. You won't be able to stop reading this invaluable guide to inner and outer success in your creative expression."

—MICHAEL BERNARD BECKWITH, AUTHOR OF
SPIRITUAL LIBERATION: FULFILLING YOUR SOUL'S POTENTIAL

"Wild success is a function of deliberate, alive choices. Through her own walk through doubts and struggles, Tama Kieves shows you how to stay 'inspired and unstoppable' in every circumstance you confront in business, living your vision, and life. If you want to stay on fire as you do your greatest work in the world, read this book now."

—JACK CANFIELD, BESTSELLING COAUTHOR OF
CHICKEN SOUP FOR THE SOUL AND THE SUCCESS PRINCIPLES

"This book is like having your own wonderful success coach. *Inspired & Unstoppable* will show you how to stay true to your personal and professional vision—no matter what—and get you where you dream to be. This is a soulful and practical book, full of encouragement and guidance that will save you years of time and pain. You're going to want to read this often."

—MARCI SHIMOFF, *NEW YORK TIMES*–BESTSELLING AUTHOR OF
HAPPY FOR NO REASON AND LOVE FOR NO REASON

"When you've got a burning mission inside you, you need to know how to stay inspired and on track. Tama Kieves shows you how to become a success warrior for your life's work. Life is short. The world needs your voice. Read this wonderful book."

—KRIS CARR, *NEW YORK TIMES*–BESTSELLING AUTHOR AND WELLNESS WARRIOR

"Tama Kieves is one of the soul-tenders, a savvy and companionable guide to honoring what she calls the gravitational pull of passion and integrity within each of us, and the power of saying *Yes!* to our lives. In her compelling new book, she brings great honesty and compassion to the hard human work of bringing our callings to life, and a vigorous torch to help illuminate the journey."

—GREGG LEVOY, AUTHOR OF *CALLINGS: FINDING AND FOLLOWING AN AUTHENTIC LIFE*

"*Inspired & Unstoppable* delivers sheer rowdy brilliance! There are truly wise, practical, and fresh methods to help you create the results you want. You'll receive expansion, comfort, acceleration, and focus for completing and living any kind of dream you can imagine. Plus, I know you'll *grin* while reading this book."

—SARK, BESTSELLING AUTHOR OF *SUCCULENT WILD WOMAN*, ARTIST, AND FOUNDER OF PLANETSARK.COM

"Tama Kieves is a woman who dives deeply into her own journey, bringing back the wisdom we all need to live true to who we are. Her desire to guide and support others in discovering and living their life's work shines in every word she writes. She is a voice that embodies the passion for the possible in our lives, in our world."

—ORIAH MOUNTAIN DREAMER, BESTSELLING AUTHOR OF *THE INVITATION*

"The words 'inspired and unstoppable' are far more than the title of this book; they are *literally* how you will feel as you are reading it. Tama Kieves is a brilliant teacher. The depth of her knowledge and wisdom is equaled only by her authenticity, humor, and candor. You will find yourself lifted, motivated, and cared for by her words. If you are seeking a deeper understanding of your life's purpose and how to actualize it, consider this book your road map." —DENNIS MERRITT JONES, AUTHOR OF *THE ART OF UNCERTAINTY*

"This is a work of genius that offers readers a hand-up to claim their inspired vision—deep within themselves—and allow it to become real. Tama has captured the essence of the ups and downs of the journey, and gives us courage to stay the course despite the setbacks and, most of all, to trust ourselves. Don't miss this opportunity to deepen both your spiritual journey and your work fulfillment. Be inspired!"

—MARCIA BENCH, FOUNDER AND DIRECTOR OF CAREER COACH INSTITUTE, AND BESTSELLING AUTHOR OF *BECOME AN INSPIRATIONAL THOUGHT LEADER*

"Tama is a pioneer in teaching you how to follow your heart and make it work in the real world. This is her 4.0 guide to doing just that. If you put this wisdom into action, you will be unstoppable and your deepest desires will become a reality. And the world will be a much better place because of you. Get to it!"

—JENNIFER LOUDEN, BESTSELLING AUTHOR OF *THE WOMAN'S COMFORT BOOK* AND *THE LIFE ORGANIZER*

"Tama tells the truth about the peaks and valleys of living the life of your dreams, and as she says, you can work hard or you can work miraculously. Which one would you prefer? Read this wonderful book and you'll come out on the other side laughing at your petty fears and ready to share your gifts with the world."

—LAURA BERMAN FORTGANG, AUTHOR OF
NOW WHAT? 90 DAYS TO A NEW LIFE DIRECTION AND *THE PROSPERITY PLAN*

"Tama Kieves has had a hugely positive impact on many lives, and I know some of them. This is a delightful blend of stories, concepts, and exhortations. Read it as you will. But ultimately, as she implies, 'do not look at the finger; see what it is pointing towards.' Go out and craft a deeply fulfilling life. You will find much help here."

—SRIKUMAR S. RAO, PH.D., MBA, CREATOR OF THE PIONEERING
BUSINESS SCHOOL COURSE CREATIVITY AND PERSONAL MASTERY AND
AUTHOR OF *ARE YOU READY TO SUCCEED?* AND *HAPPINESS AT WORK*

"In her inspiring and powerful way, Tama Kieves guides us to thrive in the greatest potential of who we are here to be. Part soul catalyst, part visionary success coach, and part encouraging friend, Tama calls us forth to live that potential and helps us believe in ourselves as never before. If you truly want to create inspired work in the world and flourish, *Inspired & Unstoppable* should be your next read."

—ALAN SEALE, AUTHOR OF *CREATE A WORLD THAT WORKS* AND
FOUNDER AND DIRECTOR OF THE CENTER FOR TRANSFORMATIONAL PRESENCE
(TRANSFORMATIONALPRESENCE.ORG)

"All artists, leaders, and entrepreneurs need to have their champion, and Tama Kieves is it! She's a brilliant catalyst and support for all those who want to live on purpose, live their dreams, and create a life of meaning. Tama shows us how to open to and apply our own inspired talents and succeed in ways that allow us to lead a fabulous and fulfilling life."

—KAREN DRUCKER, AUTHOR, RECORDING ARTIST, AND SPEAKER

"Tama Kieves has written an inspiring, optimistic, and refreshingly honest book about how to succeed doing the work you love. Her unique style of personal story, wicked humor, and practical strategies makes her book different from many in the self-help genre. Reading *Inspired & Unstoppable* is like sitting with a wise friend who generously gives you the benefits of her experiences. 'Doing the work you love is not meant to be exhausting and complicated,' Tama tells us. *Inspired & Unstoppable* is a must read for anyone looking for work that both inspires *and* pays." —AMANDA OWEN, AUTHOR OF *THE POWER OF RECEIVING*

"Tama Kieves enjoys crafting a clever phrase and fortunately has the intellect to do it in an entertaining fashion. Her persistence and enthusiasm are likely to motivate many readers to succeed at their dreams."

—ALLAN LOKOS, AUTHOR OF *PATIENCE: THE ART OF PEACEFUL LIVING* AND *POCKET PEACE: EFFECTIVE PRACTICES FOR ENLIGHTENED LIVING*

"Tama Kieves has lived and breathed every word written on the pages of this book on the way to her wildly successful life. Read it and be inspired on your way to success."

—AUGUST GOLD, AUTHOR OF *THE PRAYER CHEST* AND COAUTHOR OF *PRAYER PARTNERS*

"Tama Kieves is an inspired and unstoppable woman! She has written a book that will spontaneously ignite the flames of your inner passion. This is an absolute must read for anyone who wants to live a life full-out, sane, and wildly successful."

—DEBORAH SANDELLA, PH.D., AWARD-WINNING AUTHOR OF *RELEASING THE INNER MAGICIAN* AND ORIGINATOR OF THE GROUNDBREAKING RIM METHOD, AN INNER TECHNOLOGY FOR THE TWENTY-FIRST CENTURY

INSPIRED & UNSTOPPABLE

You are meant
to succeed in
the work you love.

Your desire will
take you all the way.

INSPIRED & UNSTOPPABLE

Wildly Succeeding in Your Life's Work!

TAMA KIEVES

A TarcherPerigee Book

tarcherperigee

An imprint of Penguin Random House LLC
375 Hudson Street
New York, New York
10014

First trade paperback edition 2013
Copyright © 2012 by Tama J. Kieves
Penguin supports copyright. Copyright fuels creativity, encourages diverse voices, promotes free speech, and creates a vibrant culture. Thank you for buying an authorized edition of this book and for complying with copyright laws by not reproducing, scanning, or distributing any part of it in any form without permission. You are supporting writers and allowing Penguin to continue to publish books for every reader.

TarcherPerigee with tp colophon is a registered trademark of Penguin Random House LLC.

Most TarcherPerigee books are available at special quantity discounts for bulk purchase for sales promotions, premiums, fund-raising, and educational needs. Special books or book excerpts also can be created to fit special needs. For details, write: SpecialMarkets@penguinrandomhouse.com.

The Library of Congress has catalogued the hardcover edition as follows:

Kieves, Tama J.
    Inspired and unstoppable : wildly succeeding in your life's work! / Tama J. Kieves.
        p.   cm.
    ISBN 978-1-58542-929-5
    1. Self-realization.   2. Success.   3. Quality of work life.   4. Job satisfaction.   I. Title.
    BF637.S4K497   2012   2012011505
    650.1—dc23

ISBN 978-0-399-16578-8 (paperback edition)

Printed in the United States of America
10   9   8   7   6   5   4

BOOK DESIGN BY MEIGHAN CAVANAUGH

While the author has made every effort to provide accurate telephone numbers, Internet addresses, and other ccontact information at the time of publication, neither the publisher nor the author assumes any responsibility for errors, or for changes that occur after publication. Further, the publisher does not have any control over and does not assume any responsibility for author or third-party websites or their content.

I dedicate this book to all of us who are trying on new creative powers: who are frightened and flying and alive and unsure.

To visionaries, healers, artists, leaders, teachers, entrepreneurs, humanitarians, career-transitioners, soul-searchers, and freedom-seekers who choose to listen to a whisper of divine intensity more than to mediocrity or collective resignation. I am awed by you. I am lifted by you. I am grateful for your kind.

And I also dedicate this book to "the tribe," the readers of *This Time I Dance! Creating the Work You Love* and my e-mail newsletters (and Facebook fans), and cherished students for your generous embrace. Your excitement, growth, and gratitude kept me believing. When I feared I wouldn't have a place in the world, you gave me a place in your hearts. Students create a teacher, followers raise a leader, and readers anoint their author. *This book might never have been written if it weren't for you.* You were fans—before there was fanfare.

Finally, I dedicate this work and all my work to the Inspired Presence and Teacher within that demanded that I be more alive than I'd imagined possible, that I love myself enough to live this life—and to do my part to help create a world of inspired and unstoppable astonishment.

What if everything you thought you needed to do to succeed
was actually standing in the way of your success?

—Tama J. Kieves

You were born with wings,
why prefer to crawl through life?

—Mawlana Jalal al-Din Rumi

CONTENTS

AN INTRODUCTION
AND INITIATION

YOUR SUCCESS PARTNER ON THIS WILDLY INSPIRED ADVENTURE

Welcome, My Courageous Friend Who Is About to Soar...

I am honored to have you reading these words. This book is a door that can open you to the most important power in your life, the power of your inspired strength. This is what I want you to know and, maybe someday, take to the streets like a liberated fool:

You're meant to succeed in the work you love.
Your desire will take you all the way.

Welcome to this amazing frontier of good.

A Bit About My Background

At the most dramatic turning point of my life, I left my career as an overworked attorney to follow my soul's haunting desire to become a writer. I had graduated with honors from Harvard Law School and worked in the litigation department of a huge, elite law firm. While there, I traded my life for societal slaps on the back, more money, and more grinding work assignments. I made partnership track. But I was desperate to be free, exhausted in my good, safe job, dying of meaninglessness, suffocating the life out of my creative soul. Finally, a friend asked me a vital question:

If you're this successful doing work you don't love,
what could you do with work you do love?

I decided to answer that question with my life. I left the practice of law to undergo the art, practice, and baptism of listening to myself in this lifetime. I wrote about this amazing journey of transition in my first book, *This Time I Dance! Creating the Work You Love.*

A Bit About This Book

This book is about wildly succeeding in your life's work: taking what you came here to do to the next level.

I don't know about you, but I didn't want to just "follow my bliss." I wanted to follow my bliss, say, to a bank, or to a bestseller list, or to some kind of explosive expression in the world. It had never been my dream to leave my law practice to end up as an incompetent entrepreneur or a starving artist. But I also didn't leave one falsely successful life, only to turn myself into a sock puppet again, swallow my spirit, and "get with the program" so I could "make it in the big time."

I was going for the holy grail of wild success, the deluxe spirit package, passion, sweetness, and inspired prosperity. I wanted creative independence *and* security, worldly fanfare *and* peace of mind, and the experience that abundance came from doing the work I came to do, *the way I came to do it.* The only problem was, I could name my desires until the cows came home—and kicked back with Netflix, cud, and apple martinis—but I wasn't sure how to create this "everything comes together" life.

Yes, I'd practiced law and maybe I *should* have known how to project business goals in the "real world." But the truth is, I have a poet-philosopher's heart and tend to process life in metaphors and fires-in-the-belly, more than data and numbers. While I'm ambitious and logical, I'm also part rebel, gypsy, and lightning-bolt bearer. That means, for instance, that when well-meaning folks suggested conventional means like business plans, I tried not to start speaking in tongues or bite them.

Still, I craved commercial success, recognition, and reach, so I turned to marketing advice, success books, and popular titles in the business, self-help, and motivational world. But the more I read, the more disillusioned I felt. I had finally found a dream that gave me life—but everything I read about succeeding in it felt soul-numbing. I just knew I had the mojo, but "the getting it out there," the pipelines to income and opportunities, seemed to be governed by a mechanical, harsh, or clannishly linear world. It didn't matter if I had twelve thousand diamonds; the jewelers wore blindfolds. Everything made it clear that real success required what *I* didn't have, and without a "mind meld" with Anthony Robbins, Donald Trump, or, say, "The Terminator" never would have.

Like so many of us, I didn't realize that I already possessed an inspired way to succeed. It hadn't dawned on me yet that the electricity that inspires our dreams also inspires the means.

But this is the truth I know now: Taking what you love into the world has little to do with conventional techniques, established reality, or the formulas of the marketplace. Following your true desire or calling is an initiation of soul. It's a rite of passage. It's a whole new game board with exciting new rules. Bring your diamonds.

This is the question that divides the paths: Will you honor your Inspired Self or will you listen to the one who talks you down from the mountain and persuades you to adjust what you desire? Sometimes the fearful, critical voice within poses as "good judgment"; it feels practical and reassuringly in sync with the prevailing culture around you. But is the opinion of an often empty, bitter, tired culture the voice of good judgment for *you*?

Let's face it. There aren't many voices in the world that will encourage you to follow your inner rock star or anointed one and get out there on the window ledge of ordinary life, mock gravity, and fly. Yet some of us are just called to fly. We won't succeed through traditional means because force, fear, and standard projections do not motivate us. We are moved by bold ideas, big love, and intuitive, flawless direction. We hear new frequencies, promise, and urgencies wailing in the wind. We did not come here to do what's been done before. We came here to expand— inspire, heal, express, create, and realize the exhilaration of being *everything* we are meant to be.

I should tell you right here that, personally, I struggled with the whole "trusting your inner-voice thing," or believing in a God, Inspired Self, Cosmic Coddler, or any energetic force beyond my five senses or the Dow Jones. A friend dubbed me "the reluctant mystic," and it's a true description. As an attorney, I'd been trained in logic and liabilities. And as a once incredulous New Yorker, I felt like anything remotely transcendental was just a crutch for those who couldn't cut it. But these days, I'd shout from the rooftops with a bullhorn, and elbow my way past the other fanatics to do it, because I see infinite possibility as a torch, and "reality" as the crutch. Still, trusting an invisible mechanism of genius or wellspring of new resources has often nettled my overindulged intellect. I suppose it's what makes me a good teacher. Because if you have a bundle of suspicions and doubts, trust me, I've had a bigger knapsack.

That's why I'd love to assist you on this journey and make sure you get where you belong. You probably have a voice of fear telling you to play it safe, heed convention, and turn back altogether. I want to represent your *other* voice, the one that tells you to *really* play it safe, by following your desire and strength. I hope you will consider me your success partner, your paper mentor, and your noisiest, most outrageous advocate screaming from the bleachers. In these pages, I hope to inspire you to live and work from your power and magnificence. Fear diminishes your strength. I plan to help you undo that fear and set free the astonishing faculties and life strategies you already have.

This book is not a cookbook of how-to steps. As a leading career and success coach, I've found it works better to share real-life experience, let someone come into the kitchen with me and feel the heat. Your natural intelligence will absorb what you need to know better this way. I don't know about you, but I've never gotten much from the "8 easy steps" kinds of books. They made things sound so simple that even a garden-variety moron could have an Internet business, and be a billionaire by Tuesday. Me, I'd still be groping through my days, wondering how I could have graduated from Harvard Law School and yet be flunking "easy" self-help programs. Turns out, I didn't thrive on "simple, practical advice" because intelligence is complex, and I'm a thinking, feeling, developing human being—not a robot. Go figure.

So I'll help you move into your brilliant power. I'll share the mental and emotional journey of this awesome ride with you; the fears, doubts, and bogeymen that arise, and how to become an unstoppable warrior for your life's work and desires. Because I know that if I can help you stay connected to your desires and shift your innermost thinking, then you will take actions like nobody's business, inspired actions that seem to fall directly out of the sky and onto your pretty plate. You will naturally outpace anything any expert could ever tell you. *You don't need the steps—when you have the moves.* Now that sounds practical to me.

By the way, I'm not saying you shouldn't have a business plan or follow an expert's marketing or financial advice. I am never negating logic, linear analysis, or any source of input that helps you accomplish your dreams. Some of you will need to listen to your business coach, lawyer, or accountant, and build temples around the columns of your spreadsheets. Others may take their cues from a late-night tarot card reading over the phone or from a neighbor's border collie who shows up in a dream with a telegram from Atlantis or an Akashic record in its mouth. Some may rely on a passage in the Bible; others on the passages of the planets. Some of you may do all of the above, repeat, and then become a life coach, I just don't know. I couldn't possibly anticipate where your direction, clarity, and power will come from, but I do know that I want your every choice to feel alive and peaceful in the middle marrow of your bones. That's your authority and my only goal. You have your own success path and I want to keep you on it.

At this point in my career, I have traveled throughout the United States and other parts of the world, offering keynotes and doing workshops in prestigious venues. I've been featured on national television, Oprah Radio, and in one of those supercool TEDx talks, and have even been noted in *Forbes*, a premier business publication. As a career and success coach, I have helped thousands of others discover their own inner voice, their own unique business and creativity consultant, and take outrageously visionary steps leading to an explosion of business, success, and happiness. Through my own personal experiences and through guiding others, I know there is another way to succeed. It's a nonlinear way. It's an inspired way. I hope you'll make it your way—because it's where the times are heading.

Remember: *You're meant to succeed in the work you love. Your desire will take you all the way.* I invite you, dear one, to use your extraordinary resources. The world awaits you now more than ever. Please know I'm holding this vision for you. I'm rooting for you in the bleachers. I'm whispering in the hard times. I'm dancing in the good ones. And though you might not feel as though you know where this is going, I do. And I'm here to remind you.

THE OTHER WAY TO SUCCEED: FOLLOW YOUR REBEL BRILLIANCE

I n conventional success books, "experts" look at the path that others took, and aim to clone the path. It's the classic Zen story. The master points to the power of the moon. Yet the students study and discuss the master's finger. They miss the exciting, guiding light. Matsuo Basho, the famously insightful Japanese poet, said this: "Do not seek to follow in the footsteps of the wise. Seek what they sought." That's the difference between linear success and inspired success.

This is the path of inspired success. I want you to study your own excitement and experience. An invincible direction already lives within you. You doubt it because you've been told there are "right ways" to make it in this world. But the authorities didn't write those strategies for you. You have never been here before. You possess an alchemical power that disrupts and alters every single prediction or traditional formula. It's the power of your spirit and it leads to wild success. Listen to me: You *are* the golden formula.

As a creative individual, visionary leader, independent thinker, soul-healer, or entrepreneur, it's your birthright to utilize other talents, insights, resources, and innate strategies. You are not made to fit into the world, make it *in* the world, but to remake the world, heal the world, and illuminate new choices and sensibilities. The problem isn't that inspired individuals can't face "reality." The problem is that they do—and they let it eclipse their instinct and excellence.

Keep in mind that today's mainstream culture sprang up from the fringes, those with different ideas, the rabble-rousers on a distant shore. Thomas Watson, the founder of blue-chip IBM, for God's sake, said, "Follow the path of the unsafe, independent thinker." The establishment always has its roots in uncertainty and the unimaginable.

In every age, alternative, bold souls have doubted themselves, have been criticized, and have struggled to forge an outlet for their brilliance. But it's only because they gave "the world" more power than their creativity. If you trust your creativity, your inspired inclination, you will discover a whole new way to flourish.

This is the time to do it. These are cutting-edge times, times of global transformation. Security is a moving target. Yet passion is your real security. Many "safe" jobs have become time bombs for your soul. Others have been downsized, obliterated, or stripped of humanity and fire. Yet just as old forms break down, new expressions, careers, needs, humanitarian causes, and industries mushroom on the horizon. Years ago, who ever heard of a web designer? A blog writer? A "green" architect? Or a life coach, for that matter. Now more than ever, it's a sense of inspired desire that will impel you in the direction of the current that's coming.

Drawing on research from around the advanced world, business guru Daniel Pink says, in *A Whole New Mind*, "The keys to the kingdom are changing hands. The future belongs to a very different person with a very different kind of mind—creators and empathizers, pattern recognizers, and meaning makers. These people—artists, inventors, designers, storytellers, caregivers, consolers, big picture thinkers—will now reap society's richest rewards."

It will take love and focus to leap into your unknown strengths. You may feel reckless for following your heart's moonlight or vapors of the

Infinite, instead of traditional career tracks or status quo business strategies. Yet that's the course of conscious evolution. That's how ordinary genius emerges. You don't need to be a Mozart, Michelangelo, or Bill Gates. Ordinary genius is just a way of discovering options, avenues, fortuitous combinations, and the untapped, unnamed exponential gifts within.

I urge you to respect your own divine chemistry. Obey your rebel brilliance. Reject advice that hobbles your nature and race toward liberation instead. Run, run, run—with everything you have—into everything you are meant to be. You deserve to succeed in your own way, unlike anyone before you, and beyond everyone's wildest imagination, including your own. And our beautiful world will surely thrive because you do.

HOW TO GET THE MOST JUICE
OUT OF THIS BOOK
(AND MAYBE YOUR LIFE)

have no way of knowing where you are on your path. But I do know this: The principles that are true in the beginning of this path are also true in the middle and at the end. That's the nature of truth. It sings on many levels. Each of these stories is multilayered with meanings, so that even if you're way further down the road, the "beginning" lessons may continue to help. Likewise, even if you're just starting out on the path of your dreams, the later stories can inspire your path. That's why you might want to read the whole thing. But you might not, and that's fine with me (well, just as long as you never tell me). Actually, I designed this book so that you can read any vignette alone. If you want to jump around this book, jump, baby, jump. This whole book is about following your instincts, so far be it from me to get in your way.

As to the order of this book, my stories leap around in time, from different parts of my professional life. I'm not really trying to tell you my story. I'm hoping to offer insights into *your* story. But just in case the poor left hemisphere of your brain tries to piece things together that aren't that clear in the book, I thought I'd just give you a bit of background here: I spent years teaching workshops, leading retreats, and coaching while writing my first book, *This Time I Dance! Creating the Work*

You Love. I self-published *This Time I Dance!* and was discovered by a "fairy godmother" who got it to the publisher of my dreams. Then I got a literary agent to represent me. A few years down the road, the publisher relaunched the book with a different cover and some new material. I think that's about what you need to know. Those are the basic facts. The rest of it is the story, the lessons, and the leaps.

Now about those lessons. Please keep in mind that each lesson is a suggestion, a fluid example, not a formula. Nothing in this book is meant to be applied in every situation. For me, wisdom always breathes. There are exceptions to everything. I believe in common sense and your uncommon personal genius. Please run everything through the unique filter of your situation. And always trust your innate wisdom, more than anything you read.

The Practices and Exercises Are at the End of the Book

(But You Don't Have to Wait Unless You Want To . . .)

I'm one of those people who reads books and feels guilty when I see exercises, especially the books that tell you not to go on and keep reading until you stop and do the exercises. I look over my shoulder, in case the author has secret superpowers. I start to feel like I did when I began making out with my boyfriend as a teenager, hoping my mother wouldn't somehow smell guilt on my clothes. So about those exercises: I think we all process information in our own way and you as an adult have the right to decide if you want to do the exercises or not, and when.

That's why I put the daily practices and exercises in the back of the book. I want you to dive into them when you feel ready. Sometimes, you may read a book that's making you think, and you don't want to lose the flow and continuity of ideas. I don't want to break that spell. You may see this book as a conversation, a deep and exciting conversation, and I don't want to interrupt it with mental calisthenics. The calisthenics will be good for you. But so is the conversation. I want to unlock the resources within you. I want to whisper in your ear, chant secret things to a secret part of you that awakens and remembers—and blows the roof off the house. I don't want to interrupt the spell.

Still, I don't know how this needs to work for you. You may need to digest each section, put it to use, build a home for it. You may need to do the exercises while you're inspired and under that spell. Please use your own navigation here. This isn't a time to be polite. We're talking about storming the world with your dreams. So please read and use this book in the way that empowers you. I'm not looking over your shoulder. Actually, I'm looking into the distance where you're going, waiting to see your sparkling face on the horizon.

Resources for Forming an Inspired Success Circle— or Just for Reading This Book

I just wanted to let you know that at the back of the book you can find a whole section on how to form an Inspired Success Circle. You can be a tribe of two. You can be a tribe of two hundred. But whether or not you decide to form a group, I wanted to let you know that you can download a great deal of free resources and support to go with this book. For example, you can go to **www.TamaKieves.com/IS/freedownloads** right now, and get a free five-minute audio download of a guided "release your blocks" relaxation exercise to help you "Open Up to Your Inspired Success," the adventure of this book, and the adventure of your lifetime. You can also download my imitation of my Jewish mother talking about "Going for Your Dreams," though who knows what that will inspire.

The Truth

I have changed some names and minor details in this book to ensure the privacy of others. The truth remains the same.

1.

OWNING YOUR INSPIRED POWER

Hello, my courageous friend—you, trying on magnificence. There's a ticket in your bones and you know it. You know who you are meant to be.

Still, you insist on doubting yourself, calling it "realism," to limit yourself to powerlessness. You'd rather "play it safe," hedge your bets, trust sweetness only some of the time. But dear one, Wild Amazing Visionary people are the new safe. We are agents of invincible faculties. And we're blazing trails of abundance.

There is nothing wavy gravy about believing in your wildest dreams. Your inspired inner voice is as real as bunions or a bouillon soup. It's not putting your head in the sand to believe in a higher intelligence than mass consciousness. It's putting your head in the game. Love is the strongest power on the planet. You want results? Trust your Inspired Self. It's a presence and intelligence that dwarfs everything else.

THERE'S ONLY ONE NOTE YOU CAME TO SING

I have this aria trapped inside me that could electrify a stadium of people, but I'm singing jingles for the local hamburger joint. I can't live with myself playing in the dollhouse, a pint-size expression of my soul. I need to give the bigger me a chance, even if I fail. I'd rather be in the doghouse than the dollhouse.

A JOURNAL ENTRY

If we all did the things we are capable of doing, we would literally astound ourselves.

THOMAS EDISON

listen to creative minds, visionaries, and entrepreneurs all day long in my coaching practice, and I am moved by the spirit that moves them. Like you, they bounce off walls with ambition, hunger, and frustration. They secretly dream big, because they are big. Still they whisper their most vivacious desires, swallowing hard, as though they are confessing, say, a small hygiene problem or a third head. "I don't even know if I'll ever have what I want," they say. But I do. I know they are relentlessly drawn to where they belong.

We don't choose our wildest dreams. They choose us. They point us toward our *natural* environment. When we're not using our deepest gifts, we can feel like trout thrashing about on a dock, desperate to find water.

It's that necessary to live our calling. It's eventually unbearable to deny our love, strength, and essence. We've said "yes" to some sacred arrangement in the ethers, and here on earth—until we live our most meaningful dreams—we ache with the pangs of blessings unfulfilled. We can golf if we want to, but it will never fill that hole. We can shop, but we can't buy our freedom. We can even hire a "life coach," but then, and I hate this part, we still have to "do" our life.

"You're just so restless," my mother, a torch-bearing worshipper of security, used to say to me. I thought wanting to "be all you can be" in life was a good thing, not a personality disorder to cover up with a *TV Guide*, or a trilevel house in Long Island. But like many inspired souls, I've often felt lonely in my consistent desire for true expression. I'd envy those who could kick back in "normal" lives, enjoy a few burgers at a backyard barbecue, and some nice, conventional success. They'd fix a garage door, buy a house at the lake, or take a cruise to Alaska, and that would be enough. They didn't wrestle with some unnameable gravitational pull, a colony of inner voices, or the secret claustrophobia of their own trapped potential. They didn't need to change the world, chant some mantra, become a brand, or win a Pulitzer or a Grammy. In other words, they could just turn on the news. They didn't need to *be* the news.

But a therapist of mine once said she believed my "restlessness" was an essential prerequisite for progress and abundance. Therapists always say these things, serving up hot cocoa for the soul and wiping our chins, which is why we pay them half our gross income. She explained how restlessness wouldn't let me fall asleep to the presence of my gifts, and the difference I could make in the world. She saw longing as a wonderful capacity to "stay attuned to what my Inspired Self wanted to become." Just so you know, this is why I've never fit in at barbecues. I just can't talk to a financial analyst or a plumber in a Hawaiian shirt or baseball cap and get the words "attune" and "pass the dogs" into the same sentence. "You want more," said my wise counselor, "because you *are* more. There's more in this lifetime for you to become."

And that's what I'll tell you. You have more to give us. You have a built-in, divine assignment to employ all your gifts and to realize your exponential capacity. Your inspired self has bigger fish to fry and it doesn't perceive any of the limitations that you do. That's why it graciously kicks you in the ribs at night and tells you to stop dreaming small. Your desire is the full moon that stirs and pulls the tide. It's compelling because it's more real than anything else. You dream of the life that calls you, because everything under the sun is hardwired to know where it belongs. You don't need reasons or evidence when your bones trill with longing. Birds and fish just migrate. Everything living seeks to unfurl its own true nature.

Gregg Levoy, author of *Callings*, says a key is made to fit one lock and only one lock. "Anyone who feels made to do one particular thing in this world but is unable to do it becomes, in a sense, an unreconciled key," he says. Your relatives might think you're going off the deep end with a savior complex or an impractical business plan, a fat head and some bad bee stings in store. Your guru or yoga instructor might think you need to banish yearning, stop "searching outside yourself," and simply find peace in this moment. But I think you are searching to reconcile your key, or even your whole paradigm key chain. You are migrating toward your destiny.

I remember talking to my friend Angela one night. I felt suspicious of my own desire to take my creativity to the next level. I wondered if I'd just watched one too many *Oprah* shows. Or maybe I wanted bigger success because I was still hunting for approval or love, admittance into some elusive club, an addict on a spree. Hey, I'd been to therapy. I'd sat on enough leather couches to know to ask myself a question or two.

"I wish I could say I wanted to help the world, like Mother Teresa and Nelson Mandela, and that's why I was doing this," I said to Angela. I did want to help, but that didn't seem to be the fuel in my engine.

"Well, why are you doing this?" she said with a voice full of love and confidence, encouraging me to sound out possible truths. She had no fear of anything I might say. Meanwhile, I cringed as I pinpointed a slippery feeling in the back of my consciousness, something crouching and uncomfortable.

"I want to win," I said to her, and it felt so ugly and unenlightened, competitive and calculating. Good-bye, Dalai Lama, enter the beast with beady eyes. "I want to win," I said again. Having confessed it, I decided to explore that naked desire more.

"It's not that I want tons of money," I said, though of course I'd welcome a padded bank account. "What is it?" she said gently. "It's not that I want fame, though I wouldn't mind the benefits that come with that," I admitted. "Then what is it?" she repeated. Finally, I felt an encrusted door swing open inside me. I looked at my friend and said, "I want to win because I think I have a home run in me." Everything within me relaxed in that moment, so I continued, "It's just the note I came to sing," I said. Then my words and tears just flowed. "I want to be big. I want to be known. It's the level of expression that I feel like my talent was made for. It's my note," I said, looking into her soft brown eyes. "I think it's the only note that will feel *real* to me." Then she repeated back to me, "It's just the note you came to sing."

Suddenly my desire didn't seem so evil or garish anymore, suddenly it wasn't narcissistic, slimy, or base. It was just the truth. It felt as natural as the inclination to write with my right hand, and love red maple leaves and coffee ice cream, or hate sauerkraut, humidity, and anyone, anywhere, who could wear Lycra and look decent. It felt neutral and ordinary and even *involuntary*. I realized then that we don't get to choose our calling. We get to choose whether or not we will listen to each nudge or flare, whether or not we will believe, and whether or not we will dedicate ourselves to this territory of homecoming within us; but we don't get to choose which doorway has our name on it, which one swings open for us, into the wild country of heightened capacities, love, and awe.

Suddenly this need for boundless expression and a sweeping life was no longer about my ego. It was about my integrity. It was about staying true to the evolving, amazing life force within. It was simple. I needed to breathe fire so that I could breathe.

I urge you to stay true to your integrity. I urge you to listen to what only you know inside. You dream big because you're called. It doesn't matter if you feel like a frightened beginner, a star-spangled fool, or a beaten, wilted cabbage in the sun. It's not about knowing how to make it happen or being "worthy." You didn't choose this dream. *It chose you.* Say yes to your only reality and unimaginable adventure. Say yes to the ride. You belong in the life of your dreams. And you don't belong anywhere else.

INSPIRED SUCCESSISMS

We don't choose our wildest dreams. They choose us.

We've said "yes" to some sacred arrangement in the ethers,
and here on earth—until we live our most meaningful dreams—
we ache with the pangs of blessings unfulfilled.

You want more . . . because you *are* more.

You have more to give us. You have a built-in, divine assignment
to employ all your gifts and to realize your exponential capacity.

Your desire is the full moon that stirs and draws the tide.
It's compelling because it's more real than anything else.

You dream of the life that calls you,
because everything under the sun is hardwired to know where it belongs.
You don't need reasons or evidence when your bones trill with longing.

Suddenly this need for boundless expression and a sweeping life
was no longer about my ego. It was about my integrity.

You belong in the life of your dreams.
And you don't belong anywhere else.

THE DECISION THAT WILL CARRY YOU THROUGH EVERYTHING

I must be suffering a spiritual amnesia. I forget my own convictions. Yesterday's miracles become like stories in the Bible, all epic, but unreachable. Who cares if the Red Sea parted 5,000 years ago? I need a check today.

A JOURNAL ENTRY

It's not arrogant to believe that you're infinitely creative, brilliant, and potentially perfect through the grace of God.

MARIANNE WILLIAMSON, THE GIFT OF CHANGE

Y ou have the power to work in this world in an extraordinary new way. When you work with inspiration, you work with a mystical *something else*, an Enlivened Presence and Wild Card Intelligence, whether you call it God, Creative Mind, or subatomic nuclear soup. You have expansive capacities and instincts that are so beautiful they will make you cry with awe and appreciation. It's as though you open a thousand new chambers in your brain and heart, and you walk on a secret grassy footpath through the world.

You discover who you really are, by following what you really want.

That's what this is all about. You are not who you think you are. You are not an ordinary human being living in an ordinary world. You are an astonishment of capacities and you are here to reach your highest potential. Nothing else will feel as good to you. Nothing else will feel right. Yet you may have been taught to avoid your desires, not to shepherd them.

"Don't get your hopes up. Don't lose touch. Don't think you'll just have everything you need," whispers the scathing voice of self-protection. It doesn't want to trust the inspired feelings of enveloping love and safety. It doesn't believe it can live a life of big freedom and security. It can muster its way through pain, but not through joy.

We all have this "false self" that tells us we are small and hopeless and bound to the reality of a cynical, methodical, and uninspired world. This is our fearful self, though it parades around as an intelligent, grounded citizen, a little big on ranting, because it doesn't want *you* to get carried away. It likes to fit in, wear the T-shirts of the day, and quote studies and statistics so that it can feel propped up and savvy while remaining out of touch with the most important power in life. This fearful self may feel familiar and real, more real than our Inspired Self. But kindergarten felt more real than first grade at first, and college seemed like Mars. We are learning to step into new territory. We are learning to speak a language we've never spoken but always possessed. We are learning to become the most brilliant part of ourselves.

You have to *choose to believe* you're called. You have to *choose* to see yourself as called to be the most alive self you can be—a self that knows you are meant to succeed in what you're meant to do. You will return to this knowing again and again. It's a practice and a launchpad.

Some of you may feel squirmy with the word "called." I don't care about the word. I care about the reality of utilizing your inspired powers. Yes, I've been on the phone with coaching clients and I can *still* see them roll their eyes. I've watched the reflex suspicion in my workshops. An engineer said she imagined being "called" as having to dig ditches in hot weather in a continent far away from Starbucks. A psychologist said he imagined a cloistered monkhood or revival tents with loud music. And an interior designer said she saw people chanting in their pajamas. And knowing her, I'd bet money they weren't *swanky* pajamas. But I see being called as the inspired part of ourselves calling to us, beckoning us to go beyond false limits and unnecessary pain and live our natural talents in the sunlight. I'm not going to say you can walk on water with this power, but I do know you can walk in this world and thrive.

Most of us don't believe we're called because we think our dreams are kind of dinky or of no use to anyone else. Maybe we don't want to feed the hungry, we just want to feed our family or our love of making Zulu-themed decorative pottery. Maybe we don't hear a bottomless inner voice, only a rustling, darting desire. Maybe we don't believe in a Higher Power, so we deny ourselves our own higher powers. And maybe we just don't believe that we could ever make anything happen with our dreams, or that we, some bits of dust living in New Jersey that never got communion or reached Samadhi or even took a tai chi class, are worth cosmic collaboration. The reason doesn't matter. Most of us *never* feel called . . . until we *choose to believe* we are being invited into partnership with a universal force, a co-creator, or the most unlimited love imaginable.

I'm asking you to *choose to believe* that you have your dreams for a reason and that an activating energy, which feels like instinct, will impel you every step of the way. You may not have conviction automatically. And you probably won't have it consistently. This is a life practice. It takes dedication to intensify trust. That's why I'm asking you to lean into this essential realization, practice it, and take it for a test-drive, even as your own revolutionary research. Here's what I know: This one core belief can rock your world. And choosing not to believe it also rocks your world, but not in a way I wish for you.

Of course sometimes it's easy to believe you're skipping along the golden cobblestones of destiny's path. Then there are the dream-shattering times when, I don't know about you, but I've wanted my money back from the "You create your reality" infomercial and I've wanted the steak knife set instead, or better yet, an ax. There will almost always be these contrasts in life. That's when we get to practice the attitudes we will base our lives on. That's the work. Let me roll out an example.

"Shall we dance?" said the e-mail. It was from an agent who was offering me a contract to represent my first book. This was the first agent who *ever* offered to represent me. Why was I hesitant? Something held me back. So I wrote back asking if we might discuss one of the details. Within hours of her original e-mail offering to represent me, my would-be dance partner sent another e-mail to me and bluntly withdrew the offer.

I opened her e-mail and felt my limbs go numb, like in one of those science fiction movies when the poisonous plant squirts the scientist into paralysis. "I do not feel called to work with you," she wrote. She continued on about how she thought I would always have more questions and that she would inevitably frustrate me. This, I believe, is agent-speak for "you're a piece of work." I was floored.

The next day I kicked into fight-or-flight mode or some out-of-body experience in which I, the one who usually needs to feel, process, and analyze, took Rambo-style jungle action. I FedExed my book to several big-league literary agents, way out of my sketchy reach as a first-time author. But I was acting in some other capacity now. I don't know if it was guidance or adrenaline, but it felt automatic and instinctive. And then it happened. The biggest-kahuna agent of them all, the one who in my mind had a backup chorus just to sing his name, and who really did represent throngs of famous authors, the one I really wanted with all my yearning baby-author heart, called back within twenty-four hours and agreed to represent me. We signed and faxed the deal that day.

Clearly, something unusual had taken place.

"You had one badass angel push that first junior agent aside," said a friend of mine, echoing my furtive thoughts. For at least a week afterward, I felt illumined. I started feeling like nothing was random, nothing out of place. I felt joined by the greater Great. I felt lifted up, protected, *seen*. I felt *assured*, solid and clear that I would never doubt my path again. There was a secret grid in place and I would always find it. If I followed my heart's desire, I could always count on being led or, if I missed the cue, shot through a cannon in the direction of my good.

Flash forward to another moment: My book has already been published and now I'm trying to promote it. I receive a form rejection letter from a big organization where I'd hoped to speak. The letterhead actually says something like "Here to Support Dreams and Inspiration" but that doesn't stop the event coordinator from writing something frigid that "supports and inspires" my defeatism. Like in a Victorian novel, this news arrives on a cold, rainy day. "Everything is so hard," I moan to myself, already groping for dark chocolate. "Everything is an uphill fight." I start to believe that I got a break, a chance, but it's not going anywhere, because I just don't know how to work things out, so, naturally, I'll have to live under a bridge. Now everything is locked doors and brick walls and there's no golden flute music anywhere in any soundtrack. I no longer believe in a secret grid. I believe in gridlock.

This is what I mean by choosing to believe you're called. In fluctuating circumstances, which perspective will you believe about your path? Facts will change in a New York City second. Does this mean the nature or intention of a co-creative Powerful Loving Consciousness changes? Do the laws of inspiration change? Is nothing out of place *ever* or can outside circumstances totally determine your success? Can your *identity* change—just because the weather does?

Which view of reality is true for you? Because you cannot be propelled by an infinitely dynamic flow and then believe "the world" or "That's just the way things are" can inhibit the onslaught of your calling. It's just not possible. If your Inspired Self is real, and yes, honey, it's more real than Kansas, then there is nothing but your regenerative path and it's always edging you toward greater freedom and expression. This is a deliberate choice of belief and focus. And trust me on this one, the more you choose to believe in your path, the more reasons you will have to believe.

I urge you to see yourself as called—meant to succeed in your deepest desires.

The wisdom tradition of *A Course in Miracles* teaches that you "can put your faith in faith or you can put it in faithlessness, but you always put it somewhere." Albert Einstein, one of the most renowned scientific minds of our times, said, "The most important question a person can ask is, 'Is the universe a friendly place?'" Perspective isn't passive and it's as crucial to your well-being as oxygen and, some might say, even dark roast coffee. Think about it. The way you choose to see the caliber of your potential . . . determines everything you see and every action you take in this lifetime.

You will have to draw your own conclusion about this sweeping adventure. Here's mine: Each of us screams with gifts and competencies we have yet to name and experience. We have barely caught a glimpse of our full tool set, the control panel of genius and exponential technology within us. We are completely cradled and reinforced, in humbling, earth-shattering ways, when we support ourselves and listen to our instincts. This is a path of unwavering good, though we may have to deepen into our awareness of that good. We are given our dreams and desires for a reason. They are the portals to inspired living. It's our work to choose this life. It's our work to choose to believe we're called by something Alive to be exceptionally alive—and to answer that call with the rest of our lives—and ten thousand actions of love, courage, and gratitude.

INSPIRED SUCCESSISMS

You have the power to work in this world in an extraordinary new way.
When you work with inspiration, you work with a mystical *something else.*

You discover who you really are by following what you really want.

You are not who you think you are. You are not an ordinary human being
living in an ordinary world. You are an astonishment of capacities,
and you are here to reach your highest potential.

You have to *choose* to be called. You have to *choose* to see yourself
as called, called to be the most alive self you can be—
a self that knows you are meant to succeed in what you're meant to do.

Do the laws of inspiration change? Is nothing out of place *ever,*
or can outside circumstances totally prevent your success?
Can your *identity* change—just because the weather does?

You cannot be connected to an infinitely dynamic flow
and then believe "the world" or "That's just the way things are"
can restrain the onslaught of your calling.

The way you see the promise of your potential . . .
determines everything you see and every action you take in this lifetime.

We are given our dreams and desires for a reason.
They are the portals to inspired living. It's our work to choose this life.

YOU DREAM BIG
BECAUSE YOU ARE BIG

The truth is more important than the facts.

FRANK LLOYD WRIGHT

Your imagination is the concept of Spirit within you. It's the God within you.

WAYNE DYER, *THE POWER OF INTENTION*

Many of us find it hard to bet our lives on things in the unseen realm. We're big on mass consciousness, agreement, and things we can stub our toes on. Besides, professionals give you drugs and labels for seeing things that aren't there. But visionaries *do* see things that aren't there, yet. Every scientific breakthrough, gallery opening, or multibillion-dollar enterprise originated as a wisp of imagination, less tangible than the colors of a dragonfly's wing. Yet most people believe more in the garbage truck passing by than they do in their own dreams. We're guided to demean ourselves, deny our inner knowing, and the embryonic encrypted code that we alone possess. Yet know this: *The life you imagine is real.*

I remember a turning-point conversation I had many years ago, with Paul—Paul who has been my steady companion in taking my work into the larger world. We stood in the living room of my tiny apartment. He held a folded letter, a job offer. It was for an office management position with a spiritual humanitarian organization, in Santa Fe, New Mexico, about three hundred miles away from Denver, Colorado, where we lived. Paul worked in the computer industry, but had always wanted to align with an organization that soulfully nourished the world. Paul possessed a big, glorious heart and a humble temperament. This fast-growing group appeared to be an answer to prayer, with thousands of people on their mailing list, world headquarters and staff, and a popular and compelling leader with books and audio programs to his name.

Paul and I had only known each other for a few months at the time, so it seemed natural that he would take the position. Still, something kept brewing inside me, some sticky tumbleweed of unexpressed raw tension. I didn't know what it was. I wanted the best for Paul, but I kept feeling like I needed to tell him something, chant something, invoke something, do something other than stand there like a cornstalk.

"I am an organization," I finally said, quietly. This seemed to fall from the sky, and to be self-evident, yet somewhat like opera and hallucination at the same time. While I had been teaching workshops for some years at this point, my "mailing lists" were more like, well, exactly like, torn scraps of paper and scribbles on napkins. For years I'd taught out of a funky Victorian studio where the neighbor upstairs seemed to be playing volleyball with a piano at all times through the day and night. I had part of my book written but no publisher or agent in sight. My staff, part assistant, part guru, cleverly disguised as a rotund gray cat, had no technical skills to speak of, but did have a thing for crumpled paper, bottle caps, and slowly dying mice. So some might say it seemed mythical to compare my work with that of an established enterprise.

Still, something welled up within me. I knew it was true. It didn't matter that it was something still to come in my future. Because it was true for all time. It was true inside me. I carried this silent knowledge like a perfect scarab preserved in a chunk of amber in a cavern in my solar plexus. I saw it in a crystal ball through the bay window of my heart. Somehow it wasn't a theory or a hope or even a dream. It was just there. I'd always been afraid to say it, for fear of sounding self-aggrandizing, or fear that I couldn't pull it off. Still, I had always known that I would write books and offer talks and workshops and become the founder of a company that would inspire and support a beautiful glowing segment of humanity.

"I am an organization," I said again, this time with a strong, clear, and even voice, a voice I almost didn't recognize. I wasn't trying to convince him of anything or prove anything to him or even get him to stay. I wasn't even sure that he should stay. We were so new in our relationship and I didn't want to make any promises I couldn't keep. God knows, I have enough issues in relationships as it is, without having to announce I think I'm a guru, visionary, or world leader, though I appear before you, at times, as a jumbled, unpublished writer. Still, I had to say the words. I knew that it would have felt wrong or bad for the rest of my life if I had stood there and swallowed my crazy throbbing truth. It would have felt like lying out loud or freezing up, like in dreams, when you know the right answer on the quiz show but your vocal cords turn into jellyfish and your face cakes into stone and a disqualifying bell rings for all time.

Of course part of me would have preferred to have just shut up and had a farewell candlelight dinner. I mean I felt pretty stupid making such a bald assertion when I didn't have a database, a business plan, a decent computer, or anything else that might look as though I was heading in the direction of a thriving business rather than the nearest compound. I didn't want to sound like some whiny, desperate, fatal-attraction kind of girlfriend either, who pulls out the "I am a spiritual organization" card just when things get rough.

Yet the moment I spoke that sentence aloud, I felt time slow down. Truth took a deep sigh of gratitude. "I am an organization" seemed to bounce off the walls, off the chambers of ancient places, and resound in my vocal cords. The truth has a magnanimous sound when spoken. When you speak the large reality about yourself it feels very humbling. Something within you discerns your fundamental nature. It doesn't matter if you can back it up with bits of facts. The authority of your soul doesn't require evidence. You know your nature in your marrow, in the soles of your feet, and between your naked eyelashes. Your essence inhabits every cell. Paul heard the truth in that moment. And the world has heard the truth since that time.

Still, the road to living your vision will challenge you. Your conviction will seem like madness or like a dream you once had, that in the morning seems like a foreign movie without editing, subtitles, or the right soundtrack. Some days, you may feel foolish just for believing you will ever succeed. But you have noble company. Remember, every one of your heroes who has ever started a business empire, a novel, the design of a room, or a nonprofit or scientific revolution believed in something that did not yet exist. They knew something then that the world would know later. And they stayed true to their truth.

I remember years ago, even before the "I am an organization" stage, I found a purple silk three-piece pantsuit in a Goodwill store. At the time, I was writing my first book and didn't have a publisher or even a completed rough draft. I imagined the woman who would wear such an outfit and she didn't live in an inner-city studio apartment and she didn't doubt her flinty instincts. I wanted to be that woman. It was more than that. I *was* that woman. Even though I had just begun writing my first book, I envisioned that someday I would stand on a stage as a speaker and this outfit was perfect: elegant, dynamic, and shouting from the rooftops: "Look at me. I've created the work I love and my life flows like this plum silk, and yours can, too!" It was kind of like "I am woman hear me roar," only it was more like "I am a self-employed artist and not broke, watch me soar."

I proudly hung that pantsuit in my wardrobe. My future self smiled. But over time, the outfit found its way into the neglected part of my closet, along with former sizes and extinct fashions. When I moved into another apartment, that same pantsuit came along for the ride. I'd begun to wince when I saw it, still hopeful in its crinkled plastic covering, never worn. Eventually, it began to moan and mutter in the dark of my closet whenever I saw its telltale fabric. It began to taunt me and shove me around like a bully in the school yard: "Oh yeah, Miss Big Speaker, oh yeah, limelight girl, oh yeah, rich and famous and way powerful, look at you." It had come to represent my unlived dream, all of my unlived dreams, half-completed projects, broken relationships, expired gym memberships, and other miscalculations.

Finally, the outfit became ridiculous. It was the poster child of another decade, with square shoulders that looked like shelves for books and trophies, or maybe some handy built-in platforms, just in case you might want to accessorize with a pair of parrots. I quietly donated it back to a thrift store, sent it back to the earth. I had never worn it. That was a banner day for my demons. They crooned their dark anthem with heinous glee. Self-judgment ruled the kingdom.

Years later, that day did come when I stood on a stage and held a microphone, held an audience, held my power, and held my own. Today, I speak all over the United States and in other parts of the world, just as I knew I would. That young woman who bought that outfit knew I'd be here. In fact, if she hadn't known that, I would never have arrived. I'm glad she gave up on the outfit, but not on the dream. I'm glad she allowed the timing to be flexible, but kept her vision unremitting. She didn't know everything about how this dream would work out. But she knew, at least on more days than not, that it would. That's why it did.

I urge you to honor your intentions, your visions, and the lucid glimpses into the future that exist for you. *The life you imagine is real.* It holds power and energy. This vision creates at a subterranean level. You inhabit it now as much as you will live it later. It's who you think you are that creates who you end up being. Your success already exists in this present moment. It's in your DNA, in the DNA of your destiny, in the fibers and filaments of your past, present, and future self. Don't deny what you know, just because of shadows on the wall, other people's opinions, or "facts" that can change tomorrow. The truth is true for all time.

INSPIRED SUCCESSISMS

Every scientific breakthrough, gallery opening,
or multibillion-dollar enterprise originated as a wisp of imagination.

I knew it was true.
It didn't matter that it was something still to come in my future.
Because it was true for all time.

The authority of your soul doesn't require evidence. You know
your nature in your marrow, in the soles of your feet,
and between your naked eyelashes.
Your essence inhabits every cell.

Every one of your heroes who has ever started . . .
believed in something that did not yet exist.
They knew something then that the world would know later.

I urge you to honor your intentions, your visions, and
the lucid glimpses into the future that exist for you.
The life you imagine is real.

This vision creates at a subterranean level.
You inhabit it now as much as you will live it later.
It's who you think you are that creates who you end up being.

Your success already exists in this present moment.
It's in your DNA, in the DNA of your destiny,
in the fibers and filaments of your past, present, and future self.

HAVING THE GUTS TO BE EXTRAORDINARY

Think of yourself as an incandescent power, illuminated and perhaps forever talked to by God and His messengers.

BRENDA UELAND

Declare that you are one with Infinite Mind. Know that you cannot get away from this One Mind; that wherever you may go, there, right beside you, waiting to be used, is all the power there is in the whole universe.

ERNEST HOLMES, *CREATIVE MIND AND SUCCESS*

Real power comes from walking on the edge, the edge of all you know, the edge of all we know as a society. You will have to discover your own amazing truth. In the meantime, you may risk not looking normal, you know, since you'll be wearing that antenna on your head and all. You may occasionally falter, because it's not that easy to learn the language of your true self, after years of ignoring your instincts, desires, and cues. But if you're willing to leave the pack behind, you will come into an inspired power that will blow your hesitations, your limits, and your training wheels away.

On vacation in Santa Fe one year during the winter holiday season, I had a mini major awakening, so to speak. I like to journal and "figure out my life" during these types of getaways. So, that Saturday, my partner,

Paul, and I steal into a coffeehouse and find a table against a brick wall. We plop down our knapsacks filled with books to read, notebooks, and journals. We look forward to settling in to write, talk, escape ordinary life, and warm up from the fire-scented, bone-stinging cold of Santa Fe in December.

Right away I see this unusual-looking individual looking directly at us and I have that sinking feeling that we have sat in the wrong place. He is tall and lanky, even while seated, has a long red beard, wears a blue kerchief, and his blue eyes gleam with a tinge of joyful madness, radical faith, or too much caffeine. I barely take a sip of my decaf Americano before he begins talking to us about prophecy and listening to the voice of the Lord God. I am polite and our friend edges closer, rubbing his olive green sweater with excitement, and boldly staring into my eyes like oncoming headlights.

He begins to preach, prophesize, and warble bits of scripture, mixed with far-reaching, unusual, personal interpretation. Part of me is annoyed and wants to get back to the business of figuring out my life. Of course, I am intrigued, too. To be honest, I welcome the distraction from myself, an opportunity to avoid writing and focusing on yet more self-inquiry, for a little longer. Besides, talking to someone even more passionate and clearly "out there" makes me feel kind of grounded, intact, and damn near status quo, and, in those days, I took my stability where I could get it. Besides, I have always believed that jewels are bestowed by the crazed and the credentialed alike.

Truth be known, I am often drawn to the fearless and the bold. My redheaded friend has no doubts about his inner voice. I ask him if he's ever had fear, and he says no. His eyes twinkle like an elf's or probably like a psychotic's. I look at his worn olive green wool sweater and wonder where he lives. Later he shows me the pages and pages of his penciled notes about "the secret war that is taking place." He is "the only one keeping track of the codes," and he's doing it in smudged pencil scratches on graph paper. It's then that I have the feeling of having entered a sad, knotty, scrambled reality. I finally beg off from the conversation to write.

But the meeting leaves me squirming inside. Because I consider myself someone who is "called" to a great work in life, too. I believe in a power that is large and invisible, potent and mystical. And I believe I am listening to that presence and walking a guided, sequenced, rapturous path. Am I another zealot? Am I a wishful thinker? Am I disassociating from reality because it's painful? I have even made my living coaching others how to discover and follow their own burning path. Like me, they believe they have something wonderful to do here, some expressive work, and some will say a mission or an assignment.

Are we like my red-bearded friend? Living in our own reality? Documenting our own private codes that do not correlate to the rest of the world? For a moment, I begin to wonder about everything I've based my life on. But I'm comforted at the rock-bottom level, that at the very least, I'm a fanatic who takes time to question herself, so that's got to count for something.

"All are called, but not everyone will adhere," says my bearded friend as he exits the coffee shop and waves good-bye. Secret war or not, I believe he's right on this one. So I decide right there and then in the middle of a Starbucks to own once and for all, or at least until Tuesday, that I *am called*. I decide that I am listening to a whole-minded intelligence, a presence of love, and an inner knowing-sense and that I will follow it. I have often doubted my internal voice as a precaution, wavered and hedged in the name of safety, second-guessed in honor of ordinary practicality. But it doesn't serve me. Yes, of course I'm perceived as rational. I'm even still welcome in some cynical, established, vociferous circles of people— people with dark circles under their eyes, who live their days and nights steeped in facts, fear, media, argument, and data. Still, I know this agreement undermines me. I'm not as powerful as I can be.

That's what I end up writing about that day in Starbucks. I decide that

I am called, impelled, nudged, loved, and carried, and I will stop trying to limit myself and my possibilities in the name of reason and stability. I am willing to go too far, rather than risk not going far enough.

I am willing to listen and to live a different life, to part the frothing seas and walk on sound ground. I am willing to leave behind common sense because I don't want a common experience. I want an extraordinary life, a life of meaning, grace, abundance, and fireworks. I am willing to be just a little too happy and trusting for your average bear because I don't believe the average bear is average. Besides, I've already walked the path of cynicism and preconceived limitation and it led me to wearing suits in a courtroom and maiming people with my words, when I had other words of hope and vision within me.

Many of us are afraid to honor the instincts within us. We are afraid to make a mistake. *But now I am afraid to make the mistake of not listening, of following the impotent path of someone else's truth.* That day in Starbucks, I decide that I need to know where my truth will lead me. I need to know if my instincts come from a Grand Intelligence, a lack of intelligence, or a part of myself that got lost on the way to the fair, looking for pink cotton candy and caramel apples, in a world of too much pain. I need to know the nature and promise of this feeling and energy inside me. I don't want to die never knowing the reach and momentum of my full potential.

Many of us are called to be artists, visionaries, leaders, healers, lovers of humanity, and ordinary business folks working with an animating clarity and perspective. We are the ones who will transcend the ordinary gravitational pull of our day and become new barometers of mass potential. Our choices raise the bar like athletes who break undefeated records. We are scientists in our own lives. By listening to the suggestions that call us from within, we research accelerated and unanticipated ways of accomplishing higher goals. We may only be trying to make a living or write a screenplay, but every time we choose inspiration over fear, we can't help but take the consciousness of humanity with us. It's a wickedly beautiful system, if you ask me.

I love what Eileen Caddy, a cofounder of the famous Findhorn Community in Scotland, best known for its miraculously sized crops of vegetables, said about daring to follow an alternative path. In *Flight into Freedom and Beyond*, she writes: "What started as a few 'cranks' doing something outlandish and suspect, has grown into a place of substance and stability that is a symbol of hope to many people in the world." It's always been those who do things differently who make a difference.

Yes, there will always be extremists who go too far or who turn a path of being visionary and instinctive into a warped path of escapism, idealism, or narcissism. Maybe we'll always have some guy with stringy hair and white robes seducing pretty women and buying real estate in the Cayman Islands with their money. But that doesn't mean that love is only for the broken or mentally impaired. We all have access to the buffet. As for me, I'm taking a second helping of inspiration. I am willing to participate in our greatest evolution, our understanding of our own faculties and powers. These days I'm ditching the idea that I'm a lunatic, and owning, instead, that I'm a lover of possibility and actuality, and the new breed of realist.

Seeing someone "called" and unbalanced upset me for a while. But then it healed me. It helped me to see this life of trust as one of strength, not weakness. It helped me to stop dismissing myself, rejecting my trust and my higher powers, protecting myself in some automatic and insidiously destructive way. At last, I came to the realization that I'll encourage you to consider as well. It's this: We are not ridiculous or fragile for believing in love, strength, and exhilarating possibilities. We are not insane just because we choose to see that the ways of fear are insane. It's not crazy to dedicate ourselves to a life that feels true, empowering, and exciting. It's just plain crazy not to.

INSPIRED SUCCESSISMS

Real power comes from walking on the edge,
the edge of all you know, the edge of all we know as a society.

If you're willing to leave the pack behind,
you will come into an inspired power that will blow away
your hesitations, your limits, and your training wheels.

I have often doubted my internal voice as
a precaution, wavered and hedged. . . .
But it doesn't serve me . . . I'm not as powerful as I can be.

I am willing to go too far, rather than risk not going far enough.

I am willing to leave behind common sense
because I don't want a common experience.

Many of us are afraid to honor the instincts within us.
We are afraid to make a mistake.
But now I am afraid to make the mistake of not listening.

It's always been those who do things differently who make a difference.

We are not ridiculous or fragile for believing in love,
strength, and exhilarating possibilities. . . .
It's not crazy to dedicate ourselves to a life
that feels true, empowering, and exciting.
It's just plain crazy not to.

YOU CAN'T PLAN AN INSPIRED LIFE

If you ask enduringly high achievers about their success, most will tell you it was a serendipitous journey.

JERRY PORRAS, STEWART EMERY, MARK THOMPSON,
SUCCESS BUILT TO LAST

Who would attempt to fly with the tiny wings of a sparrow when the mighty power of an eagle has been given him?

A COURSE IN MIRACLES

When you're following a path of listening to your true desires, you will love and wrestle with this truth: You can't plan an inspired life. You can't imagine how everything, or even anything, will fall into place. And yet, crazy, kooky, powerfully aligned you, you know it will.

Yes, of course, "if you don't have a plan, you're planning to fail." It's a popular adage boldfaced in PowerPoint in traditional corporate circles. But in case you still didn't get the memo, we're not marching the bulletpoint drill. We're listening to a dynamic, on-location wisdom, moment by moment. It's about following instinct more than dried ink. No, we're not charging into a fire without a helmet. It's a bit more like charging into all conditions, bringing the fire with us. We embody a love that creates opportunities wherever we go and whatever we do.

Now, I've heard some individuals of faith say, "God is my copilot," but I'm guessing they don't put "Him" as the cosigner on their bank loan. You see, it gets kind of awkward when you have to tell people that the core of your business strength is not your résumé, research, or strategy. It's your connection to the Universe, your empowered mind, a dazzling, expansive feeling, or The Dude. It's probably fine when you talk to your weekly levitation group, coven, or evangelical praise family, but then with other people, that rock solid trust can evaporate like morning dew. Then it can feel as though you're skydiving into concrete, without a parachute, a prayer, or a PowerPoint presentation.

I remember the night I made the decision to self-publish my book *This Time I Dance! Creating the Work You Love*. I was listening to my best instincts, my "guidance," and I was adequately comfortable moving forward without a business or marketing plan. That is, until I sat next to *her*, the Queen of Judgment on steroids. I was at an ex-boyfriend's house for a formal Passover dinner. Of course, this woman, undeniably a social Brahman, was perfectly put together. She reminded me of a china plate: showcased, hard, and trimmed in gold. As I sat down, I felt as though my hair grew wilder, my panty hose bunched up, and I'd forgotten to floss my life. I had a bad, squishy feeling inside, like sitting down on gefilte fish.

Something in her know-it-all, nasal intonation makes me feel like I simply must justify myself to her, my choices, my past with the ex-boyfriend, my latest therapist's theories, and what *exactly* I planned to do with my hair. I wish I could just pass the horseradish and shut up, but I have a little boundary problem. She keeps asking me questions and I keep drooling out answers. Everything sounds wrong, but I keep gunning forward with information, flooding the engine with gasoline, or rubbing a stain too many times, until it's worse than ever. It's bad. I am trapped at the table with unleavened bread, parsley, and the interrogator with pursed peach lips at my side. "Let my people go," says the King of the

Israelites in the evening prayer book. Suddenly, I really understand the desire for Exodus.

It doesn't take her long to drag out of me that I am a writer, and of course out comes my freshly hatched intentions to self-publish a book. Now I really want to change the subject, tell her about sex with the ex-boyfriend, sex with all my ex-boyfriends, anything but my precious book, but like a hound dog, she knows a steak bone when she smells one. My publishing plans are the evening's chew toy. "You've never written a book before?" No, I say. I manage to swallow the fact that this one has taken me twelve years of my life to write. "You don't know anything about publishing and you're starting a publishing company?" I look sadly at the matzo in front of me. I'm bonding with totally flattened bread. "You don't know anything about marketing or distribution either?" There's a pile of business books in my office, many unread. "Not too much," I mumble.

Believe me, I know how this sounds to someone rational, because I have a big, fat, logical brain. It sounds like I'm saying that I'm walking out into oncoming highway traffic with a blindfold—but it's okay because the blindfold is purple and says "I believe in miracles" if you wear it backwards, or was blessed by this master shaman, well, a middle-aged realtor, who completed the mail-in course over the weekend. Really, how can I tell Judgment Woman that I'm following an inward knowing sense and that this feels large, true, and right in bones I didn't even know I had? I can barely acknowledge this truth to myself.

"Very ambitious," she says nasally and knowingly. Very ambitious, as in, "You're a nut job, and stay away from my children."

She goes on to ask more about my marketing plans. Now, it's not like I haven't asked myself a thousand times, How will I get this book into the world? How will I distinguish it from a sea of other self-help books? But all I ever get in my journal is this immediate directive: "Just put it in the river." I know inside it means to devote myself to writing and designing the book with every fiber of excellence I have. Then putting it in the stream of life, selling it to my clients and students, and seeing where the current takes it. Still, these thoughts sound more like clumps of tea leaves or fairy tales than strategic initiatives.

Yet something in me just knows that I am meant to do this and there is no risk. I've always believed the river knows its way to the ocean and that passion, excellence, and commitment will always forge a way into the world. But I just can't choke that out to Peach Lips because it sounds like a Nike ad or the creed you'd learn at Sunny Saints church camp. I'm also not going to mention that I'm listening to an inner voice that I believe is a Creative Energy or a Supreme Power calling me to my ineffable, true mission. Hey, we're in a gated community and I want to get out of here tonight. Years later, though, all puffed up with distance, I wish I could have quoted the Sufi mystic Rumi to that insistent earth-bound woman: "Don't ask what love can make or do. Look at the colors of the world!" She may have felt her chakras open on the spot. Or she may have switched her seat.

These are the kinds of things that will happen on this path. The world will demand a reasonable answer of you. Others around you will want a predictable map of your intentions and plans. They want to hear about your research and projections, not your latest angel sighting, coaching session, or meditation. And you will be standing there with some hummingbird joy that you can't explain and that you can't dismiss. You will also know that if you turn away from this sweetness in favor of reason, you will lose your way to everything you believe in and resign yourself to a shell of a life, haunted by the truth you've denied. Let me cut to the chase and save you sweat, wasted potential, and years. It's worth a bit of discomfort to feel more infinitely alive than you ever thought possible.

This is what happened after the incident with Peach Lips. I self-published my book, "put it in the river," and started enjoying startling local success and movement. My book hit the *Denver Post* bestseller list and the *Denver Business Journal* bestseller list. Then, four months later, I got an e-mail that said: "I am the Fairy Godmother you've been waiting for." The e-mail was from a former VP of marketing and publicity from a major New York publishing house. She had read my book late one night in the midst of her own career transition and decided it was the best book she had ever read on finding your calling. She wanted to get the book into the hands of major players. She knew the president of Tarcher/Penguin—Penguin, one of the largest publishing houses in the world, and *the* company I had always fantasized about. Tarcher bought my self-published book. Not only that, but they kept the design, the title, and my writing intact, editing maybe ten sentences. May I say that again? They bought my book, the book I had written for twelve years without an agent, editor, or publisher in sight. They bought the book that my soul had begged me to write. They not only bought the book, but also offered me a lucrative contract, with solid publicity plans. Finally, I even had lunch with the president of Tarcher in New York City. You can take that to the river, and the bank.

Now how could you logically *plan* for that? How could anyone ever foresee that arc: Take twelve years to write a book in Denver, and another year to design and print it, so that just when you "put it in the river," some publishing bigwig in New York City will face her last broken, soot-covered straw, quit her job, and stumble upon your nonpublicized work? How could you make the right person fall in love? How can any rational human being plan to connect the dots this way? Yet how can any rational human being negate the impossible mastery of all those jeweled beads coming together in such an intricate and meticulous pattern that would ultimately uplift tens of thousands of people?

This kind of "coincidence" still doesn't prove anything, say the skeptics. But that's only because it hasn't happened to them. Because when *improbable perfection* happens to you, when the Hallelujah chorus sings in your bones, you know you are not alone. You know you are where you

are supposed to be. You know there is an inspired, nonlinear way to succeed. You know that just because you don't have a plan nailed down,
doesn't mean you're a loose screw. You're not choosing chaos. You're
choosing accuracy. You're listening to air traffic control instead of a map,
because if you're flying in new conditions, that's what you do.

This is what I keep learning again and again. We are loved and we are
guided. We have extraordinary faculties embedded within us. Nothing
is denied. It's hard to let go of control and guarantees and the peculiar
comfort of fitting in with people who don't really embrace a life of possibility. Yet it's amazing to allow yourself to dare your own authentic walk
in this lifetime, to listen to the love within you more than your fear, and
to discover a consistent constellation of abundance that dwarfs the scope
of any plan.

INSPIRED SUCCESSISMS

You can't plan an inspired life.

We're not charging into a fire without a helmet.
It's a bit more like charging into all conditions, bringing the fire with us.
We embody a love that creates opportunities
wherever we go and whatever we do.

If you turn away from this sweetness in favor of reason,
you will lose your way to everything you believe in
and resign yourself to a shell of a life.

It's worth a bit of discomfort to feel more infinitely alive
than you ever thought possible.

Just because you don't have a plan nailed down
doesn't mean you're a loose screw.

You are not choosing chaos. You're choosing accuracy.
You're listening to air traffic control instead of a map,
because if you're flying in new conditions, that's what you do.

We are loved and we are guided.
We have outstanding faculties embedded within us. Nothing is denied.

It's amazing to allow yourself to dare your own
authentic walk in this lifetime,
to listen to the love within you more than your fear,
and to discover a consistent constellation of
abundance that dwarfs the scope of any plan.

2.

YOU HAVE
YOUR OWN WAY
TO SUCCEED

We live in the Information Age, God help us, and we can start to believe in information more than guidance. Somewhere along the way, we started trusting complete strangers on talk shows, Botoxed with serenity, more than our own instincts. That's got to stop, you know.

Do the research, baby, because this is your original life. Ignore the changing "reality" of statistics and chase awakening joy. Get your feet soaking wet. Cherish your own signals and trajectory. Why listen to an "expert" instead of a genius? Oh, you want to do it "right." Well, I'm shooting higher. I want you to be the cat who swallows the moon.

Sure, you can benefit from others. Just don't let it stop you from learning about your power. You already have a way to succeed. Check it out, baby. It's embedded in the pockets of your ease.

EXPERTS, SHMEXPERTS: NO ONE KNOWS THE SECRETS YOU HOLD

Facts are artifacts of the past.

A JOURNAL ENTRY

I will not let you tell me what reality is. I will not let you wield your spell. I will not let your words reign true. I will not let your phrases cast shadows on my rivers, blacken the skies, or snap the evergreens of my dreams. I know what I know in my heart. I feel in my bones the life that I am meant to experience, the life force of another life, just as mothers feel the presence of their imminent children.

A JOURNAL ENTRY

hope you will not underestimate the power that limiting people can have on your potential. Many pose as experts, solicitous family members, and people who really should just chew on a sock. There's my "expert" opinion, for you. Of course, the world may even give some of these pundits the title of authority, television talk shows, branding, and bits of the alphabet after their names. But no matter what they've accomplished, they can never know what *you* will accomplish. They cannot foresee the sweep of your destiny or the evolution of your creativity. They do not know how much time, strength, and rampant love you will devote to your dream. They do not know the dispensation schedule of miracles. No one knows the secrets you hold.

Years ago, I spoke at the Aspen Writers' Conference, and watched Mr. Big Publishing, a representative from a major house, speak on a panel. He spoke to a room full of hungry, unpublished writers who would have sold their loved ones' big toes on the black market if that's what it took to turn their manuscripts into published books. I had already published my book, so I wasn't listening to how to secure an agent or contract. But then Mr. Big Publishing just casually interjected, "If a book doesn't do well in the first six months, we just punt."

No doubt, he was trying to help us appreciate the strident pace and gritty reality of the publishing industry, just in case anyone might have confused it for a nice trip to the candy store. But he used the word "punt" and sounded cheeky about it, as if marble-heartedness was just as charming as dimples. I felt as though I'd been kicked in the solar plexus. His "we just punt" triggered me. My book, while it had an exciting beginning, was definitely not going gangbusters at the time. Now I saw the terrifying premonition of my own big publisher's "punt list."

He continued, but my sensitive, creative heart contracted like morning glory on the vine. With each casually damning remark that he made, I felt as though he'd tossed a fine china plate out a ten-story window. I looked around the room at all the other writers, all of us a little bit more white-faced, shifting our feet, darting our eyes, and clutching our fine china plates to our hearts.

Later I realized it wasn't just his choice of words that bothered me. It was his tone. That know-it-all, this-is-reality, this-is-the-only-reality tone. It was a dominance that made belief seem like a lapse in sound judgment and faith seem impotent and desperate, like some lost yellow butterfly in a machine shop. In a matter-of-fact way, he said something that was not a matter of fact: that if something didn't succeed in the first six months, it wouldn't ever be a media darling or turn heads. I knew this was a common industry standard, and I knew they needed standards. I also knew that this particular individual did not allow for a universe rich with prospects. He didn't just close the doors to his publishing house. He slammed all doors.

Mr. Big Publishing is what I have come to call a Dark God. They are people who speak with false certainty. They represent "the world." They stand square with their hands on their hips, claim authority, and suck up all the oxygen around them. There are no openings for alternative points of view, the new physics, and the absolute freaky and relentless love of Divine Energy. They've discarded factors like "Thoughts create your reality," or "The Universe is conspiring on your behalf," or even "Love never fails." These Dark Gods can dismiss your world with a single comment, and feel justified, accurate, and even philanthropic in their presumptions.

Don Miguel Ruiz, a Toltec shaman and bestselling author of *The Four Agreements*, calls these types of people "black magicians." He warns us about the damning power of other people's remarks. He says, "One word is like a spell, and humans use the words like black magicians, thoughtlessly putting spells on each other."

Mr. Big Publishing was probably eating peanuts on his plane ride home, rejecting someone else's manuscript, and feeling as though he had set another bunch of loser-dreamers straight. Maybe he was just one more jaded individual, or maybe he was momentarily authoritarian because he felt threatened somewhere else in his life. But believe me, I was a sucker for anything that sounded like authority. I was all over that spell.

I drove back from the weekend writing conference with an aching, desperate heart. I ignored the mountains and evergreens, silent blessings just outside my window. I sped home in my Honda, feeling soul-bruised, angry, and defeated. I was so tired of feeling unsupported in the world, feeling as though I smashed into cold stone fortresses at every turn. Never mind that "seeing the glass as half empty" thing. I saw my glass as steeped to overflowing—with rat poison. Let's just say, I was seeing everything from the tiny, beady, all-consuming eyes of fear.

I searched through my stash of motivational-speaker CDs, the experts I did want to hear, the ones who ignited my strength and stoked my dedication to living an inspired life. I popped Marianne Williamson into my CD player. She spoke about what she called mystical power, and I loved the electricity in her voice. She talked about the strength of unseen forces, the explosive, creative power behind the scenes that unconditionally and unerringly supports our good. Just at that moment, I noticed the sunlight hit the apricot-colored canyon as I drove by. I felt a softening inside myself, a sensation of spaciousness taking over. I remembered then that my experience was not defined by someone else's predictions, positions, or even chosen facts. *His words are just words.* They did not need to be my words or my death sentence.

At last I broke out of my own dungeon and into the sunlight. I returned to my own intelligent inner voice, a voice more enduring than mountains, more formidable than a New York publisher, and more consistent than fear. It's the inner voice we all have, a voice of unmistakable truth, that voice that speaks as softly as dandelion seeds in the wind, yet girds us with strength and magnitude. This voice reminded me that I had a white-hot catalyst inside me, a creative nucleus of forces I could not imagine. Recognition flooded my veins. I broke the spell and cast a new one.

Our culture puts so much stock in experts. We revere research and data, interpretations, and "spells." But an independent mind has access to other possibilities. My father had a maddening attitude of never listening to anything anyone told him. He walked around with concrete earmuffs on, irreverent and immune, never allowing the opinions of others to get in his way. He subscribed to the religion of trying something for yourself. He insisted on laying claim to your own experience. It was an attitude that drove me crazy as a young and "follow authority" type of woman. It's also an attitude that changed my life.

In my college years, my pre-law guidance counselor told me in no uncertain terms that I should not apply to Harvard Law School. Mr. Randolph had reviewed my grades and extracurricular achievements. "Sit down, Tama," he said. I sat as he adjusted his thick glasses. "Harvard won't take you, I'm sorry." He tossed the evidence on his desk, a bulging file pulled from an army green file cabinet. "You've got all the right stuff, but no go," he repeated. "Records show that Harvard Law School has never yet admitted a Brooklyn College student other than by affirmative action."

That night I told my father, aka Mr. Earmuffs, why I wasn't applying to Harvard Law School. He snorted at the reasons. He could care less what the pre-law guidance counselor thought or concluded. I, the righteous little rule-follower and idol-maker that I was at the time, energetically defended the college counselor who had years of specialized training. "Experts, shmexperts," yelled my father, a self-made man, who had put himself through law school and now worked on legal briefs in mismatched flannel pajamas at the kitchen table. "Shmexperts," he repeated, and some other dismissal muttered in Yiddish that sounded like gargling, spitting, uttering incantations, and possibly stand-up comedy, all at the same time.

My father was adamant that I apply to Harvard, that I throw a penny in the fountain and make a wish, that I give myself that royal chance. And when I balked, he wrote the check for the application fee. I rolled my eyes as only a young woman in her twenties can. I knew it was futile to apply. But my father didn't care about the career counselor's past research. He wanted me to experience the data of my life.

I filled out the application on our cluttered kitchen table. We had had roast chicken for dinner that night and I sort of, maybe, accidentally, passively-aggressively got chicken-grease stains on that exalted law school application. My father didn't care about appearances either. "Just mail it," he said, "you have nothing to lose."

So I sent in a grease-blotched application, transparent and marred, to the mightiest Ivy League school in the country, and some weeks later,

Harvard University sent back a crisp white, crimson-embossed acceptance letter. The expert with his evidence and conclusions had been wrong. Harvard Law School had changed their admission policy history that year. The impossible had become possible.

And as my father's daughter, I'll tell you this. Dare to have your own adventure. Keep trying everything—and let experience be your only expert. The Dark Gods tell you what you can and cannot have. They chant their way. Walk past them. Walk the autonomous path of all visionaries. Vow your freedom. The Dark Gods are history teachers, and that is all. They do not understand that absolutely everything changes. They cannot calibrate the magnetic force of the love that is meant to be. They do not hear the music to come. They do not know what you do.

INSPIRED SUCCESSISMS

I will not let you tell me what reality is.
I will not let you wield your spell. I will not let your words reign true.

I remembered then that my experience was not
defined by someone else's predictions, positions,
or even chosen facts. *His words are just words.*

Our culture puts so much stock in experts.
We revere research and data, interpretations, and "spells."
But an independent mind has access to other possibilities.

Dare to have your own adventure.

Keep trying everything—and let experience be your only expert.

The Dark Gods tell you what you can and
cannot have. . . . Walk past them.
Walk the autonomous path of all visionaries.

The Dark Gods are history teachers, and that is all. . . .
They cannot calibrate the magnetic force of the love
that is meant to be. . . .
They do not know what you do.

ANY ROAD WILL TAKE YOU IN THE RIGHT DIRECTION

Start moving forward any which way—and you'll have some informa-tion about your own right way to move forward. Experience is a bus that's always available and always moving in the right direction. Questioning just takes you into analysis and paralysis.

A JOURNAL ENTRY

Your first attempts are not the measure of your possibility. They are the crusty husks of disuse. They're also the cost of initiation, the rites of passage. Face your own first efforts with patience and pride. You're on your way.

A JOURNAL ENTRY

Years ago I gave a talk to some enthusiastic college students about "How to make it as an artist in the world." They were hungry for direction, assurance, perhaps a notarized guaran-tee, and a way to paint the world without cutting off their ears in the process. They were taking notes because they wanted to get this right, and maybe avoid a divorce, an illness, a bankruptcy, or heartbreak. I wanted to tell them that life doesn't offer rubber gloves. They wanted strategy, formulas, commercial foolproof techniques, and bullet points that they could memorize.

I wanted them to take a bullet, so to speak—for their soul's true life. I wanted them to take risks, consume risks, billions of them, as though they were hungry baby birds opening their beaks for worms. I wanted them to know that everything was safe because everything would teach them and eventually activate their bionic strength and fire. I wanted them to know that openness would strengthen them more than caution and protection. I didn't say this to them, so I'll say it to you: It doesn't matter where you enter the stream. It doesn't matter how you begin. Just jump in. Get moving.

I'm not being cynical or flippant. Instead, I am confident—confident in all our abilities to find our way to our good. I want you to know that you can't screw this up and that as *A Course in Miracles* teaches: "Nothing real can be threatened." I want to feed your willingness to explore, taste, dive in, take a chance, and cultivate emotional *cojones* and a passion for your own learning and experience. Experience is the best life coach on the planet, and it will dish out anything you need to let go of your old stories, hesitations, wobbling knees, and baby fat.

The blank page teaches us to write. The stage teaches us to perform. Even surgeons have to learn on real-life patients with real-life consequences, though I hope they do that in the backwoods somewhere, and maybe only on people who don't love golden retrievers. There's no getting it right before getting it at least a little wrong. In *Grace Eventually*, Anne Lamott shares how she learned new behaviors: "I learned . . . by doing. It's a terrible system. If I were God, I would have provided a much easier way—an Idiot's Guide, or a spiritual ATM, or maybe some kind of compromise." But we don't get the compromise. We move forward or we feel the desires within us begin to rot like peaches in the sun. No one steps into "the big time" with maiden feet. All of us have to flounder through mud. It's mud that turns into stardust. Get moving.

Perfectionism, or thinking you can start only with airtight credentials or airbrushed opportunities, or the ideal schedule, is not your ally. To me, it's the fussy aunt of procrastination. Perfectionism holds you back, and tells you "you have standards." Those aren't standards. They're *issues*. They're insecurities that can heal only with mercy, patience, and moving forward in your life. Remember, conditions do not need to be "just right" for you to succeed. You have a passion. You bring the love, excellence, and secret ingredients with you. You're like one of those dehydrated meals people take on camping trips: instant lasagna, cabernet, and brownies, just add water. Wherever you are, the mojo goes with you. Everything you dare will take you where you need to go, if you stay with it.

When I first taught a professional women's group out of my old apartment, I was mortified by this gaping ugly hole in the linoleum, yes, *linoleum*, in the kitchen and some stain on the wall in the bathroom. My friends swore that no one ever noticed the stain in the bathroom. To me it may as well have been a polar bear or flashing disco ball, because I bet a movie star could have stood in that bathroom, handing out autographs, and I would have seen only the stain. I wanted to hang a sign next to it apologizing for it, and for the choices in my life in general, but fortunately my friends dissuaded me. Then the landlord promised new floors soon, so I felt appeased, but only because I didn't realize that "soon" in the language of tequila meant "sucker."

The women in this group had income levels that far exceeded mine, and they came to me for guidance and direction. They would drive to my noisy, hot, loud, hippie neighborhood in their sleek Audis and Acuras. I felt nervous inside, as I suggested places to park, where maybe they wouldn't be invited to buy some crack on their way to my house. No, I didn't have an office space with a bamboo fountain, marble floors, and a waiting area with tapestry chairs and a guest book. I didn't have that blond secretary. I had an alarmed cat. I had my small, non-air-conditioned apartment with an entrance on the side of a Victorian house. But I moved forward because I needed to teach with all my soul. Somewhere inside me, I knew I could help liberate the group's creativity, dreams, abundance, and authenticity. That's where I kept my focus.

I swear each time I taught that group, that apartment transformed into a Zen garden with waterfalls, a penthouse, a temple on a mountain, a picnic, and a party. The discussion transcended the walls and the worn floorboards. The awareness, healing, laughter, and insight became our structure and our palace. Believe me, the crack dealers would have wanted some of what we had. My inner perfectionist would still have liked to have facilitated this group in a hibiscus-covered open-air structure in Maui, right by the ocean—and only during whale season—or at least in some famous artist's cavernous loft in Greenwich Village, but I'm grateful I didn't wait. And just for the record, I have since led this workshop in a glass cathedral in Maui and at an open-air structure in the rain forest in Costa Rica. Everything takes you where you belong, if you let it.

We need to start where we are—as we are. There's always a hole in the linoleum, a missing credential in your résumé, a stain in your present circumstances, a gunshot in your neighborhood—always something not quite good enough to present yourself to the world. But take your gaze off the stain. Focus on the love you have to give. Focus on your contribution and intention. We don't care about the quality of the wrapping nearly as much as we care about the quality of the gift. You may not have experience, but you're already a natural.

Later on in my career, I had to face a fear of speaking to larger professional audiences. I maybe, sort of, definitely kept steering clear of the situation. As I got honest with myself, I realized I was afraid of failing, looking as helpless as a zoo animal in front of hundreds or thousands of people. But I realized that the longer I avoided the possibility of failure, the longer I avoided success. I had to go out there and expose myself to learning. I knew I'd hate it if an audience disliked me. But I'd never see those people again. I could steer clear of that organization or part of the world for the rest of my life. I could build a bunker if I had to, live off my own crops, and leave no forwarding address. I had options. Meanwhile, I had to live with my cowardice and stagnation every single day, in every single mirror, and watch my time and desires pass me by. "There's only one way to get past the fear," said a friend of mine over tea. "It's mileage," she said. "You've got to just do it and do it and do it and add up the mileage." I knew she was probably on to something. Because I immediately wanted to put a whole lot of mileage between me and her stupid loving eyes.

In my creative writing workshops, students often ask me, "What if I'm not good enough?" I know it sounds like a fair question. But it's the wrong question. The real question is, "Am I willing to become good enough?" Are you willing to practice, learn, sweat, shine, and dedicate yourself to growing? Are you willing to start where you are, stop judging it, get down on your knees and serve the excellence you possess inside? That excellence will take you anywhere you need to go.

Think about it. What is the need to immediately "do it right" costing you? I love how Buddhist nun Pema Chödrön discusses this devastation: "Being preoccupied with our self-image is like being deaf and blind. It's like standing in the middle of a vast field of wildflowers with a black hood over our heads. It's like coming upon a tree of singing birds while wearing earplugs."

Take off your earplugs, your shackles, and your hood. Expose yourself to the success of learning and growing. Take a step forward right now, even if you don't have the right shoes on. Stop thinking about it and shrinking inside. Your gifts are real. Your love is real. The wildflowers sing to you from the hillside. Everything you do will strengthen you. You cannot fail by moving forward. You will get to where you need to go.

INSPIRED SUCCESSISMS

It doesn't matter where you enter the stream.
It doesn't matter how you begin. Just jump in.

Feed your willingness to explore, taste, dive in, take a chance,
and cultivate emotional *cojones* and a passion for your own learning
and experience. Experience is the best life coach on the planet.

The blank page teaches us to write. The stage teaches us to perform.
Even surgeons have to learn on real-life patients
with real-life consequences.

We move forward or we feel the desires within us begin to rot.

Remember, conditions do not need to be "just right" for you to succeed.
You have a passion. You bring the love, excellence, and secret ingredients
with you.

We need to start where we are—as we are.
There's always . . . something not quite good enough to
present yourself to the world. . . .
Focus on the love you have to give.

We don't care about the quality of the wrapping
nearly as much as we care about the quality of the gift.
You may not have experience, but you're already a natural.

Everything you do will strengthen you. You cannot fail by moving forward.

CHASE GRACE, NOT GUILT

*I think this path is by invitation only. It's not a contest to prove some-
thing. This is about being moved and moving.*

A JOURNAL ENTRY

*Am I being guided by an energy or am I making excuses? Am I
respecting a solid wall inside me, a clear signal that this is not my
way or not my time? Or is this a "spiritual way" of condoning that I'm
just a skittish white rabbit and can't walk up and claim my true life
like a real contestant?*

A JOURNAL ENTRY

have coached clients who literally asked me to kick them in the butt,
twist their arms, call them names, stick dynamite into their voodoo
dolls, and make them do things they didn't want to do. But I'm not a
fan of sadism. I already worked as a high-powered lawyer in a corporate
law firm once, thank you very much. Now, I prefer love and grace. I'm
of the mind that sometimes you don't want to do something because
deep in the big sky of your being, you know there's another way, an original suggestion summoning up, or simply another day. I have no need to
micromanage the infinite resourcefulness of my clients. Still, they insist
that they're just lazy, and if only they could be jackhammered into shape—
as in, have their spirit broken—they'd be *inspired*. Yes, of course.

I've been down that twisted road myself. Here's a glimpse from the notebook of an anguished past:

"How hard could it be, to pick up a freaking phone and make the call I need to make? Anyone else on the planet could do this. But for me, cold-calling this organization feels like taking off my clothes in slow motion, in front of my entire junior high class, on some bad contest-type reality television show, like *What Thighs Not to Have*. It's so not what I love. And for once, I'm willing to consider that just maybe it isn't because I'm cata-strophically timid or inadequate at a cellular level."

Somehow I believe that I'm following a sacred evolutionary promise inside me, a knowing that I will be drawn to act when it's my right time. A lioness rests until she picks up the scent of prey and then lunges. There is no lag time. She doesn't take one breath that instinct doesn't impel. And I'm guessing she doesn't take down a gazelle just to shut up her inner critic.

The phone call is what I "should do." It makes sense to my linear mind, but I am not restricted to the tired spectrum of a solely linear world. I am walking a jeweled, soul-awakening path, and I need to allow my approach to emerge from my guidance rather than my insistence. I talked myself into freedom then, and I'd love to liberate you now.

I want you to release yourself from unnecessary pain. Following what you "should do" is an impoverished choice on a path that is original, in-spired, and inevitable. A "should" is someone else's strategy in your head. It's a rational commentary. Yet it's not an intuition or directive, an ancient gate swinging open, a holy magnetism, or an advanced sequence falling into place. Your soul has its own astonishing itinerary. What do you have energy to do? That's the stick of dynamite in this equation. Everything else is distraction. Yes, distraction.

No one taps her deepest gifts through shame, guilt, or anger. In fact, if you come from obligation, others smell the sadness in your blood and they will run the other way. Of course, if they're of the damaged variety, they may, momentarily, want to marry you, but then *you* should run the other way. You can check tasks off your to-do list, but you won't really have *done* anything. Why just "go through the motions"? You are meant to flow through ingenious channels that already exist for you.

You may have to practice having faith in yourself. Believe it or not, without that insane inner task master, a tyrant who will never be satisfied, you will not just eat Ding Dongs and read about the pets of celebrities all day. Yes, you may start there. But if you stop judging yourself, let go of the hate and resistance that feeds the behavior, you'll start uncovering an expansive, conscientious, and inspired self. You are more determined, balanced, and brilliant than you know.

Years ago, I came to see that self-acceptance does not lead to self-indulgence but to strength and self-reliance. In my early twenties I was an anorexic, who would binge-eat and then deliberately starve. I felt I could never trust myself around food. Well, because I couldn't. I admitted to my therapist one day that I secretly longed to eat coffee ice cream all day. "Would you eat ice cream all day?" she asked. "Of course," I said, "that's why I have to stay in control." She looked at me with burning brown eyes and said, "What if you let yourself eat ice cream all day and *didn't judge it*?" Let's see, I thought to myself, I wouldn't leave my bed and within weeks, I would most likely resemble a gorilla in a camisole. But something told me we were going somewhere else.

So I followed her suggestion and imagined eating ice cream all day with no mean words thought or said. That was some killer therapy right there. But after a moment of continuously eating ice cream in my mind, I had a radical new answer to her question. "Then I'd get bored and eat regular food like broccoli or *kale*," I laughed. My therapist beamed as though she had seen Glenda the Good Witch or Mother Mary sit right down beside me and offer her a high five. The revelation lit the room like sunlight. I began to cry. I wanted health. I really did want health. I really would eat broccoli. My own appropriate instincts had always been there waiting for me like soft yellow tulips beneath a winter snow. But I had been crushing them for years with suspicion and control.

Your built-in success plan begins with open-minded honesty. Listen to what feels right, without judgment, right now. You know your own next step, even if it feels uncomfortable *because* it's comfortable. I want you to know that listening to your heart isn't a gentle, sweet thing to do. It's the razor's edge. It's the gateway to quantum energy, a direct line to the technical and strategic support of a Dazzling Presence that flows more effectively without the constriction of fear. Why insist on taking an action that doesn't feel right? You were designed to follow your instincts, not to abort them. Why limit a dynamic, multidimensional intelligence to the conditioning that created the life you want to change? And why, dear Grasshopper, act from fear when you can act with love? There are infinite ways to get what you need and infinite needs you have yet to discover.

When I first published my book *This Time I Dance!*, I refused to call the organizations of popular authors to get raving testimonials for the book's back cover. Some of my friends politely suggested that I might not be getting enough iron in my diet or oxygen to my brain. Still others tried to coach me into visualizing success, seeing myself speaking to the authors' assistants and asking for what I needed with unruffled blood pressure. They surrounded me in white light, called on astral master-minds, advocates, and archangels, and told me everything would gush with true perfection. But I'm guessing that white light was on the blink that day, or one of the archangels had a bad case of acid reflux, because when my friends took off, I still felt nothing but dread. I wouldn't do it. I just knew that I could never sing an aria with an anchor in my stomach and seaweed in my mouth—and that there had to be another way for me to make it. There was.

I got fantastic endorsements for the book. Some of my students and fans pursued authors for me. Then I met an internationally famous author at a local book signing, and she generously called me back the next day with a testimonial. Then my favorite: I bought a latte from a young barista at a coffee shop in Denver who "just happened to recall" that her East Coast college advisor had written a bestselling book on careers. She e-mailed him and I had my endorsement within days. I hadn't picked up the phone. I'd picked up a latte. Now, if that doesn't speak to intelligent life in the Universe, I don't know what does.

I am not saying that we don't show up on our own behalf, but just wait around for bellhops to do our bidding. That's an advanced path, I'm sure, and you have to be kind, even to telemarketers, for an awful lot of years for that one. The one I teach, though, is taking the actions we have energy to take. You will be called to act. Sometimes you will travel on the white speedboat of inspiration. Other times, you will take actions, even difficult ones, because you feel ready to grow and show up, even with quivering chin hairs and knocking knees.

Elaine, a client of mine, confided that she felt bad about not promoting her newly minted interior design business. "I need to get out there and network," she said with a low whisper and tight teeth. Naturally, she took to her blue couch instead, "like a beached whale." But while on that sofa, surfing sitcoms and shunning a leads group, she got an idea for a side business. Something on the Home and Garden channel jogged her creativity and she flashed on a local company that might use her services. She called the company immediately, "just happened" to get the president, who never ever answered his phone, and felt as giddy as an orangutan, no whale in sight. "It all just happened," she said later, "like a perfect storm."

Here's another example. Rhonda, an aspiring actress, got a notice about open auditions for a movie. She left the leaflet on her kitchen table. It practically burned a hole in her tile tabletop, she recounts. "Every time I looked at the paper, I thought, Oh damn. I know I have to do this. I was scared," she says, "but I also felt this deeper sense of peace." That's the telltale sign. When you're listening to your soul, you feel the bass guitar of integrity. You don't feel bruised, shoved, or threatened at gunpoint. The core of you knows it's time to do this, even though some part of you will begin bargaining like a merchant at the end of the day.

Pay attention to how you feel before you take action. Is a bully shoving you around, or is your inner advocate encouraging you to show up? Move with your heart, not your head. Face fear when you feel *ready*, not when you feel guilty. It's time to leave the emotional baseball bat behind in the evolutionary Dark Ages, along with the bed of nails, and dial up and step into the new dawn of trusting yourself and the power of your calling. You want what comes naturally to you because it's better than anything else.

INSPIRED SUCCESSISMS

I'm of the mind that sometimes you don't want to do something because
deep in the big sky of your being, you know there's another way,
an original suggestion summoning up, or simply another day.

I'm following a sacred evolutionary promise inside me,
a knowing that I will be drawn to act when it's my right time.

I am not restricted to the tired spectrum of a solely linear world. . . .
I need to allow my approach to emerge from my guidance
rather than my insistence.

A "should" is someone else's strategy in your head.

What do you have energy to do?
That's the stick of dynamite in this equation. Everything else is distraction.

No one taps his deepest gifts through shame, guilt, or anger.

I came to see that self-acceptance does not lead to self-indulgence
but to strength and self-reliance.

Pay attention to how you feel before you take action. . . .
Move with your heart, not your head.
Face fear when you feel *ready*, not when you feel guilty.

YOU DON'T NEED A THOUSAND WAYS TO SUCCEED

I've recently had the thought that improving myself was kind of like "I'm proving myself, proving that I can do the things I'm not good at." Maybe that's not where I want to put my energy.

A JOURNAL ENTRY

What should I do first? Should I focus on networking or visualizing success or creating a website or finishing the eight thousand projects I've started? I feel like a piece of honey on the ground being swarmed by ants. Details peck at me and guilt decays my bones. More ants pile upon me and soon I can't even see the sky. I can't feel anything sweet anymore and I have no energy. This isn't the life of living my dreams.

A JOURNAL ENTRY

There's a jungle of success strategies out there: e-courses, programs, quick tips, surefire techniques, and little-known secrets, so little known, by the way, that they're broadcast all over the Internet. It's easy to feel like a child on a busy street in New York City, not knowing which way to turn, sirens screaming, vendors hawking, horns honking, and thousands of focused people rushing by you. Relax. Ignore the hysteria and hoopla and listen to the hum of all you know inside.

Creating the work you love is not a path of doing everything right.
Creating the work you love is a path of doing everything right—for you.

I listened as Carol, a friendly web traffic guru, "a dynamo" a friend recommended, babbled on about establishing an Internet presence, marketing campaigns, and other avenues to succeed. She was trying to help me. "It's easy," she said, then plunged into garble speak. I watched her mouth move and her perfect little teeth glint as she gushed on about the right steps to take. But her suggestions cost more cash, time, and drive than I had in my emotional budget. I tried to nod my head and not look too much as though I'd just seen the end of the world. I felt sick. Secretly, I had wanted her to say, "Hey, you're just so darn cute, you don't have to do anything at all!" Or maybe something like, "Just push this paper from one side of the desk to the other," you know, something I could finesse and maybe even, well, *later*, have a film crew document for others. But instead, I left with piled slabs of concrete in my arms and a map of a trail that scaled a mountain.

It's not uncommon for the most ambitious people to feel the most frustrated. My friend Rich and I sat at the South End Bistro. "I have so many things to do and I keep falling behind on things," he says. He assaults the pasta on his plate. "You are doing so much, though," I remind him. "Yeah, but I can't do all the stuff I *need* to do," he says. He tells me about his lists of marketing tasks and all the informational e-books he has loaded on his computer. He is under siege with information. Ambition beats a drum in his mind as soon as he wakes and when he tries to sleep. Rich checks the NFL scores on the computer or plays solitaire into the night. I can see why procrastination has become a sweet and treacherous friend. Creating the work he loves is now a nonstop obligation and imprisonment.

Information will often kill inspiration. You can bury yourself alive in the best intentions. Please put down that crazy shovel. Doing the work you love is not meant to be exhausting and complicated. Stay light. Stay breezy.

Pick one or two strategies that feel natural to you and ignore the rest. Yes, I said that. Ignore the rest. When you have a rocket ship, you don't need a thousand rowboats. Sweetheart, you're an astronaut. You have Houston at your back.

Sometimes your "rocket ship" is so natural to you that you don't think it counts. I once had a marketing expert sit down with me to strategize my business. "What's worked for you in the past? How have you gotten business so far?" she asked. I told her that I taught classes at an adult education center. I told her that whenever I did public speaking, people recommended me to other organizations, or sent their friends to workshops, or called to hire my coaching. "Well, then do more of what works," she said calmly. "Don't worry about networking, getting publicity, or increasing your web presence right now. Just start speaking more." I looked at her blankly. I had wanted some edgy, fast-track, breakthrough approach, something hot, new, and different. "I don't want to make you different," she said. "I want to find what effortlessly works for you." I'm sure my mouth hung open. I'm sure I wanted to ask her if she did relationship counseling, or if maybe she felt like getting married.

Years later I met a very financially stable and happy graphic artist who had run her own business for over twenty years. I asked her how she found her clients. She smiled coyly, and I knew somehow I wasn't going to hear about leads groups or advertising campaigns. "I realized long ago that I hated marketing," she said. "But I also knew I loved creating dinner parties. So I throw dinner parties here and there and I tell my guests that I'm looking for new projects. It's weird, but it works for me."

In her book *Work Less, Make More*, Jennifer White, a business expert and syndicated columnist, writes about how most people try to get too much done. She suggests picking a maximum of three important focuses. "Spend 80 percent of your time on the three most important activities that will bring you the greatest results." Yes, there's always so much more you could be doing. But "the more" comes out of insecurity, superstition, some kind of vestigial belief in entrepreneurial original sin, and definitely from "trying to make it happen." I want you to create a life that you could not make happen. This isn't about your industriousness. It's about your consciousness. It's about having the courage to trust that you have your own inspired success strategy.

"Purple people don't wear gray suits." It was a punch-drunk line that shot up in my journal one day when I'd been having a glacial meltdown with myself. I'd been trying to wheedle myself into being a marketing harlot with a cheeky bulldozer personality, something I naturally assumed would boost sales. I told myself that I was looking into this sadistic strategy because it was time to conquer my white-bellied weaknesses. That actually sounded reasonable. But later I realized that even if it was reasonable, which it damn well wasn't, I wasn't on a "reasonable" path. Being "reasonable" and "on fire" are two different tracks. I've created the work I love by obeying my own wild guidance. When I've tried to play it safe or realistic, by popular criteria, anyway, I was not inspired and guided. I was tired.

See, on the inspired success track, conventional strategies are usually about as useful to you as damp confetti. You are an agent of original genius coaxing atoms into form, following an intelligence that exceeds the limits of your mind, training, and evolutionary perspective. There are no statistics on the miraculous. It's not predictable or uniform. Business-people say, "I don't want to reinvent the wheel." Yet wild success is all about idiosyncratic innovation. It's about discovering your own footprints in an emerging world. It's about writing your own ticket.

Many alternatively oriented, brilliant individuals inhibit big results, inexplicable dexterity, and prophetic timing by trying to work "according to the world." I call it pulling down the kite—instead of letting flight uproot all obstacles. Laura, a coaching client of mine, birthed a remarkable idea over popcorn and Merlot with some friends for a web-based greeting card company. They brainstormed and shrieked with excitement, taking down notes and sketches through the night. When Laura shared the ideas with her husband, a very successful executive, he put on his business hat and grilled her. The suits took over the party.

He started talking about profit shares and loans and asking her to graph things out. She stumbled on her words, the sketches wilted in her hands, a thousand magical ideas flitted off like startled birds, and she felt cold, frightened, and naive inside. The jolly genius of the night before abandoned her throne and ran out of sight. Her husband was just trying to help. But it was the wrong paradigm. He thought that if she couldn't answer some hard-core linear business questions, she would obviously fail in the marketplace. But just because she didn't have linear answers didn't mean she didn't have power. She had her own ride to the store.

Renee started her life coaching business because she loved helping people speak their truth. She hired a marketing person to grow her business. "She pounded it into my head that I needed to know my target audience. I needed to have a value proposition. I started getting more self-conscious and way less creative. I hated it," she says. "All the defining and targeting took me right out of the spell. I lost the feeling of having fun." Renee continued, "It's my passion that attracted clients to begin with." When Renee stopped enjoying her business and started focusing on "building her business" instead, she thought she was being responsible. But her bottom line collapsed with her joy. "I realized then that I had to do what made me happy. It's my happiness that sold my clients, not my slogans and brochures."

Joe is the president of a multimillion-dollar publishing house. I talked to him about success, over lunch in SoHo. He is a visionary, and also a master of the bottom line. He told me that one quarter he studied all the "how to be a success" books and started making systematic decisions based on them. "I had the worst sales that quarter," he said, and laughed. "Then I chucked the books and ultimately followed my gut and passion, what made me do this work in the first place. You'll love this. My sales doubled." I do love it. It makes sense to me. Purple people *can't* wear gray suits. The traditional "fast track" is the inspired person's dead end. I am not saying you can't use strategies that have worked for others. I am saying that you can't use strategies that don't excite you.

Remember, sustained passion always beats a program. Let go of "the right way" to do things and follow your automatic strength and involuntary joy and direction. The Universe has a billion ways to succeed. And you have the authority of a way that works for you. Ditch the oars and fly. Houston, we have launch.

INSPIRED SUCCESSISMS

Relax. Ignore the hysteria and hoopla,
and listen to the hum of all you know inside.

Creating the work you love is not a path of doing everything right.
Creating the work you love is a path of doing everything right—for you.

When you have a rocket ship, you don't need a thousand rowboats.

Yes, there's always so much more you could be doing.
But "the more" comes out of insecurity, superstition . . .
and definitely from "trying to make it happen."
I want you to create a life that you could not make happen.

This isn't about your industriousness. It's about your consciousness.
It's about having the courage to trust that you have
your own inspired success strategy.

Many alternatively oriented, brilliant individuals inhibit big results,
inexplicable dexterity, and prophetic timing
by trying to work "according to the world."
I call it pulling down the kite, instead of letting flight uproot the obstacles.

Purple people *can't* wear gray suits.
The traditional "fast track" is the inspired person's dead end.

The Universe has a billion ways to succeed.
And you have the authority of a way that works for you.

YOU WILL FALL,
BUT YOU CAN'T FAIL

Okay, spirit, I am willing to take your hand. I don't know when the timing should be. I don't know what this should look like. I know you love me and want me to blossom inside my soul. I know you've reminded me that I don't need to push the waves or blow on the wind. I need to relax. When I am struggling I am trying to force something too small. So help me get out of the way.

A JOURNAL ENTRY

I have to be willing to accept the outcome I don't want. If I am at peace with the unacceptable outcome, I'm free. No investment, no weights. No weight, no barriers. Then the divine can rip right through like the notes of a trumpet.

A JOURNAL ENTRY

Y ou can't claw your way to *inspired* success. There's no platinum ladder to a grand slam on this path. In fact, I think there's a lounge chair. And it's mandatory. In other words, you have to chill out. You have to approach this life a little bit more like a well-fed basset hound and less like the new guy on the SWAT team. You have to be *free* to succeed. Let go of proving, striving, panting, and always, always, *always* needing to win. You may have to let things go awry while still belting out love songs to yourself as though everything is fine, because it is. What I'm saying is this: To be free to succeed, stay with me here, you have to be free to fail—at times.

All right, so every kitchen-table shaman, savvy business coach, hip therapist, and anyone who's worth their salt in the burgeoning human potential movement will tell you to chase your heart and "to let go of your attachment to the outcome." It's one of those sayings that's passed around like bread at the dinner table. It's one of those sayings that can drive you nuts when you're mashing your stomach muscles, and needing your outcome like a strung-out addict just might "prefer" a trough of crack. How do you "have no attachment" in how things turn out when you're plunging your life, blood, credibility, and child's college money, not to mention the possibility of your next meal, into these shining dreams? Well now, that's a tidy little question.

One evening, just a few months after *This Time I Dance!* had been in bookstores, I realized I was no longer in a buoyant—newly published— "come what may" mood. Instead, as I thought about trickling book sales, I felt like I had a thin dagger in my heart and was spurting life fluids, while writing chirpy e-mail responses to my lone ten readers. I wanted success. No, I *needed* success. Let's just say I was breathing hot, rank breath down its glittering golden neck. I was like a desperate girlfriend calling her cheating boyfriend's answering machine for the fortieth time, "just saying hi," in way too high a voice. I really did want to be casual and trusting and visualize world peace no matter what happened on this path, but frankly that was just way beyond my ambitious, covetous, and wired personality.

I felt like a *loser*. Yes, that was the ripping sensation in my heart. My book was only in a scattering of bookstores. The major chains had stopped stocking it on shelves. It wasn't selling quickly enough and "the machine" had spit it out. Meanwhile, I saw other, and might I add in my humble, nonjudgmental opinion, lesser, ridiculous books taking their unwarranted place on the red carpet of life, enjoying gushing reviews in national magazines, radio spots, and privileged placement in window displays.

So how did putting my passion and contribution into the world turn me into feeling like a loser? I took this question into my small green meditation room. I sat and squirmed with the feeling until an insight hit me. Finally, I understood I'd been focused on the wrong thing all along. I'd glossed over my wildly adoring fan mail and new speaking opportunities. Friends and colleagues remarked on how often I discredited the sweet spots, the building momentum and increased income, and made every accomplishment seem pygmy-size and unremarkable. It was true. I kept a relentless gaze on my empty nets. I wasn't focused on the joy of succeeding, even one little bit. I was obsessed with *not failing*.

Just in case you might not know this, fear of failing creates hardened arteries, soul damage, headaches, traffic jams on the astral planes, and barriers to good of every kind. It is not the recommended course of action here. It's kind of hard to stay open to the nuances of genius, sideways opportunities, and the joyride of it all, when you're focused on the shopping list of what you didn't get. You also get more of what you think about, go figure. A part of me didn't trust in my ultimate success, so the breeze of the butterfly wings in the garden could set me on edge and make me think another speaking opportunity had fallen through. This vigilant part of myself always found reasons to believe in imminent danger because that's what it looked for, shopped for, visualized, and found. The problem wasn't what was happening outside of me. It was a teensy-weensy dire problem of mental focus.

Most inspirational teachings urge us to focus on the result we want, not the circumstances that we do not want. Because I was terrified of failing, I found myself unconsciously erecting shrines and altars to disillusionment. I made my disappointments more real than my progress. I had my success strategy backwards, like playing a game of chess, plotting possibilities in the wrong direction. Ernest Holmes, the spiritual founder of the Science of Mind tradition, taught that when we find ourselves facing unpleasant circumstances, we need to "drop the undesired thing from our thought, forgive ourselves, and start anew." He continues, "More and more we will come to see that a great cosmic plan is being worked out, and that all we have to do is lend ourselves to it." But see, that's the thing. We don't know there's a cosmic plan because we're busy. We're busy trying to manage things, manufacture results, get things under control, and snag the gold every single time so that *then* we can relax and trust the journey.

"You have to learn to fall before you can fly," said the bronzed ski instructor in a beginners' ski class. The memory flashed before me in my meditation room. This demigod could certainly scram down a mountain. His philosophy sounded Zen-like and expansive—that is, until I imagined the shattered bones, body cast, and little bland green peas rolling around on my hospital dinner tray. I'm not doing the peas, I thought. So I ignored his noble instruction and skidded down the mountain like a mummy in a scarf, supple as a flagpole. I watched other skiers cascade past me like twigs on a river. My muscles throbbed with vigilance. I slid in every direction and fell hard and, to my horror, more often. Eventually, and painfully, I understood that it was safer to relax and fall than to try to prevent all falls. In skiing as in life, there will be falls. They don't mean a thing. And the more you relax, the more alert power and energy you have to negotiate success. I love the Japanese proverb that defines success: "Fall down seven times. Get up eight."

So that night in my meditation room, I give myself some breathing room on this path. I decide to focus on enjoying my experience rather than treating it like a virus in need of containment. I also undertake the unthinkable. I give myself permission to "fail," as necessary, in my business. It's the only way to proceed. I can't hold back the sea. I can't prevent the rain. I need to allow the natural to occur and I don't know what every single outcome needs to be. I let go of the need for constant reassurance. I free myself from a control-junkie mentality. I know I won't be in a situation where each effort instantly takes off, all horizons deliver, every market wants me, clients stay forever, and Oprah begs me to come over to dinner, *nightly*. This is an inspired life path and I will allow the creative energy to grow and develop and assume the matrix it needs to take.

Sometime later, I wrote myself a "permission to dare" statement. Here's part of it:

I am willing to respect and advocate myself no matter
how my work is initially received; I know I will grow in strength,
clarity, and magnetism as I go along.
I am willing to focus on all that is going right, explore more of
what is going right, and talk a lot about what is going right.
So much is going right.
I am willing to partner with a dynamic, intelligent force that I do not control.
I am willing to recognize that I do not know how or
when my destiny needs to unfold.
I am willing to give things breathing room and know that nothing can stop
the power of my soul aligned with the Power of a Brilliant Universe.
I am willing to remember that every disappointment is a misperception and
is nothing compared to the trauma of not daring my dreams at all.
I am a huge success already, because I am on this path,
dedicated to this evolution, growing continuously,
giving myself more love, and moving in the right direction.
I am succeeding just by being on this journey.

It's fun to let go. It's fun to be free. It's fun to go through life with mindfulness and receptivity instead of ulcers, gas masks, directions to the nearest soup kitchens, and suspicion. I can't even describe how astounding it is to stop attacking yourself at every turn and to start being open to the moment, a capable cosmic plan, and the expanding adventure of soul-inspired success.

Go ahead. Lose a client, a contract, or a contest. But do not lose sight of all the good that you have already experienced, and the knowing that you are meant to complete what you came here to do. Trust your inevitable success and let the good, and only the good, times roll.

INSPIRED SUCCESSISMS

You can't claw your way to *inspired* success.

To be free to succeed, stay with me here,
you have to be free to fail—at times.

It's kind of hard to stay open to the nuances of genius,
sideways opportunities, and the joyride of it all,
when you're focused on the shopping list of what you didn't get.

Most inspirational teachings urge us to focus on the result we want,
not the circumstances that we do not want.

We don't know there's a cosmic plan because we're busy . . .
trying to manage things, manufacture results, get things under control . . .
so that *then* we can relax and trust the journey.

Eventually, and painfully, I understood that it was safer to relax and fall
than to try to prevent all falls.

I know I won't be in a situation where each effort instantly takes off,
all horizons deliver, every market wants me. . . .
This is an inspired life path and I will allow the creative
energy to . . . assume the matrix it needs to take.

I am succeeding just by being on this journey.

3.

MOJO MASTERY: WORKING THE INSPIRED WAY

Now, I know you think the path of inspired co-creation is when the Universe does everything you want, like, maybe a good virtual assistant. Then again, you're the one who's suffering, so you can't be right.

So here's another option. Stop trying to control the rain. Love is what makes this train roll, baby, not just action. Love everything or go home. No amount of work puts the flutter in a butterfly's wings. Things move when you're moved. If nothing astounding is happening through you, it's not going to happen to you.

Here's how co-creation really works. Slow down, ditch agendas, and cruise into the connected zone. Now, let's talk about going places. . . .

YOUR FANTASY IS IN THE WAY
OF THE FANTASTIC

The trick is to keep exploring and not bail out, even when we find out something is not what we thought. That's what we're going to discover again and again and again. Nothing is what we thought. I can say this with great confidence.

PEMA CHÖDRÖN, *WHEN THINGS FALL APART*

Appreciate the moment and give it everything you have. That's the secret. Our minds will tell us, oh but this circumstance isn't that great. Our minds work in terms of big deals, small deals, good, bad, right and wrong. The heart works with now, only now. The heart does not evaluate. It connects and transforms the space.

A JOURNAL ENTRY

Every now and then my clients find their "doing the work they love" journey going south of mayhem and haywire. It's not. It's just that their fantasies of perfection are based on, how should I say, a control freak's über-tiny menu of preferences. See, their inner chef may not have gotten around much, may favor only chives, or may be missing a few ingredients in his kitchen, head, or heart. Their "ideal" circumstances may not be inspired ones. From where they stand, they may not know how to dream a higher dream.

Fortunately, the inspired life will have its way with you, and leave you sautéed, curried, and astonished in the end. It will ignore your scripts, show up unannounced, expose your wounds so you can heal them, and rearrange the scenery. It will rearrange *you*. Just consider it a bit of divine madness, an Artist in ecstatic frenzy, splattering lime green over your cherished still life. It's not a mistake, an accident, or a devastation. It's part of co-creation. This life is alive. It's going to call you to be a shaman in every situation, knowing nothing is ordinary or casual. Let go of your trifling fantasies, demands, and tiring expectations. Enter the fantastic.

I remember Susan, who saw me for a relationship issue, and who struggled with the loss of a whirlwind love affair, but most of all with the loss of her idea of how this part of her life would all turn out. She sat on my couch, cried, and blew her raw pink nose again. "He had no right to say those things to me," she said. "He said he wanted to spend his life with me, and I thought this is why I was single for so long." I handed over the tissue box. "'This was so meant to be,' he said." They'd popped corks and stopped time. Then he stopped the movie, did a 180, and moved to Oakland to be closer to his really needy, not-really-blond ex-wife. That was meant to be as well.

In our careers, we have romantic ideas, too, the dark chocolate and cherry stories, great yellow balloons that coast through a cloudless blue sky, wine and cheese, and throngs of customers and followers depositing their life savings into ours. We see the "perfect" picture. Some of us have even built it into business plans or visualized, affirmed, treasure-mapped, paid psychics to tell us the minute details, and written about it for years. But then, things don't go the way we dreamed.

Your daughter has an emotional crisis, or doctors say a chemical imbalance. Your car breaks down, your computer crashes, and your checkbook is imbalanced. Reality stomps in with thick mud on its boots, rejects your novel, or your one great client takes her business elsewhere. Right about now, you may just want to join a cult, take up a new hobby like drinking, run off with the guy behind the deli counter, who either has a tic or who always winks at you with the left side of his face, or take a nap in an abandoned grotto for at least eight hundred years. But I'm going to ask you to trust your life—more than your script.

You are always where you need to be. It's not like the Universe dropped your call. Your wise eternal inner self didn't fall asleep at the wheel or start playing for the other team. You're still plugged into power and flow. But the experience before you doesn't look like *your idea* of bliss, grace, or any ride at the circus you've ever heard of. You take your marbles and go home. You stop treating this moment as though it's precious. You rage against this circumstance, this life, and everything coming down the pike forevermore. Your tantrum gets in the way of your birth. Closing your heart is your only problem. Closing your heart stops the deluge of everything you desire.

I understand that this moment may seem like annihilation to you, but it's only to the small self. I promise you—it's not a pathetic movie made in the basement of a student director who is clearly on his way to becoming a sociopath. You are still loved and every situation has purpose. Try not to shut down. Your response to the scene creates your movie. Your response will determine who you become in this life.

Years ago I did a hiking and inspired living class and I had a healthy number of people registered for the event. But on the day of the hike, I got a flurry of surprise cancellations. Out of nowhere, droves of people decided they couldn't come. It was like some kind of plague. Someone had a flat. Someone had a stomachache. Someone had a visitation from the mother ship the night before. I don't know. I can't even remember all the sudden causes and reasons. There was such an avalanche of them. Of course I took the news like a professional and murmured some encouraging sentiments. I stayed reassuring and enchanting on the phone. I did not once call them liars, scaredy-cats, or losers, despite what the lunatic in my head politely suggested. But after each call, I hung up and cried.

This wasn't the day I wanted. I had been preparing for a huge gathering of people, a chance to teach to the masses, or at least a full class, and also, finally, fatten up my anemic bank account. I felt sabotaged by the Universe, as though I'd been getting ready to sink into a honey milk bath, and found myself easing into Dead Sea brine instead. In just minutes, I went from bubbles to bones, and you know how that goes. "Yeah, just think about the money you could have made," whined the lunatic in me. "You should call those people up and see if their toddler really has the flu." Fortunately, I hustled my sad mind into meditation instead. From a more centered place, I decided to let the day I had planned dissolve into the day that *was* planned, the tide of occurring events. I opened my heart to myself, and then to the circumstances that lay before me. I resolved, with everything I had, to walk forward in love, or at least not to spit.

Let me tell you, a strange thing happened on that hike. Only five participants showed up. Every one of them was a woman. Every one of them was a woman wearing a purple T-shirt, including me. And on that clear and sunny day in the cedar-fragranced mountains, one woman felt safe enough to begin to grieve a recent death in her life, and the rest of us instinctively circled around her like medicine women holding back the wind and inviting her voice. That day on the mountain, we the chosen ones had a deep, raw, and otherworldly experience, and it was clear to me that we had been destined to be there and the others absolutely needed to clear away. During that entire hike, I could see the hand of a Great Love, impeccable, unpredictable, and sacred. Obviously, this day had never been about having a well-attended class. It was about encountering an original, alive, anointed experience and the honor of serving with grace.

I invite you to live a life of being called. Make the decision to show up for every moment. Make the decision to be alive for it all, and let Spirit decide the way it wants to move you forward. Your job is to show up as a love warrior, arms wide open and chest on fire, even when circumstances look bleak, broken, or "beneath" you. Do not be fooled by events. The

truth is always present. Everything is moving you closer to your true desires. You don't know which circumstance is the big one and which one is
small. You don't have the tools with which to measure the creativity of a
Presence that shatters and cultivates your understanding at the same
time. This chef runs a completely different kind of kitchen. Lightning
strikes where lightning strikes. Nothing follows precedent, though nothing is by accident.

When I first decided to launch my work nationally, I decided to put
everything I had into every workshop I did, no matter how many people
showed up. Once while in Sacramento, I offered a women's retreat day to
just eight women. "Woo-hoo, you're a national author now," said the belittling part of myself that thought only big crowds reflected success. But
my inspired self vowed to stir the energy wherever I planted my feet. In
my journal, it instructed: "Keep cooking up the magic even if you're in
the corner of someone's basement. Magic is magic. Where there's energy,
there's something alive."

So I showed up. I really showed up. I showed up as if it were the last day
of my life, the only day of my life, the one chance I had to offer my gift. I
showed up as though everyone there was a messenger, a healer, and a cosmic aerobics instructor sent just for me. And, this being California, practically everyone *was* a healer. I gave the best retreat I knew how to give,
spread my wings and flew. I stayed true to my calling and not to my fear.

A year later a woman called me and asked if I'd like to put on a retreat
at the world-famous Canyon Ranch, the exclusive six-star spa that attracts
celebrities the likes of Julia Roberts and Oprah. I gripped the phone
tightly. My heart began racing. This was the kind of work I longed for,
but had no clue how to go about putting in motion. This was the kind of
thing that happened to other people, accomplished people, people who,
for instance, have clean backseats in their cars, even when no one is
looking. "Ohmygodyes," is what spilled out of my mouth. It felt like an

Olympic-level teaching opportunity, a shifting tectonic plate, and a nod from central casting. This was moving into a sphere I'd barely allowed myself to dream of, without so much as moving a pinkie finger to make it happen.

And get this. The amazing long-haired woman who organized this retreat for me happened to take a women's workshop of mine. It had eight women and took place in Sacramento. "It was good that the group was as small as it was," she said. "It gave me the chance to see what you're all about." I am so grateful that I showed up instead of shut down. That small class led to world class.

Remember, you do not know what's behind any circumstance. This is a co-creative, inspired journey. It's a clarifying, mystifying, and vivifying ride. This is not a walk down Main Street. Expectations are the recommendations of the uninformed. Expectations are *your* arrows, markers, and suggestions for a trip *you've* never been on. Don't limit your flow for anything. When you're on a co-creative journey, everything is inspired. Meet all of it with love.

INSPIRED SUCCESSISMS

Let go of your trifling fantasies, demands, and tiring expectations.
Enter the fantastic.

Trust in your life—more than your script.

You are always where you need to be.
It's not like the Universe dropped your call.

Your tantrum gets in the way of your birth.
Closing your heart is your only problem.
Closing your heart stops the deluge of everything you desire.

Your response to the scene creates your movie.
Your response will determine who you become in this life.

Your job is to show up as a love warrior, arms wide open and chest on fire,
even when circumstances look bleak, broken, or "beneath" you.
Do not be fooled by events. The truth is always present.

You don't know which circumstance is the big one
and which one is small. . . .
Lightning strikes where lightning strikes.
Nothing follows precedent, though nothing is by accident.

Expectations are the recommendations of the uninformed.
Expectations are *your* arrows, markers, and suggestions
for a trip *you've* never been on.

BECOMING A MOJO MAGNET

Actions without excitement are hollow. They are empty bowls. There is no nut underneath the shell and everyone knows it. Efforts like these fall on deaf ears. Everyone can hear what's real and what's not.

A JOURNAL ENTRY

Not by might, nor by power, but by my spirit, says the Lord.

ZECHARIAH 4:6

am going to put this out there right now. The Puritans could not have led a life of wild success. Wild success is not about hard work. Just about anybody—even in a frock—can roll a rock uphill. But not everybody can rock and roll.

Here's what I know from coaching thousands of creative individuals and visionary entrepreneurs. It's all about the *mojo*. The *mojo* unleashes the electricity that turns a lamp into an obliteration of darkness and an act of God. Wild success isn't about going through the motions. It's not even about staying in motion. This isn't about your legs. It's about the light in your eyes, the fire on your tongue, and the sweep of your heart. When you're bouncing off the wall with voltage and star power, and as long as your hair looks good, nothing can withstand you for long.

So study your *mojo* meter. Here's how to pay attention. Do your actions stem from desperation or inspiration? Are you coming from fear or love? Because, dear one, where you come from is where you'll go.

Otherwise, you can take all the "right steps" and still end up in a ditch, miles from the festival and pots of gold. I witnessed this with Leslee, a conference organizer, who stomped through life in a red silk suit and lugged around a day planner that weighed more than a championship bowling ball. She produced radio spots, back-page ads, and thousands of perfect leaflets. She was insanely methodical, aggressive, and impressive in a kung-fu-meets-marketing kind of way. But Leslee wasn't on fire. She was on adrenaline.

The woman was obsessed about money and couldn't breathe, connect, or sit still for a second. I once asked her what *inspired* her about the conference. She looked as though I'd asked about her thong collection or the full, unabridged history of dodo birds. "I have no idea," she snapped. "I need to market this thing."

Leslee is one of the gurus I hold in my mind when I am tempted to think, when the sun slips behind the clouds, that I should definitely be employing more guerrilla-style tactics or "practical" actions in my business. She appears in her red suit, rips out pages from her day planner and pleats them into origami swans, and croaks, *"A thousand actions is less effective than a true connection."* In real life, Leslee blanketed an entire city with seeds. Yet nothing took. She ended up in catastrophic debt and disappointment. She taught me this: You can force actions. But you can't force attraction.

So throw out superstition in favor of inspiration. The Puritans believed in hard work to brace themselves against the devil. I want you to believe in love. I want you to believe in fun. I want you to revere the supernatural force of just being natural.

Years ago, I attended a huge holistic trade show looking to meet magazine editors, radio talk show hosts, and others who could ramp up exposure for my book. I hadn't "worked" a trade show before and I felt nervous.

I dreaded starting spontaneous conversations for completely calculated purposes. Looking around at endless aisles, I imagined everyone else signing major talk show deals, making insanely beneficial arrangements, and "pitching" their shiny little hearts out. Meanwhile, every time I even thought of showing someone my book, I felt like a carnival huckster in a scratchy, used suit, twitching under hot bright lights.

I dared some false starts, introducing myself to someone who seemed like a "connection," but it went flatly, terrible really, like meeting a rock star and singing to them, off key, and drooling with your eyes. This stargazing, crystal-carrying woman, with a bead on her third eye, looked at me like *I* was from another planet. I limped away, scarred, and bought a jumbo-size coffee. Coffee always makes me stronger.

Finally, something inside me invoked, "Relax, dear one. You will always meet the people you need to meet. You can't force connection. Follow *your* natural enthusiasm." So I decided to visit some major booths, and then drop my agenda. "Pay attention to people you feel a connection with, rather than sizing up people as connections to something else. You won't relate to anyone if *you're* not having fun," instructed my inner voice. So I decided, as an experiment, to let myself be drawn, chosen, and receptive to the next direction that stirred my attention.

Of course, this led me to shopping. For jewelry.

I beelined to a display of purple and teal fused glass earrings and sundries. The artist, a clinking, laughing, creative siren, unraveled the story of one of her designs. That led us to talking about creativity, making a living, and hormone-management issues. We didn't say anything to impress each other, and at one point I sprayed her with saliva while laughing, and she laughed harder, the universal code of marking a true friend. Later, that artist helped me get one of the most coveted speaking engagements of my career. She knew the program director of a high-powered organization. She sang my praises until the director booked me. Yes, I felt ridiculously lucky with the outcome of all this, like a Bingo winner for a night, but I have to tell you, I also felt led. There were thousands of people at that event. I walked over to the one I needed to meet. And everything was laughter.

A friend of mine and I call this phenomenon "sideways magic." It's when you take your eyes off the straight line of your perceived goal, *ahem*, obsession, and allow yourself to be present to the energy that's available. Something is always available.

Often when I teach this, students will tell me they can't just follow a flow. They say this as though I'm suggesting they chase butterflies instead of prospects. They have to make payroll, house and car payments, or they have kids in expensive schools, they say. But I'm not suggesting chucking responsibilities as much as meeting them. Dynamic energy makes money. When you feel relaxed and engaged, clients drop down out of the skies, cherry trees blossom in your wake, invisible geishas do your bidding, and the producer of the *Today* show calls, or somebody does. Joy is power. When you obsess about needing to make money or have specific results happen, you drain your concentration, stamina, and creativity, and muck up your pipeline. Life will always reflect back to you your true motivation. When you're coming from fear, people start running from it.

Fear is not a magnetic business strategy, even if you call it "getting results." I once worked with a businesswoman who told me she could teach me to sell. Her exact words: "sell like a freaking maniac," which I'm telling you, at the time, acted like an entrepreneurial aphrodisiac. If memory serves, I think I started fondling her booklet. "Mention your products after every point you make," she said. "Make them need those products more than they need their own blood." I must have winced, because the sales tycoon snapped at me, "Do you want to make money?" I was feeling small, fearful, and as soft as sea grass at the time. I nodded like a soldier.

That evening I taught a workshop with a glint in my eye. Setting up products for sale, I kicked my shyness to the curb and marched into the abundant tide pool, as a take-no-prisoners, but do take Visa and Master-

Card, business mogul. That night I smelled dollars. That night the class smelled me. While I doled out all the benefits of my offerings, spoon-fed every feature, I barely sold a book. But it was worse than that. I felt horrible, like I'd bashed someone over the head with a credit card machine when they came to me to ask for help. I wanted to apologize and buy everyone a small gift, say ten years of therapy and a car, except I couldn't even make eye contact as they left the room.

The next night I taught a different workshop. This time I abandoned all sales strategy. I chose to love the people in front of me, offer kindness and encouragement, and make forty new best friends. I wanted that classroom to be an ashram, a temple, a holy site, even though I was teaching a creative writing class in an office building after hours. I just wanted to be available to those specific individuals in that exact moment in time and see what they desired and how I might help in any way.

Of course, at the end of class I mentioned the resources I had to offer, because I cared about these individuals and I wanted them to have tools and support. But I didn't try to sell them anything. I just shared naturally because I felt safe with them and they felt safe with me. When the seminar ended, everyone just lingered. I don't think anyone wanted to leave the Shangri-la we'd created. We were pretty close to setting up a commune in the parking lot. That class bought everything I had. I sold out and took home orders to fulfill. Referrals poured in for months after.

There you have it. Take it for a test-drive. Love sells. Joy sells. Connection sells. Great energy draws abundant opportunities to you. It's just natural and inevitable. You don't have to make things happen. You invite them to happen by being available to what's already there. You're just irresistibly attractive when you're naturally attracted.

INSPIRED SUCCESSISMS

This isn't about your legs. It's about the light in your eyes,
the fire on your tongue, and the sweep of your heart.

Do your actions stem from desperation or inspiration?
Are you coming from fear or love?
Because, dear one, where you come from is where you'll go.

You can force actions. But you can't force attraction.

Pay attention to people you feel a connection with,
rather than sizing up people as connections to something else.

Joy is power. When you obsess about needing to make money
or have specific results happen,
you drain your concentration, stamina, and creativity,
and muck up your pipeline.

Life will always reflect back to you your true motivation.
When you're coming from fear, people start running from it.

Love sells. Joy sells. Connection sells.
Great energy draws abundant opportunities to you.
It's just natural and inevitable.

You don't have to make things happen.
You invite them to happen by being available to what's already there.

LOVERS SELL MORE
THAN CRITICS

*I need to stop trying to get something from the person I'm supposedly
here to give to. The customer doesn't have to be nice. They're not the
bellboy or my therapist.*

A JOURNAL ENTRY

*The rain pours on every seed and does not wait to see which daffodils
make use of the gift. The rain moves on to other buried treasures, other
hills, other gardens below the earth waiting for love. We really never
know who receives our gifts.*

A JOURNAL ENTRY

t's a tricky thing, this having a dream or a vision. By nature, we have to
at some point believe that we have the greatest thing since running
water or Google, a gift from the gods, an expression or service for mankind. But then we have to let people have *their* opinion. It's called free
will, natural selection, and joyous, abundant business practice.

You have amazing gifts to give. Still, that doesn't mean everyone can
or needs to receive them at this exact moment. Some will stare at their
shoes, even while you offer them the heart-stopping meaning of the universe, not to mention the free blender and a money-back guarantee. Some
will moan with reasons, hauling you through a gluttonous confession as
though you have a novena up your sleeve and a day pass into Heaven.

But here's what I want you to do with all the people you meet. Set them free. Love their decisions. Love their indecision. Love their spirit. Love their fear and rigidity, their skepticism, frugality, or imperfect choices. Set them free. They are not here to stuff your bank account, soothe your ego, or launch you onto the talk show circuit. Acceptance increases the chances for connection. And connection is the law of success.

I used to get frustrated when I taught workshops and participants didn't respond more: hang on my every word with dewy, grateful eyes; throw credit cards, blank checks, and gold bullions at me; or flail with ecstatic revelation. Really, a simple screaming standing ovation would have been fine. So it was a little disappointing to have some participants stare at me with nonresponsive, tired eyes. "Get a life," I'd think reactively, until I realized that maybe that's why they had signed up for my "find your passion" workshop in the first place.

Back in those days, I was "giving" with a psychic fishhook big enough to land the state of Texas. I told myself I was "giving my love to the world," but that was just bait. Really, I wanted everyone to love me, save me, and make me rich so that I could finally feel as though I deserved to have both feet in this world. It's a grabby way to do business and most people will get the message loud and clear that you need your own love, more than they need anything you have to offer.

Here's the thing. *You can't judge people and touch their souls at the same time.* You just can't spit at people on the mental airwaves and then expect them to nuzzle up to your contribution. People are funny that way. They may not even know what you said or did. But they always know how they feel around you. And just so you know, the wallet bone is connected to the heart bone.

I learned this lesson many years ago in one of my first speaking engagements. I was hired to speak to a group of engineers at Lockheed Martin. They were older men in white shirts with pocket protectors and striped ties and I felt all girly and young when I walked into the hushed conference room. I rippled with self-consciousness. No matter how professionally I dressed, I felt as though I slithered about in ruffles and glitter, maybe with a little pink tiara and a wand. I guess I just couldn't shake the fear that despite the designer black suit I wore, they'd still think, okay *know*, that I was too touchy-feely, algebraically challenged, or just *other*.

One night I was teaching a class on "Right Livelihood" and I knew I wasn't reaching these men. I felt my words rebounding off a shield of Plexiglas. They sat like stones, and I badly—though for educational purposes only—wanted to hurl huge rocks at their heads. Only it wasn't so secret. The energy in the room brewed thick and ominous like the minutes before a thunderstorm. I knew everyone could feel that strain; they knew I could feel it, too. It wasn't like I was expecting a riot to break out or anything, just because they couldn't name their life purpose. Actually, I was thinking more about one of my shadow life purposes at the time: looking good. You're going to get really negative evaluations, I thought. The achiever part of me froze.

During the break, I took some deep breaths and tried to collect myself. My inner voice, always ten steps ahead of me on the staircase of emotional evolution, said, "Give them love. Pour your love into the room." But how could I *love* them? I thought. I don't like them. They don't like me. They want to pull out their calculators and measure things and build energy chips and rocket ships. I want to live in a world of haiku and watercolor gardens and mythology. And, yeah, maybe I *do* want to wear sparkles. I wanted to run out of the building. I had closed my heart and I wanted to close the door behind me.

"Your judgment is separating you," said my inner voice. I knew the break would be ending soon and I did not want to walk back into the same room. I want to stop judging, I resolved. "I'm willing to see this situation differently," I carefully chanted inside myself. Really, because on top of everything else, I didn't want to be seen as talking to myself out loud now. Immediately, I felt this softening inside. In a flash of insight, I no longer fixated on the engineers' lack of enthusiasm, but instead recognized their courage.

It dawned on me that many of these men had been working at the same job for more than twenty years. This one career had been their mainline of self-esteem and identity. Naturally, a class on reinventing yourself at this stage of the game might be daunting and uncomfortable. Still, they were taking notes. I felt moved by their curiosity and guts.

Then something else struck me. I remembered how in the "you're on a desert island and can do anything" exercise we'd done together, many of them had wanted to be helpful. Some wanted to build bridges and others wanted to purify the water and devise storage systems. I smiled to myself as I glimpsed their souls' desire to contribute. Before I had looked at these interests with disdain, hoping to hear that someone wanted to write a novel, for God's sake, or belt out a solo on Broadway. But now I saw how similar we were. We were all about the business of making our world an even better place.

After the break, I spoke to the class with respect and appreciation and soon the room buzzed with questions, brainstorming, gales of laughter, and breakthroughs. That night I got glowing reviews about my teaching, but I took home the biggest lesson: Judgment begets judgment, and love begets love.

I saw this same dynamic again while walking through the Pike Place Market on a Thursday afternoon. This time I was the consumer. At one of the stalls, I tried on a purple wool hat that had stolen my heart. A small Asian woman, obviously the proud mother of the hat, clucked at me for putting it on with the flower on the side. She called me over, and then shoved the flower to the front, the "right way" to wear the hat. I felt hot and unglued inside, as though someone had finally clued in that I really don't know how to wear hats and that maybe, in general, I am embarrassing myself in more moments than I know.

You might think she was neutrally suggesting another way to wear the hat. Oh, but not with that energy. This was militant. She shook her head, and it was clear she would have to call upon the ancestors for purification, just to avoid the nightmares of having seen that hat worn inappropriately. The woman didn't speak a word of English to me, but I felt yelled at. I gave her back her hat, fled her booth, and took my money with me. Hey, I never said I'm the most grounded human being out there. But neither are your customers.

Later that day at the Pike Place Market, I walked by a thin young man with stringy blond hair playing the guitar. He was singing the ABC song to a toddler in a blue stroller. "ABCDEFG, now I know my ABCs," he sang, with such joy and purity that, though I am an honors graduate of Harvard Law School, I felt ridiculously proud at that moment to know my ABCs. Then he invited everyone within earshot to join in his genuine delight. "Come on, everybody, sing," he called out, and as I walked down the market singing "ABCDEFG," my voice was joined by a large Hispanic woman singing, and then a man and a woman singing and smiling at me as they strolled by.

I marveled at this far-reaching magic. This young man had adults singing their ABCs on a Thursday in a fish market. And we all felt sort of like we belonged to each other in that shared moment, and to a bigger, sweeter community that we had just remembered. Everything in life felt better. This is the power of love. I wanted to stuff his guitar case with as much money as I could, because I was so grateful for the love and exhilaration that came through him. His generosity of spirit called forth mine.

That brief encounter with the ABC crooner confirmed something I've come to understand about doing the work we love and offering it to others. It's not enough to just love our vision or our art or our service. It's our job to extend our love, *to stay in our hearts*, offer ourselves unconditionally, and benefit humanity, one encounter at a time.

This is the secret of abundance. We don't infuse our gifts with the impoverished energies of obligation, resentment, or desperation. We don't decide who needs to receive what we have to offer or when they need it. We give with grace. We give with fullness. We give with gratitude for our gifts and for this life and for every single human being who walks this earth. We stay connected to the highest frequency possible and it shines through our eyes. Laurence Boldt says, "The wealth of the Universe comes to you through people. No matter what kind of work you do, you are in the people business."

Besides, stay with me here, we're not worried about where our seeds land. We know that we will be received by all the right people in the right time. The world is hungry for our gifts.

INSPIRED SUCCESSISMS

Here's what I want you to do with all the people you meet. Set them free.
Love their decisions. Love their indecision. Love their spirit.
Love their fear and rigidity, their skepticism, frugality,
or imperfect choices. Set them free.

Acceptance increases the chances for connection.
And connection is the law of success.

Most people will get the message loud and
clear that you need your own love,
more than they need anything you have to offer.

You can't judge people and touch their souls at the same time.

Judgment begets judgment, and love begets love.

It's not enough to just love our vision or our art or our service.
It's our job to extend our love, to stay in our hearts,
offer ourselves unconditionally, and benefit humanity,
one encounter at a time.

This is the secret of abundance.
We don't infuse our gifts with the impoverished energies
of obligation, resentment, or desperation.
We don't decide who needs to receive what
we have to offer or when they need it.

We're not worried about where our seeds land.
We know that we will be received by all the right people in the right time.
The world is hungry for our gifts.

YOU WILL HAVE YOUR PEOPLE

The truth reverberates and will always be discovered. Gurus "market" from caves in foreign lands. Truth and power travels fast.

A JOURNAL ENTRY

For others do I wait ... for higher ones, stronger ones, more triumphant ones, merrier ones, for such as are built squarely in body and soul: laughing lions must come.

FRIEDRICH NIETZSCHE

Chances are that if you're doing something different with your life, you can feel like the odd duck out, a very odd duck out with peacock feathers, though all the rage with therapists. Mavericks are misfits. But of course, what makes you different can also make you exceptional. You may stand alone. But you will call your own. Become an invitation, a lighthouse, a leader, and a pioneer. If you fit into your own skin, you don't need to fit in. You will have your people.

I remember years ago trying to find a way to package my workshops and talks for corporate America. Betsy, a corporate trainer, had generously agreed to coach me over lunch. Within seconds, I felt that old familiar "I am a weed in the garden of life" feeling, and I knew I didn't click with my new perfectly coiffed business mentor. Instead of gobbling up her information, I choked on my salad. "Damn it, this is where the money is," said a demanding voice in my head, hoping I would finally lie prostrate before this woman's feet, or at least take decent notes. But I felt irritated and bored trying to figure out ways to change myself. I tapped my feet under the table with salsa rhythms, and tried to imagine what Ms. Power Beige would look like in a Guatemalan poncho, a nose ring, and dreadlocks. It was that or drink.

I couldn't help it. The woman was velvet-voiced and condescending. She spoke as though every word was plucked from Mount Olympus, though I found her to be a little bit more like slick processed cheese than all that. See, Betsy wore the standard-issue beige outfit and chunky onyx jewelry from the socially acceptable outlet store, which, I'm going to bet, looked just like that on the mannequin, when Betsy knew she had to have it. Her hand gestures were choreographed, and her words painfully manicured. Really, I wanted to throw this woman into a river, into an ice-cold shocking breath of nature. I wanted to say, "Wake up. Be real. And go easy on the trite sayings." But then, Bullet-Point Betsy was making thousands of dollars telling people, in packaged presentations, "how to love their life," and I was here, hating mine. Besides, the woman had come here to help me, and she did look kind of cute, in a Barbie-goes-to-the-office-and-becomes-VP kind of way.

Truth is, I was jealous and threatened. I envied her ability to find an easy place in the known world, a label, a ticket, a nice three-lane highway that proceeded directly into her bank account. She was a corporate trainer and business consultant with a brand, a logo, and something she could say with a straight face, over a martini at a party. For lack of any better term, I was a career and "life coach," heaven help us all, and someone who was trekking through a swamp, hunting for meaning and a definition, a niche, and even just a trace of market share. Betsy took off for her next appointment and I whipped out my journal and wrote: "I feel deflated and sick."

"You will have your people," said the steady voice of my guidance. *Yeah,* I think to myself, *all seven of them in the world. Oh, wait, they're weird like me, so they can't pay me.* I couldn't help but feel like the runt black lamb in a herd of white cows. I hadn't asked to be different. I wasn't consciously making a statement. I wanted to fit in at the ranch and have direct access to the easy chow. But I knew I couldn't trade my spirit for a corral. It's not that I wasn't willing to learn new ways to reach new audiences. It's just that I couldn't stay on fire with what didn't excite me. I could adjust, but certain compromises would compromise my stamina. I hadn't asked to be different, but I had answered to it. I had committed to never ignoring my spirit again. I finally believed, or was determined to believe, that some-how, some way, this great vast Universe could provide a place for me.

It takes stubborn originality to make it as an artist, entrepreneur, in-novator, or change agent of any kind. You are a channel for inspiration, a new artery of the extraordinary, and it's your role to tend, trust, and birth this expression, not to deny it, twist it, or make it seem like everything else. It's not like anything else. And that would be the point.

Thank God, integrity isn't just good for the soul. It's also great for your pocketbook, and I, for one, just love it when that happens. Michael Port, author of *Book Yourself Solid,* urges entrepreneurs to avoid choosing their target market based solely on logic, or what they think will make more money. When his clients have done this, he says, "The end result is that they're bored, frustrated, and struggling to book themselves." He says, "If you're not passionate about what you're doing . . . if it doesn't have mean-ing to you, you are not going to devote the time and energy required to be successful, and you'll never, in a million years, be able to convince people in your target market that you're the best person to help them."

You may fear what you will lose by not fitting in. Yet there is great abun-dance you can lose *by* fitting in. I remember sitting on a plane next to a large woman who was a hard-core pro-life, hates-Muslims-Jews-and-gays, Bible-thumping kind of gal. The moment we left the ground, she asked me if I liked flying, but I knew this was foreplay and that we were heading toward Scripture. When she talked about Jesus, she sounded like a thirteen-year-old girl talking about a rock star coming to town. Ever the people-pleaser at that time in my life, I casually and even eagerly nodded my head, and had a little fabricated bonding time with the chatty Fundamentalist. She beamed at me with brotherly love, and hoped we'd be roommates in Heaven. I just didn't bother to tell her I was Jewish, unmarried, and having lots of sex.

Then I noticed the man sitting next to her, a delightful-looking soul with bright blue eyes and a worn backpack and a literary novel, just my type of yummy human being. He probably wrote poetry, ran eight businesses, and worked for humanitarian causes when he wasn't meditating and reading Rumi. Naturally, he did not agree with the intolerant evangelist between us, and politely and exquisitely said what I wish I would have said. I wanted to scatter rose petals at his feet, and even give him my extra package of airline salted peanuts. He was one of my own. But I lost that opportunity to know him. For years afterward, I wondered what I had sacrificed in that casual betrayal of my integrity.

Follow your calling. People will tell you it's dangerous to walk out on the edge. But baby, it's dangerous to stay in the middle. Find your true, inviolate voice. You have a power in you that is not of this world. That power will awaken the creativity and resourcefulness of other people, people you don't even know yet, people you may not even know you want to know, people who can get things done. You will have your people.

When I wrote *This Time I Dance!* I left a prestigious legal career, my identity, and everything that had originally had value to me. Maybe that's what gave me the courage, when writing, to ignore the trends and follow my instincts. Some literary agents urged me to position the book as memoir. Others advised cutting the personal stories, doing more research, and conforming to the formulaic self-help market. These tracks sounded sensible to me, but sensible, as in wearing thick-soled shoes or listening to an actuary do a lecture on annuities. I wanted to write another kind of book. It burned within me, though I could find no label for it or marketable track. I wasn't writing to wedge myself into a category, but to answer a hunger, name a storm, and find my way to oxygen. Finally, I ignored the industry and leaped into the fire.

You know the rest of this story, but I have to say it again, because I want you to know "you will have your people," and they will hook you up when the time comes. Having worked up the guts to self-publish the book I needed to write, a former publicist at a large New York publishing house found it and connected with the work so deeply, she recommended an unknown writer to a major publishing house. She heard the same call I did. Maybe it's everything that the new physics and the old mystics have been saying all along. Like energies attract one another on the cosmic grid, linked at the heart, soul, profit centers, and crossroads of destiny.

Then the big publisher e-mailed, asking big, scary, big-publisher questions, about previous sales of the self-published book, as in bald statistics and no adjectives. My partner, Paul, and I stared at cases of unopened books. "We need better numbers," said Paul. My usually Zen-calm partner sounded a little like he might need to breathe into a paper bag. "You need to get out there and sell like a freak," said a friend in marketing, mincing words, she told me later. The situation suddenly required bomb specialists. My big dream was about to detonate. The miraculous connection couldn't hold. The facts would do us in. Then something came over me I will never forget.

"It's not about the numbers," I said, as though speaking in a different voice, I'm thinking the kind of voice Moses used just before he parted the Red Sea and got his Grauman's Chinese Theatre star in Bible history. "If this is my publisher, they will connect with the power of the work." Then I said it again for myself, because, believe me, I was hearing it as much as I was saying it: "*My* publisher will connect with the *energy* of this book and my energy, my fire." And that is exactly what happened. The publishing house moved quickly, responding to something other than our lukewarm facts. Somehow it seemed ordained, natural, alive, and complete.

Somerset Maugham says, "Almost all the people who've had the most effect on me, I seem to have met by chance, yet looking back it seems as though I couldn't but have met them. It's as if they were waiting there to be called upon when I needed them." Your people are out there. Stay true to what lights you up, and those who have work to do with you can find you, even when it's dark.

INSPIRED SUCCESSISMS

Mavericks are misfits.
But of course, what makes you different can also make you exceptional.

If you fit into your own skin, you don't need to "fit in."
You will have your people.

It's not that I wasn't willing to learn new ways to reach new audiences.
It's just that I couldn't stay on fire with what didn't excite me.

I hadn't asked to be different, but I had answered to it.
I had committed to never ignoring my spirit again.

You are a channel for inspiration, a new artery of the extraordinary,
and it's your role to tend, trust, and birth
this expression, not to deny it . . .
or make it seem like everything else. It's not like anything else.

People will tell you it's dangerous to walk out on the edge.
But baby, it's dangerous to stay in the middle.

You have a power in you that is not of this world.
That power will awaken the creativity and
resourcefulness of other people . . .
people who can get things done. You will have your people.

Like energies attract one another on the cosmic grid,
linked at the heart, soul, profit centers, and crossroads of destiny.

IT TAKES A BREAK TO HAVE A BREAKTHROUGH

Here is a big, bold, ugly and very true truth: I am afraid of intimacy with myself. I am afraid of having time. I am afraid of feeling my feelings. I'm so busy working and afraid to stop. If I stop, I'll feel that deep loneliness from having ignored myself for so long. But I know my feelings are the lifeblood of this journey. Where I stand inside myself will determine where I stand in the world.

A JOURNAL ENTRY

From the beingness comes the inspiration and from the inspiration comes the genius and from the genius comes the power.

A JOURNAL ENTRY

When I work with a new client, I will often ask them if they have a spiritual practice or a way of breaking free from ordinary consciousness. Some look at me as though they would prefer that I *return* to ordinary consciousness. So I explain that there are probably all kinds of people who succeed in the work they love without believing in an inspired source. But I'm not one of them. I can't imagine making this happen on muscle and strength. I'm a sucker for the joy of quickening and ease. I've worked really, really hard in my life. And let me tell you, nothing compares to working *miraculously*.

That's the thing about creative work. It's not about work. It's about the pouring out of love. It's about being a divine chute for inspiration and clarity. But there is no spilling out when there is no pouring in.

Now I'm all for patience and persistence and staying with a project. But I've had to learn to walk away when I'm bone-dry verging on bitter. If I'm doing the writhing-in-agony thing, I'm nowhere near the conversion experience of limitlessness. There will be no cinchy magic. I'm like someone with low blood sugar, who needs an apple, not an algebra problem. I'm having a spiritual or emotional hypoglycemic moment. I need to nourish my soul.

The soul loves breaks. The inspired self likes to hang out in the Jacuzzi of your mind, turning up the jets and kicking back in bubbles of ideas. You may need to stroll barefoot in the Japanese garden, take a nap, or do a crossword puzzle. You may need to leave the house or office, meet with a friend and eat pad thai, french fries, or homemade brownies, or all of the above, until some natural order of goodness is restored in the universe. It usually begins with a sigh, and the sound of a thousand tiny bells tinkling on the hillside, as you surrender, drop your burdens, and enter the realm of love and *beingness*. Self-care calls back your spirit.

Some of us meditate or do yoga. Others go to temple or worship before the forgiving paws of a golden retriever. Others allow their own wellspring of wisdom to whisper to them in their journal or on the trail, or in an admission to a treasured coach or therapist. However we do it, we leave behind the world we knew. We do the hokey pokey and we turn ourselves around. That's what it's all about. We gather back to the part of us that is bigger than details, stronger than days, the one that can take us through any forest, not lose sight of the trees, and breathe with more than just our lungs.

I curl up with a novel and I feel as though I've stolen something, like I should put this hour back on the shelf. I should be working. I should be making progress. Yes, I know it's great that I'm self-employed and *can* read a novel at two p.m. on a Wednesday in my stuffed chair with my cat, but nobody I know really *does* that. My cat stretches and yawns and looks at me like a small, tawny King Tut, regal and clearly insulted by my gaze. He hasn't checked e-mail once in his lifetime. He communes with all the sun spots in my house. I hear my to-do list bleating and snarling from my office. I should answer calls and e-mails. I should send out packets and proposals. I should work on my new book or the blog or fill-in-the-blank, and I assure you there is always a blank.

Instead, I turn the page of a well-written novel, words from the candy store. I feel rash, intentionally choosing leisure over guilt, as though money is hemorrhaging out of my bank account with every minute, or I am permitting a bonfire to blaze upon my desk. It's unsettling to go from being a hyper-driven type A to downshifting, just pausing and enjoying a moment, like some kind of normal or healthy person with a life. I secretly believe that if I don't stay busy and focused on my work, this plump chair in the sun will turn me into a marshmallow or a memory. I will never move again. I will demand to be put on a chocolate drip and tabloid life support. All hell will break loose because I've allowed myself to taste a sliver of heaven. But the real truth is, all hell is breaking loose—and that's why I need to taste some heaven.

A week later, I just happened to teach one of the most amazing seminars of my life. One of my students commented, "I was sure you were channeling straight from God. The whole room was still and electric." Others said, "Your eyes were on fire and everything you said felt like you were reading minds." I had to admit I had been "on" and funny and alive and saying things off the top of my head that sounded a little bit like Robin Williams meets Kahlil Gibran meets LSD. It was what I absolutely loved about teaching. I had become this transparent membrane for the group's energy and a higher, brilliant consciousness played jazz piano on my brain in words, concepts, and vibrations. It was alive and raucous, unscripted and unrepeatable. I loved that feeling. I also know from experience that workshops like these create word of mouth, and word of mouth means income, opportunities, and jelly beans.

Later, it was obvious how I'd gotten there. It started with reading that novel. Then a few days before that seminar, I had collaged a vision board, burned a lemongrass-scented candle, and listened to several new CDs, stopping to dance like a maniac in the living room and show my cat and dog that, indeed, I was not leashed to my computer screen, and, hey, I knew where the biscuits were. I'd taken a long sun-filled walk with a good girl-friend. I had tossed up my arms and released things I was desperately try-ing to make happen. I had put extra honey in my tea, thank you very much.

In short, I'd broken the chains of bondage. I bathed on the emotional realms. I restored myself to goodness and to being capable of receiving good. Then, in the big block letters of hindsight, it seemed ridiculous that I had been trying to make wonderful things happen in my life—by *limiting* my joy.

My client Peter, a Wall Street maniac turned work/life balance trainer and consultant, a driven, sharp businessman, calls taking time for yourself the "heavy lifting." He says that taking ordinary actions on the hit list is easy. But the heavy lifting is taking time for yourself and reflecting, asking the tough questions, drilling down into what's really going on. Peter takes time every week to inhale books and articles that engage him. They tickle his brain and pretty soon he's writing e-zines and blogs and jumping on the phone with people with new ideas for joint ventures. He's found that time-out fires up his creativity and creativity animates his business.

I have another client who writes screenplays for Hollywood. "I've learned that downtime is part of the process," she says. "It's almost as though I have to slow down enough, before I can tap into this other vi-bration. If I can tap those resources, the scenes write themselves. I'm ten thousand times more productive."

Still, many of us feel as though we're spinning too many plates to take a break. Edie is a lawyer and speaker, building her empire of one. We are talking one day and she has lost her faith. She has lost the sense that it will all work out. She is scared and tired and feels as though she has blisters on her feet the size of coasters, and thousands of miles to go, uphill. I tell her to take some time out to drop it all, ride her bike, journal, and connect with her deep, original, knowing sense. There is dead silence on the phone. The moment I said "drop it all," I might as well have said "drop acid, pretty mama." Her sense of urgent responsibility kicked in. "But Tama, I have all these things I've got to get done. I don't have time to take time for myself," she says finally. Now, I understand that if you're in the middle of a brain surgery maybe, it's not a great idea to take time out to feed the ducks. But short of that, I vote for sanity over hysteria every time. Take a break.

Yes, it's hard to value "feeling good" when you feel like you're under pressure. But feeling good is part of your work to do. It's a professional responsibility. Otherwise, I ask you, *who* is doing the work? If you're not nourished and connected to your own flow, what grim pickings are you drawing from? I don't much see the wisdom in having a tired, hostile mind meeting with clients and making the most important decisions of your life. I'm not sure you ever have too much to do to take some time to open up to the other dimensions within you. When you're refreshed, you're present and alive, people beat their way to your door to help you, and light whizzes through your tasks. You may not even get everything done you originally intended, but that's because your intentions came from tiny mind and now *big mind* is on the scene.

I suspect I am a workaholic by nature. But I have chosen to have an astonishing life instead. Thankfully, I know some of the rules now. I know that if I don't take the time to slow down, I will work from a barren and distorted place. I will feel abandoned by the magic kingdom within me and all that is alive and precious. I won't experience my natural resilience. I will convince myself I have to work harder, as a result. I will lose my sense of sacred companionship, buoyancy, equilibrium, and the expectancy of abundance. I cannot feel the support of the Universe if I do not support myself. Neither will you.

You have more abilities than you know. Discover your full palette. Take a break and beckon a breakthrough.

INSPIRED SUCCESSISMS

That's the thing about creative work. It's not about work.
It's about the pouring out of love.

I've had to learn to walk away when I'm bone-dry verging on bitter. . . .
The soul loves breaks.

Self-care calls back your spirit. . . .
We gather back to the part of us that is bigger than details,
stronger than days.

I restored myself to goodness and to being
capable of receiving good. . . .
Then . . . it seemed ridiculous that I had been trying to make wonderful
things happen in my life—by *limiting* my joy.

It's hard to value "feeling good" when you feel like you're under pressure.
But feeling good is part of your work to do.
It's a professional responsibility.

If you're not nourished and connected to your own flow,
what grim pickings are you drawing from?
I don't much see the wisdom in having a tired,
hostile mind meeting with clients
and making the most important decisions.

I'm not sure you ever have too much to do
to take some time to open up to the other dimensions within you.

If I don't take the time to slow down,
I will work from a barren and distorted place. I will feel abandoned. . . .
I cannot feel the support of the Universe if I do not support myself.

4.

THERE ARE NO OBSTACLES

What if I told you, you have no problems? I know, you might just like to Facebook my dealer or M.D. Well, I'm not on drugs, but I do have medicine: There are no obstacles on this path.

There are wild stories and nightmares you tell yourself. There are crossroads where you will make defining decisions. There are opportunities for awakening clarity, and, yes, maybe just a few more visits to your favorite therapist, rabbi, or witch doctor. But most of all, there is the ridiculous misunderstanding that something outside of you can stop you or make you weak. It cannot. It will not.

You are safe and you are loved. Nothing has changed, even when everything changes.

SLOW TIMES ARE GROW TIMES

Resistance can kill a dream or unleash its primordial power. That choice is ours. Hard times push us up against the wall and compel a decision.

A JOURNAL ENTRY

Underneath the emotion, I have this deep knowing that all is well. I am more than these thwarted efforts. I am more than my fear. I am this greatness, too. I am this love and resolve. I also believe I have a partner in this work, a very silent partner, an ultimate energy that sustains my work.

A JOURNAL ENTRY

Many of us will hit fear season, the winter of our work. It's when things go inky, evaporate, slow down to a crawl, or simply collapse on the side of the road. It's when insecurity whips up like candy wrappers in a tornado. Most of us see the slack times as the pink slip of self-employment or some bad plague from which we will never recover. Poet W. H. Auden captured the fear of everyone who needs the phone to ring or ideas, cash, and energy to materialize. "We are afraid of pain but more afraid of silence; for no nightmare of hostile objects could be as terrible as this Void. This is the Abomination."

But every creative success story seems to require that secret ingredient of "abomination." It's the emotional jalapeño that wakes up the creative grit to succeed. It's when you call up your willpower, leave chance behind, and summon the immensity of your own unspeakable strength. Nothing is happening on the surface. But know this: There's a surge of growth mounting within you.

When I've hit dry skids in my speaking and coaching business, I have often gone on wild red alert. You would think the aliens had finally arrived, closed Starbucks, and brought the end of civilization with them. Friends say comforting things like, "The land needs to be fallow before it yields new crops. It's all a period of gestation." But I am gestating demons, bankruptcy, and new strains of anxiety attacks. I am growing crops of hallucinations. I'm not so good with this passive little time-out, say, for supposed spa days and redirection.

For weeks I felt all these doors slamming on me. No one wanted to hire me for a speaking engagement, not even the scrappiest organizations where the honorarium was three slices of bread and an apple. No one wanted to publish any of my writing. They had budget cuts or they'd just done that subject in their last issue, or the editor had just shot her husband or a hundred other bad bounces of the ball. "It doesn't mean anything about my future," I'd tell myself. Even so, I felt the termites nibbling away at the beams of my faith. I'd compulsively check voice mail to see if something new had come in. "Everything happens for a reason," chirps a friend of a friend, naturally, someone with money, not to mention that good-looking husband with bright blue eyes, who just got another promotion. Deep down, I know she is right. Still, enlightened wonder that I am, I imagine giving her a tiny little kick in her shins, *for a reason.*

I tried more marketing and focus. I tried brainstorming with colleagues and friends about how I might do things differently. I try hanging on to my clients' arms as they leave, casually cajoling them to do more business with me, because *they* have issues. But nothing sticks or works.

Finally, I realize I have done what I can to change the situation. Now, just as in bad dreams, I have to turn and face the monster. I know it's no longer about changing my circumstances. It's about healing this terror inside me.

There are times when we must feel our pain so that we can also know the relief that comes from just being honest and not resisting the mysterious healing powers of the truth. Buddhists call this "leaning into the sharp edge of the sword." It sounds bloody, but trust me, you will bleed diamonds and pearls. So I close the door of my meditation room and I imagine a beautiful, kind woman who sits down with me and listens. "I am really, really afraid," I tell her. She nods and I continue. "I'm scared that nothing good is ever going to happen again." She nods. Now the tears come. The feeling of helplessness spews out of me. I am as fragile as a petal, no warrior here.

Finally, I am sobbing with the intensity of an island downpour. It feels right and freeing. Because underneath this hot broth of emotion I've been pushing away for weeks, if not lifetimes, I feel this presence of neutral strength. It's just there. "But I'm supposed to do this. This is my work to do," says a quiet voice within me. I am surprised by this even intelligence. It's not posturing. It just feels as true as wool. This is faith. It's a bedrock power that has nothing to do with external reality.

Remember, we are fortified by a miraculous force. We are not playing the lottery. As in many spiritual paths, there is a lesson in A Course in Miracles that says, "God is the strength in which I trust." It's about letting go of what we can't control and trusting in the powers of a Presence that loves us with a panoramic intelligence and takes us through necessary terrain and consciousness-changing turnstiles. The lesson goes on to say, "If you are trusting in your own strength, you have every reason to be apprehensive, anxious, and fearful. What can you predict or control?"

In times when everything feels out of our control, it's comforting to remember that our small, fear-brained self doesn't need to make something happen. We can allow this dynamic transformation to play out. We trust in the Playwright, the consistent nature of a loving universe, and the shifts and wonders we've already experienced. This journey isn't about getting lucky here and there. It's about walking through anything, knowing that Perfect Love walks beside us.

In my office, I have a picture of a Native American Indian canoeing by himself through a mist in the dawn. He is creating the current of the stream with his oars and his will. He is not a twig on a river, bouncing on this current, floundering on that one. He knows his path. He rows his path. He finds medicine in silence, strength inside the core of his being. He remembers where creation comes from. He is not a victim of powers beyond him. He calls up powers within him and his movements create swift passage across the water.

During one of the dead winter times in my career, I begged anything divine or other for immediate assistance. As usual, I sought understanding in my journal. My wise Inner Teacher wrote back that day: "Dearest, I have no interest in making you a superstar so that your small self can sigh with relief. I am interested in your complete healing. I need you to know your true power. Then you will walk in this world in safety and as a beacon."

I knew that I still lived portions of my life like a shiny barking seal, doing flips and tricks for external validation. If people called me or paid me, I believed in my work and slept like a baby. If they didn't, I doubted my worth and every choice I had ever made, right down to the fact that I'd always chosen magenta from the crayon box in kindergarten, and *clearly* that didn't bode well for a future in business. I was at the mercy of circumstance. I wavered at every shadow. But I knew in my heart there would come a day when I wouldn't ride the roller coaster anymore. I knew there would be a time when I understood and trusted the infinite power of my calling. Sometime later I found this quote from the sage Sun Tzu and I knew it described this path. "Victorious warriors win first and then go to war, while defeated warriors go to war and seek to win."

Face your winter times with compassion for yourself and conviction in your strength. Silence is not abandonment. It's a catalyst. In facing the void, you increase your potency and capacity. It's a version of the Native American sun ceremony. Warriors endure the fierce ritual to give birth to their true identity and solidity. Likewise, on this path, you will go into these dry times, deep into the desert or dark woods, and emerge with a new authority, vision, or pair of wings, and finally you will write less desperately and spasmodically in your journal, your dog will sigh with relief, your therapist can fire her therapist, and all will continue to be well.

What do you know about yourself and your path in the silence? This is the only question that matters. Where does your power come from? Will you listen to the command of an authority that speaks from the depths of the earth and the ascension of galaxies, or will you listen to the scratching terror of a thousand small and disempowering thoughts? What you believe will prevail.

When we can't change things externally, then it's time to stir the cauldron of our governing magic. It's time to go to church, hire a coach or therapist, or pray like monks and meditate until we see stars. We have to find our way back to the stars. There are no guideposts in ordinary reality. Inspired lives depend on staying connected to the higher love and power that weaves our threads together, the dissolver of limitations, the force and knowing of our own irrevocable will.

Finally, we will emerge from the bowels of these times resolved and whole. I love that word "resolved." It's like we face the same mystery and challenge again and we re-solve it. That's exactly how this works. We remember that we are not alone. We feel empowered and determined. We no longer fear the world, and the phone starts ringing, the work starts coming, the ideas return, the doors open, and the void time ends. It has served its purpose. We are ready to handle more than we ever have before.

INSPIRED SUCCESSISMS

Resistance can kill a dream or unleash its primordial power.
That choice is ours.

Every creative success story seems to require
that secret ingredient of "abomination."
It's the emotional jalapeño that wakes up the creative grit to succeed.

Now, just as in bad dreams, I have to turn and face the monster.
I know it's no longer about changing my circumstances.
It's about healing this terror inside me.

In times when everything feels out of our control,
it's comforting to remember that our small, fear-brained self
doesn't need to make something happen.

This journey isn't about getting lucky here and there.
It's about walking through anything knowing that
Perfect Love walks beside us.

You will go into these dry times . . . and emerge with a new authority.

What do you know about yourself and your path in the silence?
This is the only question that matters.

The void time ends. It has served its purpose.
We are ready to handle more than we ever have before.

MEETING UNCERTAINTY WITH WARRIOR CERTAINTY

One rejection does not mean no one will ever buy your work, loan you money, or offer you a contract. Nor do thirty slamming doors. You won't have to eat cat food because the price of gasoline has gone up. Stay in the moment. Pay the bill. Show your work to someone else.

A JOURNAL ENTRY

Ambiguity. Uncertainty. Volatility. They're part of free agent life. Projects collapse. Money evaporates. Customers go wiggy. Get over it. That's the way it works.

DANIEL PINK, *FREE AGENT NATION*

People who live their dreams have big, wide-open hearts and the rapier focus of a secret agent on a precarious mission. They do not sweat in heat. They do not run because of a tabby cat's shadow in the alley. They no longer fear disappointment or disruption. They meet uncertainty with certainty. They keep moving in the direction of their dreams and they don't turn back. It's a constant redirection of the mind. And it works.

I remember talking to my good friend Catherine on a cold, gray November day. She lit a fire in her living room and we traded tales of recent challenges. I was upset because my business was slow. She was upset because it didn't look like a particular literary agent would represent her novel. We both congratulated ourselves for how well we were sulking with creative maturity and flair. Sensitive, transparent, touchy souls that we were, we had both grown into the deliverance and necessity of thick skins.

"This kind of thing would have killed me in the past," she said. "I'd have to get into bed, eat a pound of Belgian chocolate, journal, and lash out at my man," she laughed. "I just don't have time for that now. I have deadlines for my business." I smiled, though I did begin to pine for that chocolate. "Well, I certainly know how to wallow like a pig in mud," I chimed in. "In the past, even just one client cancellation could ruin my whole day." We giggled. We knew the secret of success now. Whine, soothe, and burn up the road. Winston Churchill, the military dynamo, who battled exhaustively with depression, said it this way: "Success is going from failure to failure without a loss of enthusiasm."

I had a therapist, Katelyn, who used to madden me with a philosophy I have come to bless. To each catastrophe I would report, she would sigh and say, "Oh well." "Oh well," as in "I guess you'll live anyway." I would embellish the horrors I'd faced. I wanted a gasp from her, a "how horrible," maybe just an overwhelming desire to faint or organize a small revolution on my behalf, or at least a handsome little tortured facial expression. Still, Katelyn would look me in the eyes, pierce me with a gentle lance, and reiterate, "Oh well." I couldn't help but think that for the money I was paying, I deserved more than two words. But I was wrong.

My neutral counselor was not coldhearted but kind and wise. In sessions, I'd pound my chest like a gorilla or flare up with emotional skunk stink, flaunting my newest crisis. But Katelyn took *me* more seriously than any difficulty I perceived. She remained certain of my strength and wingspan, unruffled by the fanfare of my current drama. Katelyn saw me as a golden warrior, a strong being with a strong mission. She didn't worry about passing circumstances because she knew I had a fire and a light that would prevail.

Years later I thought of Katelyn when I found this quote from spiritual activist Marianne Williamson: "Who we really are is a power bigger than all our problems, both personal and collective. And when we have remembered who we are, our problems—which are literally nothing other than manifestations of our forgetfulness—will disappear." Katelyn had reassuringly and militantly refused to buy into my spiritual absent-mindedness.

As a holistic therapist, working in Boulder, Colorado, a known metropolitan hotbed of personal growth, I'm sure Katelyn had heard it all. She understood that life would always roil with challenges: rejections, Mercury going retrograde, sluggish days, small jealousies, huge jealousies, insurance premium hikes, brain fog, alien invasions, faulty meditations, and client cancellations. She offered me "oh well," the warrior's serene acceptance, a response that naturally beckoned solutions. Katelyn wasn't interested in my tales of villains, traitors, and idiots. She wanted to hear about next steps. She wanted to hear about how I would continue to express my love. That's when her eyes grew bright and rapt with attention.

Katelyn encouraged me to pay attention to the kinds of "stories" I told myself. She believed, as I do now, that how I saw events shaped the events and would create the foundation of my life. I've seen this with my own clients. We live the stories we tell ourselves. When you really start to get conscious about this, you realize there are no neutral viewpoints. The narrator of your story may be your guilt-gushing mother, Chicken Little, or the Marquis de Sade. Remember, all stories are creations of a storyteller. That's why it's best to borrow a narrator like the Beloved Within, Jesus, or your aunt Sadie, who'd pat your head and say, "Everything is going to be all right, dear. You're a bright little boy. Want a brownie?" A loving narration leads to a loving life.

I remember when I first left my legal career to write. I was writing articles and living on next to nothing and mustering up all my faith in this journey. One day I had lunch with a friend downtown. Between the animated conversation, the drunken noodles, and the insanely cute waiter, I lost track of time, space, and the tethers of daily life. Finally, I floated back to my car. Then I remembered—I'd completely forgotten to feed the meter. The words Official Citation affixed to my windshield jammed me back into the cold "real world." I swear it started to rain right then.

That flimsy square piece of paper did me in. The tears came without warning, just like the ticket. I was already feeling meager and vulnerable. Earlier in the week, I'd received a Harvard alumni magazine and fantasized about my financially serene colleagues who owned investment villas and who never had to worry about the cost of the water bill or of getting new tires. I studied my new $15.00 liability. If you'd seen my face at the time, you would have thought I'd seen a ghost or discovered an explosive in my gas tank, or maybe even had to spontaneously recite the periodic table in front of a panel of chemistry teachers in order to save my life. It wasn't the cost of the ticket that rattled me. It was that it was an "unexpected expense." Suddenly the world teemed with unknown dangers: snipers, diseases, more bills, global warming, and everything I couldn't predict and control.

How many other unforeseen charges would there be? Why didn't I have more savings? Why couldn't I stick with a real job with a real paycheck? Why didn't I own a villa? Why didn't I at least know anybody rich who could fund my dreams? And while we're on the subject, why didn't I have thin thighs? Okay, that wasn't really the subject, but when you're thinking painful thoughts, it's not like you're being scientific. It's more like the big pain ball starts rolling and picking up all kinds of scrambled information from the past—the first test you failed, your ex-husband's sneer, and things your mother said when you were prenatal and couldn't fight back.

Oh, but what if the winters in Denver were cold when inevitably I found myself homesteading under the bridge? What if I couldn't afford Thai food? What if the other homeless people didn't want to have a support group with me? It didn't take long for a parking ticket to end in a sick and tortured death on the streets. My life would end with a shameful eulogy with my uncle George, the big shot conservative engineer in the family, bowing his head and prodding my humiliated father, "I told you it was a mistake to let her major in English."

Finally, the reasonable part of myself grabbed the reins. "Do you have fifteen dollars in your bank account?" it demanded. "Fine, then you can pay this parking ticket. Deal with the future in the future. Let's move on." I shoved the ticket into my coat pocket and drove into my life. Man, the Dalai Lama or somebody would have been proud.

One event has nothing to do with the breadth of your life. Pay attention to the sneaky glum conclusions you draw from things, which sound like reality, until you realize, again, it's just a point of view. And, for the record, if that point of view doesn't empower you, it doesn't serve you—so it couldn't possibly be reality. What are you making this situation mean about yourself or your life? It's never the facts that send you over the edge. It's always the story. Here's my suggestion. Deal with the real. Everything else will take care of itself.

Oh, and speaking of telling stories, people who succeed don't waste time in blame. Ranting eats time. You have dreams to live. You can't be cataloging other people's flaws, policing the fairness of all that is, entertaining the masses in your midst with the miniseries of melodrama, and moving forward in the same breath.

We who are visionaries take steps and continue to believe in our dreams no matter what. We believe with eyes open, knowing that certain things will fail, but believing anyway, trusting in a greater good anyway, because it's our one road out of hell. Trust allows us to proceed. Grievances and frustrations may make for vociferous conversations over cocktails in some circles, but those are not the circles in which anything changes. We are about the business of change.

Let go of the ridiculous, inflated, sad story. Create the real story. The sooner you say, "Oh well," the better. You need your precious energy. More good is on its way than you could possibly imagine. Dare to live that story.

INSPIRED SUCCESSISMS

We knew the secret of success now. Whine, soothe, and burn up the road.

It's best to borrow a narrator like the Beloved Within,
Jesus, or your aunt Sadie, who'd pat your head and say,
"Everything is going to be all right . . ."
A loving narration leads to a loving life.

One event has nothing to do with the breadth of your life.
Pay attention to the sneaky glum conclusions you draw from things,
which sound like reality, until you realize, again, it's just a point of view.

What are you making this situation mean about yourself or your life?
It's never the facts that send you over the edge. It's always the story.

Deal with the real. Everything else will take care of itself.

People who succeed don't waste time in blame. Ranting eats time.
You have dreams to live.

We who are visionaries take steps
and continue to believe in our dreams no matter what.

Let go of the ridiculous, inflated, sad story. Create the real story.
The sooner you say, "Oh well," the better.
You need your precious energy.
More good is on its way than you could possibly imagine.

YOUR WORK IS MEDICINE

There are some days when you feel like none of this is real and that you've just been singing yourself some lullaby all along or telling yourself a whopping fairy tale.

A JOURNAL ENTRY

I think I might just be a fraud. How can I accomplish something good when I feel so broken and doubtful? Okay, so I'm forgetting that it's the light in me that holds the power. I am willing to step forward and that is my gift. That's my part. I am willing to trust a greater love within me.

A JOURNAL ENTRY

Sometimes you don't think you're fit to do your work because you're having a bad hair day of the soul. You feel half-hearted or foul. You think that maybe you've been insanely mistaken about your abilities and that clearly it's overly optimistic to get out of your pajamas. Maybe someone canceled an appointment, a check bounced, or your competitor just had a runaway success, not that that matters to you, of course. Now you feel just too second-rate to show up. But fortunately you have technology within you that makes you more resourceful than you know. You've got the power of a mission. Perfection is not a requirement for your service, expression, or contribution. You don't even have to be in a good mood. It's not you who empowers the gift. It's the gift that empowers you.

In *Success Built to Last*, authors Porras, Emery, and Thompson talk about how a cause or calling has a life force that is bigger than the individual. They share the example of a former addict who formed a center to help other women get off drugs. Her cause, the best drug on the planet, motivates her to show up no matter what. The authors report: "Even when her emotions are descending into darkness, the light of her conviction reassures her that what she is building is bigger than she is. Fretting about whether or not she's up to the task gets overshadowed by the urgency of the need."

There have been days when I'd prefer to not look my students in the eyes or pick up the phone and have the nerve to do a coaching call. It doesn't matter that I've had standing ovations, thousands of zealous fans, or television talk shows in the past. Suddenly, my spirit lags and I doubt everything, including my ability to keep my own candle lit. There are days when I'm secretly carving a bigger slice of victimhood pie. I'm about ready to argue with clients, "You think you've got it bad? My God, with all those great circumstances, you're still whining?" Then I secretly want to ask them for help, just a little encouragement or compliment, a book they could recommend, or even a big fat stock trading tip. These are days when it's downright embarrassing to know I live in the same skin with this person. Still, I've discovered, these are important days for me to do my work.

Because doing my work is an honor and a prayer. It's medicine. It's a correction of soul. When I use my gifts, I call upon my strength. I open up to another dimension of beingness, intelligence, and even joy, and I tower larger than my ordinary self. I embody the truth as I impart its fire and tenderness. Love reorders the tenor and success of everything. It's why we do the work we do.

I remember when I first started coaching. My first ever client came over and sat on my beige couch. I was so amped up about changing the way we live our lives, and I just kept going on and on. Finally, she peered at me, fidgeting, after three whole hours, and said, "Tama, don't you think we should stop? I have to pick my son up from school." I had completely lost track of time. The energy of the work had just catapulted me into a state of seamless potentiality. Our gifts take us into other dimensions. They help other people. But they transform *us* completely.

Now let me share a little bit with you about the power of showing up, even when, say, you want to crawl off into the desert and lie down with the snakes. Years ago, I had to teach a class at one of the worst moments of my whole life. Driving to the speaking engagement, I sobbed inside my car. I can't do this. I just can't get in front of people now and start talking about the power of our attitudes. I don't believe in the transcendent power of love. I don't believe anything I've ever taught. I feel like issuing a recall notice, just like the big car companies do when they've found out about a defective part. I had discovered that *I* was that small piece of metal that disintegrates when the temperature hits a certain degree.

A few weeks before, ordinary life had come to an end for me. I was ordering chicken teriyaki at a diner, it figures, when the emotional atom bomb hit. My boyfriend closed his menu and told me he was leaving for another woman. Let me correct that. My prince, guru, and love incarnate had decided to ditch me, without warning, after seven years, for another dish on another menu. And might I add, just for further clarification, because certain friends just had to tell me this, the "other woman" had large breasts.

It was then I wanted another God. It was then I thought the cosmos should issue a recall notice on the not-so-super superpower that didn't stop insane travesties like this from happening. Nothing made sense to me. My heart slid out of its little silky pouch and the world tilted off its axis. In the days that followed, I couldn't believe that people were still buying Slurpees from 7-Eleven. My dental hygienist chirped on about a vacation to Aruba. Everyone was acting so normal. But for me, the world had spun into radio silence and the vacuum of a black hole. Grief coated everything in gunk, just like garden furniture you haven't used for twenty years.

Anyway, I was on my way to teach a class at a popular adult-education center. It was "Introduction to *A Course in Miracles*," all about living in love instead of fear. I was so disappointed in God that this had happened. I couldn't believe that I could go from having a normal, happy life to feeling as though an unknown undertow had hurled me out into cold, dark, savage waters that took my breath, will, and ground away. Then, as though drowning in broad daylight wasn't enough, I still had to earn a living. I was a single woman in a metropolitan city. Also, in a few days, I'd have to face Thanksgiving, a nice big fat holiday where I could share my *gratitude* for all this "good fortune." I wailed in my car the whole way to the center. When I parked, I dried my tears and got ready to teach about how to live an inspired life of peace and freedom. I briefly checked for mucus. When you get paid for speaking, as I do, you have to at least look as though you're a little further up on the food chain.

I dragged myself into that workshop. I may have felt like a zombie, but never let it be said I'm ever anything less than an up-to-the-minute professional. Those students had paid good money to attend this workshop and I was not going to let them down. I told myself to be present for them. That's, of course, how I hit the jackpot. Because this amazing thing happened. I started feeling better as I was talking about what I loved, almost sort of normal, almost as though I was going to get through this class just fine and maybe even get through my life just fine. Talking about the principles of *A Course in Miracles* and my work, I felt grounded and lifted at the same time. I felt this strength come through me and make everything right in the room.

Then, of course, because I'm me and often do not seem to have a shred of self-containment, I ended up telling the class about my life, my heartbreak, the rogue, chicken teriyaki, and where I was and how I was trying to use the principles to keep me focused on the right things. Some of the students looked at me as though I'd gotten up from a car wreck, stumbled into the room, and decided to offer a little inspirational lecture, while the blood and body fluids dried. You could tell the therapists in the room wanted to slip me their cards, rates, and emergency hours. Still, most everyone left that seminar feeling more connected, and reminded of their own ability to choose empowering perspectives.

Then two women came up to me after class and were the most loving souls I could possibly imagine. These two "strangers" gazed at me with the fire, peace, and compassion of angels. "You're so brave and courageous," they said. Their soft words wrapped around me like a cashmere shawl. Both women, total strangers, urged me to come to their Thanksgiving dinners respectively. I felt myself being healed, by doing the work I am born to do, *no matter what.* I had felt so alone in the universe the night before the class. Yet in that moment, I felt as though my gift would always give me a place to stand, a place to belong. I felt bigger than myself, connected to strangers and angels, graciously tethered to strength, purpose, and even faith again.

That night I learned something very powerful that has changed my life and has empowered many of my clients. I learned that our gifts are impersonal. I don't have to be in the right mood for truth. What truly moves my soul will always move my soul. Even when I'm in a different place, there is a part of me that is strong and sure and knows its way. I can feel as small as a pinpoint, but a pillar of holy fire resides within. This enormous presence gets activated when I offer my talent and service to others.

In the Alcoholics Anonymous twelve-step program, this is common wisdom. If you feel like you want to take a drink, it's good medicine to help another alcoholic who has less sobriety than you. There is universal healing in that guidance. Focusing on your strength, hope, and experience fills you with strength, hope, and experience.

You will know when it's not ethical for you to show up and do your work professionally. That's something else altogether. I'm just trying to remind you that most times when you *feel* as though you have nothing to give, you still have everything to offer, and everything to receive.

INSPIRED SUCCESSISMS

You've got the power of a mission.
Perfection is not a requirement for your service,
expression, or contribution.
You don't even have to be in a good mood.

It's not you who empowers the gift. It's the gift that empowers you.

Doing my work is an honor and a prayer. It's medicine.
It's a correction of soul.

When I use my gifts, I call upon my strength.
I open up to another dimension of beingness, intelligence,
and even joy, and I tower larger than my ordinary self.

Our gifts take us into other dimensions. They help other people.
But they transform *us* completely.

My gift would always give me a place to stand, a place to belong.

Our gifts are impersonal. I don't have to be in the right mood for truth.
What truly moves my soul will always move my soul.

Focusing on your strength, hope, and experience
fills you with strength, hope, and experience.

EXCITEMENT ALWAYS LEADS YOU SOMEWHERE, IF YOU KEEP GOING

Hope is itself a species of happiness, and, perhaps, the chief happiness which this world affords.

SAMUEL JOHNSON

Things do come out of the blue. They come out of the blue to remind us that things do come out of the blue, and that life could get crazy good at any second.

A JOURNAL ENTRY

Many of my clients often experience something big coming down the pike that goes down the drain instead. It's disappointing and disorienting. It happens to everyone. I don't know why it happens, that's another department, but I do know this: You can benefit from everything. The independent, creative mind will choose to benefit from everything.

I once met an energetic PR person at a conference and she had an "in" to a rather famous national TV talk-show host. My new best friend Robin knew she could get me on that show. "It's almost done," she assured me, radiant smile and lilting voice. The stars had finally aligned, the cosmic committee factored in how hard I'd been trying all these years, the host would be given my package, and I positioned myself to jump into my newly appointed life. Then the bonanza lost steam, just like a flat tire, no explanation. Robin backpedaled, sent one-line e-mails, and eventually slid into the ethers of the unavailable. I felt more disappointed than ever before. Life had teased me, dangled an eagle feather, then snatched the prize away.

I remember having coffee with my friend Ted back in Denver, squalling about the injustice. First, this is what you need to know about Ted. He is an eternally positive, loving, believing soul. I'm quite sure he's part leprechaun, part doorman, and part knight. He's also been married three times, so the man kind of grooves on possibilities. I asked Ted, "Why does the Universe set up things, show us possibilities, and then take them away?" I thought he'd tell me I was blocking the energy with some deep-seated childhood wound and would need to bankroll some pricey energy healer in Sedona.

See, but this is what I love about Ted. He doesn't go shopping for darkness. He likes the light. "So why do these kinds of things happen?" I ask him again. He grins and says this: "Can you imagine if those things didn't happen? What if possibilities didn't keep arising? How would *that* make you feel?" Now that might not do anything for you. But it smacked me between the eyes, hey, like maybe in my third eye, like bush lightning.

I've been in business now for over two decades and here's one thing I know: Possibilities keep us alive. They are vitamins. Even if they don't turn out the way we hope, their energy gets us somewhere. Just thinking that something will work out helps us approach the point where something does. It keeps us going, still brushing our precious little teeth and answering e-mails. In some thick psychological tome, this phenomenon is probably flagged as *delusionitis helpfulitis*. But let me tell you, for our purposes, it's the free trolley ride.

I have a favorite example of this. When I was in law school, my study partner John and I planned to go dancing on a Tuesday night at Spit, a popular downtown Boston dance club. This was a big deal, kind of like staging a personal insurrection, since, at any other time, we were both barnacles affixed to Harvard's law library.

In my dorm room, I slipped on tight black pants and danced with a fantasy stranger with soulful eyes who, with any luck at all, would think torts were pastries. John called again to confirm "operation liberation." When we added having dinner off-campus to our plan, we actually found ourselves bubbling with giddiness, light-headed, even cracking non-legal jokes, and basically one step away from foaming. You would have thought we'd booked a flight to Mardi Gras or the Spanish Riviera.

Huddling in down coats, we scampered to the warm cove of the Indian restaurant in Harvard Square. Among sequined cushions, we feasted on nan, green curry, lamb vindaloo, chai, and rice pudding. When we finally left the restaurant, the arctic Boston temperature had dropped and it felt as though the blood in our veins would freeze. The air stung like a fresh paper cut. We both felt like huge full moons, hung low and sleepy from our meal. With guilty smiles, we mutually decided not to take the train into the city and go dancing after all.

I always remember that night fondly. In fact, it's one of my favorite experiences from law school. It was the best night of dancing . . . I didn't do. I'd gotten so much out of anticipating our plucky expedition. That Tuesday, I strode around campus knowing I was going dancing. Even the law library seemed brighter than usual, what with those disco lights circling our heads and all. I swear I could hear thumping rhythms while I squirmed in contracts class. I got a crazy amount of studying done in advance, and tried on images, conversations, and alternate sultry lives in my tiny dorm room mirror. Later, it didn't matter that I never stepped foot in the club. No one and nothing could take back the fun from my bloodstream.

These days, when the merest possibilities come through in my business, I intentionally use my excitement. I make phone calls or appointments because I know I'm blazing. I approach power brokers or difficult relationships with new mettle because I have aces in my hand. I fling e-mails like Frisbees across cyberspace. Maybe it's just a placebo, but sugar pills have been known to cure people. I enjoy every ounce of magnetism while I'm plugged in. It's fun to have high-speed Internet instead of dial-up.

Excitement always leads you somewhere, unless you dismiss its value. In the early days of my would-be writing career, I hoped to make it as a freelance magazine writer. I sent in query letters and I interned at a small local women's publication. I remember driving back from my first "real" profile interview with a successful maverick entrepreneur. I just kept saying, "Yes! Yes! Yes!" to myself because I had a fireworks-show-for-one going on in my soul.

Speeding in my pint-size crème-colored Honda Civic back from the foothills, I felt as though I was floating across the empty plains into that coal sky. I kept reliving the interview. She sat in a white silk pantsuit on her leather couch and told me everything about how she'd started in the exotic fashion industry. Acting like I'd interviewed a thousand other multimillion-dollar women in plush living rooms, I braved my first questions, gulped mineral water, and casually destroyed my lime.

Driving back to Denver, I dreamed aloud, maybe I could sell the article to *Cosmopolitan* magazine or *New Woman*. Maybe I'd write a syndicated column about successful, adventurous women. Maybe big-name magazines would make me their go-to girl with these kinds of features. Maybe I would start a magazine or a chain of them. I could barely keep myself seated in that car. I recalled Brenda's comment to me as we said good-bye. "I said things tonight I didn't even know I felt," she'd remarked. "You really have a way with asking questions." In that moment, I stood as a writer, a professional freaking writer, on top of the highest mountain, at the tip of the world; I knew I had a gift and that everything good would come my way.

I never sold that profile to a glossy newsstand magazine. In fact, during that period of my career, I never sold any articles to big-name magazines.

Yet the outcome of that article didn't matter as much as the outcome of that evening. In that moment, my cells realigned. I knew I was born to write. I had a stand-up-straight-and-be-counted feeling of recognition. I knew my life and this gift would come together. I just knew this couldn't be wrong. It could never be wrong to feel this clear and exhilarated.

When later I decided to write a book instead of magazine articles, I did not discard the meaning of that inspired evening. Instead I chose to see it as a life raft that got me to the five-star cruise ship. "You never did any-thing with that article," my pitchfork-toting inner critic jabbed. But that's not true. That evening remains in my mind like a clasp to a jeweled neck-lace. It closed the circle. It purged my insecurity at that time. It gave me permission to trust my inner conviction and follow each cue wherever it led.

You are on a dynamic journey and your evolving creative life is bigger than just one designated point along the way. It's not about the literal out-come. It's more about how an encounter makes you feel, the truth it ignites within you, the possibility that becomes real through you, and how you use and express that energy.

You will have many "Yes!" moments on your path, too—times when lightning strikes for you and you know that something within you has shifted for all time. These moments may come apart at the seams later. They may not lead to job offers, clients, deals, or cash, but they do lead to transformation. And transformation will take you everywhere you want to go.

A "Yes!" moment is a moment of success unto itself, a milestone mark-ing your journey. Focus on the feeling you experienced when in the thick of your desired circumstances. That feeling is real and irrevocable. It has power and vibration. That reality contains potential and direction. Re-ceive the energy. No one will snap your picture and write you up in the paper for it. Still, you know the truth. Own it—and then ride that trolley as far as it will take you.

INSPIRED SUCCESSISMS

The independent, creative mind will choose to benefit from everything.

Possibilities keep us alive. They are vitamins.
Even if they don't turn out the way we hope, their energy
gets us somewhere.

Just thinking that something will work out
helps us approach the point where something does.

When the merest possibilities come through in my business,
I intentionally use my excitement.
I make phone calls or appointments because I know I'm blazing.

Excitement always leads you somewhere, unless you dismiss its value.

It's not about the literal outcome.
It's more about how an encounter makes you feel,
the truth it ignites within you,
the possibility that becomes real through you,
and how you use and express that energy.

You will have many "Yes!" moments . . .
times when lightning strikes for you
and you know that something within you has shifted for all time. . . .
A "Yes!" moment is a moment of success unto itself.

Focus on the feeling you experienced
when in the thick of your desired circumstances.
The feeling is real and irrevocable. The feeling has power and vibration.

THERE ARE NO GAPS IN INFINITE GOOD

I can stuff my pockets with shells and sand, but I can never hold the ocean. In the end it's not the evidence that I want. It's the experience.

A JOURNAL ENTRY

Never place a period where God has placed a comma.

GRACIE ALLEN (MAGNET ON FRIDGE)

As many spiritual teachings suggest, I have come to see that when something falls through, something else emerges. A Loving Life Force just keeps giving and giving and giving. But every now and then you might just want to return the gift to the Customer Service Department in the Sky. It isn't what you ordered. It has a higher price tag. It's not your favorite color. But trust me, those are the packages that will really jump-start your lagging potential and empower your life. Sometimes divine intelligence really is divine.

One day I talked to my novelist, mystic, moon-watching, gardener friend. She had just been working on another draft of her novel, the final version to send in to an agent. She is a freelance editor and marketing writer by trade. She told me of the time when she was working on her novel and her business slowed down. No one called. The voice mail was empty. "I felt like this cove got created around me so that I could do my real work," she says. "The very second I completed the manuscript, people started calling me again."

I was thunderstruck by her trust in the events before her. Some people are like this and I covet their serotonin levels. She saw a cove—not a sinkhole or a maximum security prison. She imagined herself nestled in with a purpose. She didn't envision drifting in black space where you can advertise, send e-mails, and cry out, but your attempts just bounce off meteors and gooey constellations, proving once and for all that no one really does hear a tree fall in the forest or a radio ad. She didn't grind her molars to calcium dust or sweat one extra bead. She *enjoyed* herself. She baked organic oatmeal cookies, I kid you not, and finished another chapter of her novel.

Lily, a client of mine, owns a financial services empire that hit a slump one year as the summer months began. She began to freak out just a teensy-weensy bit, and joined about thirty high-end networking meetings and strategic fundraisers. Yet the more she tried to amp up her business, the more exhausted she felt, especially as the poor results undermined her checkbook and her confidence. Then one day she realized this: "You know, I began my company because I wanted to spend more time with my teenage daughter before she leaves for college." Lily brightened as she fantasized about lounging by the pool with her daughter, reading trashy novels, sipping raspberry iced teas, and talking about hairstyles, boys, and her daughter's imminent passage into adulthood. The network groups couldn't hold a candle to this suddenly revealed cornucopia. It was time to grab her new "opportunity." By early September, Lily had a radiant skin tone and a priceless connection with her daughter. She hummed with real exuberance. Business picked up again, as it always did in the fall, and she had the energy to meet it.

Business guru Daniel Pink, acknowledging the fluctuations in work and business, writes about how important it is to take advantage of the slower times. "Don't squander this downtime worrying about going broke. Instead use this time to clean your office, take a trip, plant flowers, or have some fun. When the mania begins again, you'll be glad you did."

Yet sometimes we just can't see the opportunities. Sometimes we can't pinpoint the grace. It doesn't look like apples for apples. To some of us less-evolved people, it looks like apples for dung, the short end of the stick, and a bunch of runty lemons that couldn't even make a thimbleful of lemonade, not to mention the half-empty glasses everywhere. I don't mean to sound negative. I mean to sound *hostile*, because that's how it feels when you're having one of those times.

Thankfully, I have a technique for seeing the true possibility in front of you, no matter what: *Stop seeing the story of what you're losing.* Wipe the slate clean and look at this moment with inquisitive, engaging eyes. What opportunity am I being given in this moment? That's the question. Something is being "taken away" so that something else might be experienced. What is that new something?

Sometimes the opportunity isn't something else to do. Sometimes it's something else to *feel*. When I first started promoting my book, I strained to get speaking engagements, book signings, and exposure any way I could. This often demanded investing in myself and hitting the road. I would pay to fly to another city and try to sell enough books, CDs, and follow-up programs at a talk to pay for my trip. Early on, right after a boatload of rejections, I landed a speaking engagement in San Francisco, a chance to speak at a prestigious women's wellness conference. I felt so excited that finally something from "the good life" had come my way. Then just a week before my trip, I received a crisp e-mail letting me know the conference coordinator had canceled the event. By then I'd already bought my airline ticket and scheduled a small free workshop at a church. It was too late to back out or change plans. I was out the airline ticket, hotel bill, car rental, and time. I felt sick.

"Just make it a vacation," said friends, but I didn't *want* a vacation. I wanted to move a pawn on the chessboard, make a next move, and see something productive set in motion. I was desperate to grow my business and expand my work. I felt knocked down, like a toddler taking a few wobbly steps only to be smacked down by a powerful ocean wave, shoved back into my small, so not happening life.

But I decided to "make the best" of this expensive, unnecessary excursion. At the time, I'd been reading a beautiful book called *Beachcombing at Miramar* that I'd picked up at a garage sale. I brought it with me on the plane from Denver and then made the coincidental discovery that the beach in the book was a beach near San Francisco. Some part of me giggled softly. For something to do, I decided to visit that beach and make a day of it, since, of course, I now *had* a day.

I spent a day walking on the beach, watching waves, and writing. The expanse of the place started to seep into my veins. I was surrounded by soft damp air, the haunting sounds of a lighthouse, jade plants sporting bright pink blossoms, and the voluptuousness of the shining Pacific Ocean.

Finally, walking along the beach, I gave in to the unabated generosity of just being alive, really alive in that moment. It was beyond success and failure. As I relaxed, I felt my soul's presence overshadow my momentary identity. I was lifted out of strife, out of pain, out of the fierce and frenetic need to succeed, to make it, to prove something and get to safety. In that moment I didn't need book sales or clients or anything else. I felt alive and connected to my True Self, my fearless, grateful, ravishingly free self.

I started thinking bigger instead of bitter. I laughed lavishly in the face of my fears, even though I knew they still had a rusty iron grasp on me and would surface again, maybe even in five minutes. Here's what I wrote in my journal that day:

"I am never going to make it in the world with a petty mind, an uptight, counting, calibrating, fearful mind. I see an old woman clucking in the back room, counting pennies and dimes and desperately grieving the one that rolls away. I see the Universe laughing mirthfully, fitfully, squandering dollars, fistfuls of coins scattered, like crab shell confetti and glittering particles on the beach. The Universe laughs with abundance. It is not so concerned with making every single opportunity work. It always has more in the pipeline. Losing an 'opportunity' is no big deal. There are infinite opportunities."

It felt good to let go of my frustration and breathe into the continuous profusion of possibilities. That day the Universe knew that increasing my business was not my greatest need. Yes, my mind hungered for vetted rock-solid proof of success, increased visibility, and climbing income. But my soul needed to tap into a deeper feeling of bounty and healing. That was the real deal. I'd been knocked around and felt raw and sad and I needed nurturing more than I needed to pound the streets. I needed to know that circumstances couldn't stop me, because I would always have an amazing unlimited ability to generate more abundance. I needed to tap back into the bigness of life and remember the indescribable confidence of being inspired. I needed to swell from within so that I could carry that love into the world.

Sitting on the beach for most of the day into the early evening, eating organic strawberries and a peanut butter sandwich, I realized that a Loving Intelligence had given me a precious gift I had almost not received. I had been bitter, rejected, and deprived, when I was being given a gift of spirit, mercy, and generosity. I would never ever have taken this time for myself. I would not have rested when I burned to gun the gas and prove to myself that I was going to make it in this life. So that keen coyote, the Divine Friend, set up the perfect scam for joy.

The Presence of the Wondrous is *always* giving us love. Its nature doesn't change just because our moods and views do. Sacred love is consistent. We may not see the kindness or potential for expansion. Like children, we may feel punished or denied. We may spit out the medicine or continue to wail for matches, knives, or poison. Sometimes it takes growth to appreciate a higher love. Until then, we may see ourselves as victims. Still, let's claim another experience. Life always presents us with the best possibility for progress at the time. We are "victims" of grace at all times.

INSPIRED SUCCESSISMS

When something falls through, something else emerges.
A Loving Life Force just keeps giving and giving and giving.

I have a technique for seeing the true possibility
in front of you, no matter what.
Stop seeing the story of what you're losing.

What opportunity am I being given in this moment?
That's the question. Something is being "taken away"
so that something else might be experienced. What is that something?

Sometimes the opportunity isn't something else to do.
Sometimes it's something else to *feel*.

I am never going to make it in the world with a petty mind,
an uptight, counting, calibrating, fearful mind.

The Universe laughs with abundance. It is not so concerned with
making every single opportunity work.
It always has more in the pipeline.
Losing an "opportunity" is no big deal. There are infinite opportunities.

The Presence of the Wondrous is *always* giving us love.
Its nature doesn't change just because our moods and views do.

Life always presents us with the best possibility for progress at the time.
We are "victims" of grace at all times.

5.

TIMING WILL
TURN ON A DIME

I know you want to speed things up a bit. Well, I don't. Hey, you're in the dream birth canal. I want to make sure you develop lungs and kidneys and nose hairs and every one of your precious reaching toes.

Of course, I'm not suggesting you just wait. I'd prefer you step out of time altogether. Stop counting seconds or years. Fall in love with the task in front of you until you remember who you really are and you tremble and burn with freedom. The results are not in the future. They're in you—this second.

There is no place to rush to. Believe me, a dead body on a fast train will never arrive in the Promised Land. Timing is about awakening to another state of mind, letting go of numbness, fear, and limits. You don't get somewhere new. You become someone new. And everything you need comes to you.

TIME IS LOVE

When I'm chomping at the bit to "get there" already, it's my ego and fear. It's insecurity that is eager to prove itself, get somewhere, and be somebody. The truth is serene within me. It smiles as big as the sky. It knows the outcome.

A JOURNAL ENTRY

It does not astonish or make us angry that it takes a whole year to bring into the house three great white peonies and two pale blue iris.

MAY SARTON

Have you ever seen Chia Pets? They are some kind of instant plant mix sprinkled onto terra-cotta pots in the shapes of animals. The ads say something like, "Just add water and watch them grow." They repeat these ads on television late at night, when most viewers are sleep-deprived, stoned, or drunk and most likely to think that an instant plant-covered lamb is just what they need to relieve their money or marital problems. I admit it is an attractive offer.

I mention Chia Pets because I think a lot of us want what I call "Chia Pet success," just add water and be quickly entertained as you watch fast growth. But inspired success isn't like a vending machine, where you put your currency in and then push a button for the instant exchange of energy. It's more like a pilgrimage or a vision quest, or a sacred marriage, where you commit to the process through flood and fire and you're grateful for the opportunity in this lifetime. It's not about paying your dues. It's about devotion, the freedom that comes when you've given up your clawing angst, and you know you're going to give this ride everything you have, one way or another.

Do yourself the smartest favor imaginable. Relax. Take the long view. Settle in for the duration. Give your dreams all the time they need. Time is love. And your love will survive the avalanches, cross the desert and seas, climb the mountain backward and forward, singing a thousand and two names for beauty, and even sell your services.

I've seen many individuals give up on beautiful aspirations far too soon. Looking for quick results, they abandon their gold halfway out of the mine. They tell me, "I don't have time to waste." They want to be VP already, have their foundations funded, or win the Oscar, just for *thinking* of the screenplay. Real life is just too slow for them. They're looking for the Chia Pet.

I sit with Patty, who's decked out in power red. She's the former head of human services for a major company who now wants to offer feng shui workshops for women. Today she is in a snit, she's got her chakras all up in a ball. She has just offered a free class and no one signed up for her follow-up paid event. "So that's not going to work," she says, on the very next day, disposing of the marketing idea, the joy of the class she just taught, and even her passion to pursue this dream. She sets her teacup down like a gavel. She calls this clarity, but I see it as insecurity in a suit. Defensiveness is not self-respect, nor is crumpling like a silk shirt without starch. Patty tried one free workshop and it didn't take off like brush fire, and now she's tired. She thinks she's worth more than that. She *is* worth more than that. That's why I urge her to give herself more chances, more time, and more of an opportunity to be free of the exhaustion that comes when you haven't fully committed to your dreams.

Believe me, I know what it's like to feel like you're not "getting anywhere." I know how it feels to have things just sit there on the runway of life, like dodo birds, wounded eagles, or a thousand pounds of orange-and-plaid garage sale furniture. I've given free talks and talks I had to pay to give, and I've lectured to groups that responded to my work with as much enthusiasm as cows staring at a passing bicycle. I've had clients cancel, classes cancel, and the phone go quiet, horribly, wretchedly quiet. Still, my career has blossomed anyway, blossomed into a large, dynamic, international following that not only rocks my world but rocks *the* world. Some things took off. Other things didn't. Yet everything took me somewhere. Many beginners think that the lack of *instant* results is the lack of results, but that's a sad and senseless assumption, and lead in your dancing shoes.

Of course I'm not advocating martyrdom, absurd suffering, or constant bad networking meetings as a ticket to CEO or entrepreneurial heaven. I'm also not saying you should just be a pit bull and ignore the communication of the marketplace. By the way, I'm also not saying that you won't be one of those people who bypass all this education and simply succeed in the blink of an eye. You might. And I will hate you for three seconds and then applaud you. But here's my point: If something sticks to your soul, stick with it no matter what. Your dreams are worth the industrial brand of emotional Velcro.

Yeah, here comes *The Sound of Music*. Hey, it's not my fault if the great truths in life became musicals. Remember when Mother Superior sings to Maria in a voice as big as a canyon, "Climb every mountain. Ford every stream. Follow every rainbow, until you find your dream." See, that's the point. Your dream is worth every effort. It's what you're here for. Now, maybe you're thinking that it's taking too much time. Hey, let me ask you, what else is on the docket? What else besides taking steps toward your dreams and shedding limits *are* you here for? If you can find another life that makes you more crazy-fulfilled, then by all means run to it as fast as you can. But if this is the dream that lights up your switchboard, then active devotion will save you years. Only avoidance, in all of its alluring field trips, wastes time.

Where did we get the idea that great things happen at great speed? Train wrecks happen at great speed. "Nothing in nature tells us that rapid growth is good, and certainly nothing in human biology," says author Paul Hawken in *Growing a Business*. Prodigies and airbrushed pop stars aside, most of us require time and experience to get impeccable at what we do. We live in a world of instant messaging, but that doesn't mean we have an instant message. It's okay to explore, practice, and deepen your craft. Even the big boys in business give things time to grow and succeed. Sergey Brin, cofounder of Google, said, "We knew that Google was going to get better every single day as we worked on it, and we knew that sooner or later, everyone was going to try it. So our feeling was that the later you tried it, the better it was for us because we'd made a better impression with better technology." It's good to take your time. In the long run, you'll go further on quality than velocity.

When my business didn't go national immediately, I saw it as a condemnation. I got all nervous that I would never hit the commercial stratospheres that I dreamed about. "Just take the steps you can take," I'd journal to myself. But I questioned these. They felt like making little rodent scratches, and I wanted swashbuckling, billboard success. I couldn't imagine how my "baby steps" would take me anywhere significant. Now I know that there's no such thing as baby steps. Every step is courageous and heroic and ushers you into unimaginable growth. Every step you take to support your talent or gift activates a divine serum within you and a stream of good coming your way.

Years ago, while giving my first spa retreat at Canyon Ranch, the famous spa in Tucson, I found myself wondering how to continue to get my work into the world. I sat by a fountain created from a tower of rocks, called "Intention." As I gazed at the sculpture, I could tell that each rock had been meticulously placed with a brain surgeon's precision and a Zen master's calm. If even one rock had been slapped or forced in there, the communication would have lost its hypnotic vibration. As I studied this amazing cairn, I realized what it would be like to build a masterpiece with love. "Greatness is about cultivation, not sensation," whispered my inner voice. I felt understanding and peace flood my body. I realized that I was growing my enterprise one rock at a time, loving or benefiting one student, organization, or fan at a time, placing one stone upon another. I was building a brand of excellence and consistency. I was dedicated to quality, not velocity. I believed in the endurance and the expanse of the sublime.

I reflected on how two of the participants at this very retreat had seen me speak at a conference five years ago. And while they had received my mailings and brochures, they had not responded in any way, not a peep, not a purchase, not a nod, until now, *their* right time. I reflected on all the people I'd spoken to since that time. I realized that many of them were getting ready to show up in their right time, maybe a week from now, maybe in four years. I decided, then and there, that I'd be there when they were ready.

Finally, I dropped my shortsighted view of cause and immediate effect. I was growing a spectacular worldwide garden, and some plants would come up early while others would require further cultivation. It was my work to love and tend the pregnant ground, see through its bare appearance, and nurture the thousands upon thousands of seeds growing in their own right time—and mine.

As you go forward, dare to know this truth: Your success is a given. This is where you belong. Why waste time looking for quick fixes when you have been given a guarantee all along? You will succeed in what you are meant to do. Just add devotion and time.

INSPIRED SUCCESSISMS

Inspired success isn't like a vending machine,
where you put your currency in and then push a button
for the instant exchange of energy.
It's more like a pilgrimage or a vision quest. . . .

It's not about paying your dues.
It's about devotion, the freedom that comes
when you've given up your clawing angst,
and you know you're going to give this ride everything you have.

Take the long view. Settle in for the duration.
Give your dreams all the time they need. Time is love.

Your dream is worth every effort. It's what you're here for.
Now maybe you're thinking that it's taking too much time.
Hey, let me ask you, what else is on the docket?

If this is the dream that lights up your switchboard,
then active devotion will save you years.
Only avoidance, in all of its alluring field trips, wastes time.

There's no such thing as baby steps.
Every step is courageous and heroic and ushers
you into unimaginable growth.

I was dedicated to quality, not velocity.

Why waste time looking for quick fixes when
you have been given a guarantee all along?
You will succeed in what you are meant to do.
Just add devotion and time.

YOU ONLY RUSH YOURSELF
INTO STAGNATION

Infinite patience brings immediate results.

A COURSE IN MIRACLES

*Is your goal taking up so much of your attention that you reduce the
present moment to a means to an end? Is it taking the joy out of your
living? Are you waiting to start living?*

ECKHART TOLLE, THE POWER OF NOW

watch many of my clients struggle with "how long things take."
Whether they are designing a website, creating a new software program, or hoping to get cast in a leading role, I hear the mental sighs
and whimpers of *frustration* and frenzy. When will I get that big
break? When will things move quicker? When will I get there? I can't
help but think of children who wriggle in the backseat of a Chevy rolling
down the highway en route to Magic Kingdom. "Are we there yet?" they
demand every two minutes. And in two-minute intervals, the road
stretches on like homework, or like opera.

The path to wild success, or *any* success, is all about what we mentally
focus on. Frustration is a big, unsupervised self-attack fest. When I'm impatient, should *that* ever happen, I'm replaying how far I have to go, my
days disappearing off life's calendar, tasks crushing against one another
in a stuck and crowded elevator, prizes I never won lining up and dancing like chorus girls, and my accruing age sitting down in the middle of

the road. Then for added self-defeatism, I toss this on the grill: Some people actually have fat budgets, flat stomachs, and a flair for time management. It's all too much to bear. Fortunately, it's optional.

Because whenever I'm floundering in my own frustration, I'm not focusing on what there is to experience right *now*, this unprecedented little deity of a moment. Yet spiritual traditions, healing practices, quantum physics, and executive peak performance programs (and they cost a chunk of change so you'll listen), all demonstrate that the real show takes place in the moment. Good things don't happen in the future. They happen now. Linear time focuses on the past and the future. But the good stuff, the high jolt of liberation, is now, baby, now.

You may sense a growling urgency to *finish* your masterpiece soon, soon, before you die perhaps, or get a brain disease that makes you forget just which one of those eighteen projects you were working on anyway, or before yet another person jabs a pin in your voodoo doll by publicizing their latest box office hit in life. All you need is just a little multibillion-dollar business or a Pulitzer Prize. The cruel irony, of course, is that that tiger pacing in the cage of your brain actually blocks your progress. Its massive weight crushes every seedling, fairy tendril, and wisp of imagination. The faster it paces, the slower you move. Impatience is a form of anger, and creation is a path of love. Only love will move you forward.

When you hunger for velocity, the hunger below the hunger is to fall in love with the work before you, to stumble across the threshold "into the zone," that elusive magic rush of being present. Take a deep breath. Apply your neutral attention. Continually let go of your judgments. What if this moment were the highest pinnacle in your career? How would you look at the work before you then? What if this was your last breath? What if everything in your life depended on this moment? It does. It absolutely does.

Years ago I jogged regularly. I was committed to running a certain distance weekly and, if truth be known, keeping certain body parts in check. Many times I would focus on just wanting to get the run over, and achieve my goal. I'd focus on the distance I had to run, and that would often make the experience empty and brutal. My running practice taught me that I could gain distance by forgetting about miles and focusing on scenery, forgetting about the task at hand and, get this, distracting myself with actually being alive. The impatient, demanding, groaning voice in my head would start, "How far do I have to go? Eight miles will take forever! My knee hurts and the sun's too hot this morning and I have a lot of work to do at home and I think I have a headache and I didn't get enough sleep and . . ." Can you imagine running any distance with this endlessly fascinating companion? No wonder the miles seemed eternal.

Then as I turned my mind to noticing a magpie shuffling its feathers or an aspen tree slithering in the breeze, effort and time evaporated from my consciousness. Sometimes on really great runs, even my awareness of myself blended into a red berry or the varnish of a leaf. I found it exhilarating to "disappear" and become the parade of my experience. I awoke miles later.

Then I even noticed this strange phenomenon. When I relaxed my pace into luxuriousness, telling myself "I never want this to end," the run itself appeared to speed up. Being done was often a surprise and even a subtle disappointment. Being present squeezed out anxiety, boredom, sluggishness, and every other life-debilitating form of self-judgment. With a mind immersed in tall grasses, magpie feathers, speckled leaves, awe, exhilaration, and outstanding gratitude for being alive, there were no thoughts of measurement, comparison, minutes, or a desire for anything else.

Discover the leaves, birds, and vibration of your craft. Captivate yourself. Keep it simple. Focus on the single undertaking before you. You won't find any aspect of your work boring or time-consuming once you're consumed. As we channel all of our mental energy into this time and space, we blaze through the ordinary into the magnetic divine.

Attention flings open the doors to new dimensions of experience. In this state of connection, the struggle disappears. We're talking altered consciousness, winning the lottery of the mind, and discovering new capacities, bells, and whistles. And that's how we get hooked on doing what we love. Sure, we want money and fame, but truth be known, we're in this for the naked joy. We're in it because showing up for the work we love uses us like nothing else. It's a place where we can lose ourselves and find ourselves and tap resources within us we didn't know we had. And here's the day when everything changes: It's the day we realize that we're not doing our work to *get* somewhere, as much as to *be* somewhere right now. We're no longer desperate to land. We're just crazy for the magic carpet ride.

I suggest you buckle up and ride the ride. Break the project or timeline down into small, manageable, nibble-size tasks and then lunge in. William Blake discovered the universe in a grain of sand. Walt Whitman realized selfhood in a blade of grass. Okay, it's true, poets always seem to explode with ecstasy when confronting something simple and pure. They're just masters of attention, showing us how it works, because most of us think we need the whole deluxe fireworks display or the moon on a silver platter before we could peel off the numbness. We keep looking for the brownies, but this is a path of bread, sustenance in the everyday activities, rising in the task at hand.

Tell the tiger to pace elsewhere. Choose this moment, as though it's the moment you've always wanted to be in, even if you feel dull or frustrated or so far behind where you hope to be. You can have an adventure right now by choosing to be present. The quality of your life is not the amount of things you get done. Quality depends on how much *beingness* you flood into each experience. The high points of life sweep you up because you lose a sense of self-consciousness, of time, hunger, limits, grievances, ambitions, or memories. But these moments don't have to happen on a mountaintop with the wind whipping through your bright red hair or in the middle of a wine-and-sweat-soaked romantic encounter. They can happen while calling your client back or crumpling a form rejection letter. Now, personally, I wouldn't try this one at home by myself, but I'll bet you the

Dalai Lama knows a little slice of nirvana just dealing with his Internet provider.

I'd like you to consider that there is something that needs your attention right now. It's not as though you're being deprived of your good. It's not as though the Universe, "if it really wanted to," could drop you off at the corner of Party Central and Success, with engraved invitations to the black-tie celebration. This is a process of answering your own invitation to all that you are meant to be. No one else is holding up the show. What do you need to focus on right now? What cries for your devotion and attention? When you show up, so does everything else. It's a crazy simple formula, really. *When you get here, you'll get there.*

A Course in Miracles offers this mantra: "Let all things be exactly as they are." That's a painful invocation when you're kicking inside, aching for things to be different. But it's not just some holy-minded pacifier, like how to *spiritually* kill time while you're waiting in the cold for the bus. It's a focus that helps you let go of your resistance to the situation before you. Resistance causes pain and separation. Resistance is the part of you that "wants things to be otherwise." The lack of resistance frees up more resources. When you accept what is, you can begin to love what is. Love moves energy.

This is what I've come to understand about slowing down into my work of writing, teaching, coaching, marketing, putting one foot in front of the other, and tending even the pieces of lint in the belly button of my business. When I settle into and blaze *where* I am, I finally know *what* I am. I taste my bigness, my love, and the exhilaration of my own nature. When I know what I am, I have so much less pain and fear. I have nothing to prove or make happen. A client can cancel and I'm still on cloud nine, not because I'm in denial, but because I'm in reality. When I know what I am, I can't help but enjoy success right now. The feeling of being crazy on fire and at ease is its own culmination. It's everything I want from living my dreams.

INSPIRED SUCCESSISMS

Good things don't happen in the future. They happen now.
Linear time focuses on the past and the future.
But the good stuff, the high jolt of liberation, is now, baby, now.

Impatience is a form of anger, and creation is a path of love.
Only love will move you forward.

When you hunger for velocity, the hunger
below the hunger is to fall in love
with the work before you, to stumble across the threshold into the zone,
that elusive magic rush of being present.

You won't find any aspect of your work boring or
time-consuming once you're consumed.
As we channel all of our mental energy into this time and space,
we blaze through the ordinary into the magnetic divine.

Here's the day when everything changes.
It's the day we realize that we're not doing our work to *get* somewhere,
as much as to *be* somewhere right now.

The quality of your life is not the amount of things you get done.
Quality depends on how much *beingness* you flood into each experience.

When you get here, you'll get there.

When I settle into and blaze *where* I am, I finally know *what* I am.
I taste my bigness, my love, and the exhilaration of my own nature.

THERE ARE NO DEADLINES
ON INSPIRED TIME

In the moment that a new-and-improved version of life is born out of the life you are living, you have the option of aligning with the new idea or resisting it.

ESTHER AND JERRY HICKS, *THE ASTONISHING POWER OF EMOTIONS*

There is no measuring with time . . . Being an artist means not reckoning and counting, but ripening . . .

RAINER MARIA RILKE, *LETTERS TO A YOUNG POET*

There's a difference between "getting something done" and giving birth to an explosive new self-expression. It's a whole different game show. It's the kind of difference that can make the smallest task seem like crossing a desert on stilts, while listening to some time-management evangelist in your head. If you have the wrong expectations, you will feel lame and hobbled.

It's admirable, really, and so very endearing, this desire for efficiency and control. But do you know how to change your beliefs at a cellular level, order up the timing of world events, or make lightning strike? Let me ask you, can you really know what the perfect timeline is for forging one extraordinary life? How long does it take to heal inside, learn to breathe large, and meet the world unconditionally with love, conviction, and talents you didn't even know you had? Of course, I understand, you thought you were just trying to set up a meeting or write a book proposal. Yeah, I see, but action is the last step, because it's the last snowflake on the tip of the iceberg. Meanwhile, everything has to line up deep down inside you first.

That's why you might want to take your idea of a timeline and shred it into little bits of confetti, and sprinkle it around your room. That or you could set a date on your calendar, same thing. Because like it or not, you are not in charge of the Genius Department. And the head Big Dog is moody, flippant, thorough as hell, and sometimes, it's true, gets weeks and centuries a little mixed up.

My client Karen has put together a business plan for her dream to open an Internet store and portal for yoga practitioners. Each week she creates a to-do list that looks like the instructions for building a small country, and each week goes by and her to-do list is still congested with tasks. "I don't feel like I'm moving forward," she says. But that's not true. It's just more involved than she realized it would be. Every step begets a hundred micro-decisions that command her concentration as much as threading tiny needles in dim light. On the surface, things look basic and simple. But underneath every action lies questions. What does her brand represent in the world? Does she believe in what she's offering? Is she making the wisest choice for her website's shopping cart and for the infrastructure of her business, her life, and her future? Every transaction feels like an Olympics relay race for her psyche and soul.

Then of course there's our personal emotional barricades, you know, those precious opportunities for *more* healing. "I find all this resistance coming up," says Steven, a client of mine who has decided to finally take his video work to the next level. It's this resistance that's stopped him his whole adult life. There's the voice of his dismissive mother standing at the gateway of every action. There's a reason he waited this long to go after his dreams. Now the doubts and old stories are surfacing one by one for healing. What if I fail? Do I deserve big success? Can I trust myself? "This stuff

never came up for me even when I headed up a major division for a Fortune 500 company," he says. Of course it didn't. Working at a job he didn't
love was emotionally safe. Going after something he believes in, infusing
his essence into every detail, that's where the shaman meets the demon.
Then try telling that to all those noses pressed up against the window of
your life, asking you, "Did you get that website up yet?" Try telling them
you're working on another set of inner demons right now, and that search
engine optimization is the least of your concerns.

One of my clients had a personal power outage because, at the urging
of a professional, she set a strict timeline for writing a book. Her former
business coach was all about accountability. Why didn't she have the chapter done? Wasn't she serious? Every week she paid to confess her sins. She
felt worse about herself because he prodded her to set all these goals,
which she didn't meet. I asked her if he was a writer or involved in any
creative projects himself. "No," she said. "He'd been a manager for a mega
corporation. I thought he could help me get down to business." Instead he
just helped her get down.

To me it was obvious that he didn't understand the nature of this electrifying transformation. Soul time is different from linear time. It's a time
of birthing, redefining, asking fundamental questions, surrendering to a
mystical creative force, and healing any place within us where we have
failed to champion and forgive ourselves. People who don't work in creative time have a bit more of a simplistic view, and they like to tell you, just
when you're feeling something like a jellyfish tangled in seaweed, that it
really is easy to get things done. It can seem awfully tempting to believe
them, especially because they get things done, and have time to clip cou-
pons, clean out their car, and criticize you. But look deeply into their eyes,
and glimpse the flatness of their gaze for just a moment, and you will remember that some never question the value of *what* they're getting done
or at what cost.

Ellen is a weight loss expert who helps men and women take back their health. She has three different projects that she is working on and she hasn't finished any of them. She feels like a failure. "Why can't I finish this?" she says, and she secretly waits to hear that I think she is a deadbeat loser waste of time and that she can't finish things because they are not worth anything and the Universe knows this and deliberately blocks her for the good of all. That thought really hasn't crossed my mind. I'm not sure what to think, so I ask more questions.

As we explore together, she tells me she can't finish the book because it doesn't present the information the way she wants. She wants a multimedia thing going on—cyber bells, beads, fireworks, and dancing girls. She wants to use the Web to experiment with taking men and women into a whole new kind of experience. As she elaborates, her voice quickens, and she goes from guilt to excitement in about two minutes. Talking through it, she realizes that writing the book has taken her into another dimension of her creativity, and that to just finish the book isn't really the point. She hasn't finished the book because that wouldn't finish the project.

I call this artistic integrity, following where your energy and mission lead you. It may look like hopscotch to others, but it takes an enduring commitment to honor your inspiration as it evolves or crystallizes. Danielle, another client, kept changing her business ideas almost weekly, and with them, her potential market. "But with every change, this business is getting to be more of me," she said. I loved her willingness to track the scent of her true desire. She wasn't being irresponsible, but doggedly responsive to her soul's communication. With artistic integrity, it's not a matter of getting things done. It's about feeling complete.

Sometimes we're working on things we don't even know are in the works. After I published *This Time I Dance! Creating the Work You Love*, I felt hideously slow in selling books and workshops and establishing a national presence. I was a butterfly pounding on the walls of my cocoon. Then one day a friend of mine poked a saber through that cocoon. Knowing that I was hoping to write this next book on being "wildly successful," she said, "How could you really write the book on how to succeed if you hadn't hit some walls and failed? What would you have to say?" Suddenly I saw everything I'd gone through as useful rather than as a pathetic reflection or really sad breaks. I realized it was part of my mission to teach myself and others to access their true power, in every kind of circumstance. Everything felt alive again. My experience hadn't kept me behind. In fact, it was moving me forward.

Set timelines if you like. Just know that sometimes your rope will be too small for the wild bull you're trying to lasso. On that note, I just can't help but think of the classic Zen proverb that goes something like this: Three blind men approach and touch an elephant. The one who touches the tusk declares the beast is surely a horn. The other grasping the trunk imagines some kind of snake. The story goes on and reveals that all of the men guessed wrong. They had felt only parts, insisted on a partial reality, and had not discovered the whole.

It's hard to know the timing when you don't really know the goal. I urge you to have the conscious courage to guess wrong, change your mind, change your goal, and, in the end, bring a different animal to the table and to our world.

INSPIRED SUCCESSISMS

There's a difference between getting something done
and giving birth to an explosive new self-expression.

Can you really know what the perfect timeline is
for forging one extraordinary life?

Action is the last step, because it's the last
snowflake on the tip of the iceberg.
Meanwhile, everything has to line up deep down inside you first.

You might want to take your idea of a timeline
and shred it into little bits of confetti, and sprinkle it around your room.
That or you could set a date on your calendar, same thing.

Every step begets a hundred micro-decisions
that command her concentration
as much as threading tiny needles in dim light.
On the surface, things look basic and simple.
But underneath every action lies questions.

I call this artistic integrity, following where
your energy and mission lead you.
It may look like hopscotch to others,
but it takes an enduring commitment to honor
your inspiration as it evolves or crystallizes.

With artistic integrity, it's not a matter of getting things done.
It's about feeling complete.

It's hard to know the timing when you don't really know the goal.

TIMING WILL TURN ON A DIME

Some things arrive in their own mysterious hour, on their own terms and not yours, to be seized or relinquished forever.

GAIL GODWIN

Patience is natural to the teacher of God. All he sees is certain outcome, at a time perhaps unknown to him as yet, but not in doubt. The time will be as right as is the answer.

A COURSE IN MIRACLES

great saxophonist senses the exact millisecond to belt out a note. He also knows when to wait and safeguard his golden-winged lung power for the opening where it counts. Perfect timing is about two sides of the same coin, the faith to act, and the faith to wait. The wisdom tradition in *A Course in Miracles* teaches that "those who are certain of the outcome can afford to wait, and wait without anxiety." Wait without anxiety? Valium and Xanax aside, most of us don't even know how to *think* about waiting . . . without anxiety.

But what if you knew you were on the right train, right on track? What if you knew you would be given everything you need at your ideal time to receive it? Yes, I know you think *now* would be nice. But remember that darling hunk who never called back, the one you later found out robbed another woman's antique jewelry collection, gave her herpes, and ran over her flower bed as he fled the state? Or the job you had to have that later turned into the job you had to extract yourself from, with the help of a therapist, a crane, a psychic, a shaman, and finally that strange little ritual in the wilderness? Still convinced you know exactly what should happen and when? Maybe not.

I know I would have saved a lot more time if I had less fear. I'd have paid attention to the moment in front of me, as though it offered me a once-in-a-lifetime opportunity or training course. Because every moment does. Yet part of me always wanted to rush the process, hitch a ride that wasn't mine, speed into the center of glitz town like a gambler desperate for a win. Now I want only the gold that comes delivered to my door. Finally, I know my opportunities have my name on them and I don't have to shake the tree to get them, or hurl myself out of the nest before I've grown wings. Timing is natural and instantaneous. When it's time to expand, my instincts nudge me, and a next wind current comes. I am meant to fly in my own bright time.

Years ago, when I first self-published my book, I had a famous author write a testimonial for me. Then she absolutely shocked me. She called me—little, self-published, unknown-author me—and left a beautiful invitation on my message machine: "I think you should send your book to my literary agent and get it published by a major publisher. I'll tell him about your work." You would have thought I'd start chanting in ecstasy, but for some reason I felt a hesitation about sending it to the agent. I felt this squishy heaviness in my stomach. Do you know the feeling of trying to make yourself be in love with someone or something? I wanted to be giddy, decisive, and grateful. Yet I felt oddly ill at ease, as though I'd gotten onto the wrong elevator.

"Am I just afraid of success?" I wrote in my journal. This question lunged its pitchfork into the softness of my white belly. "Come on, admit it, you're just scared. Here's the big time delivered to your door and you're cowering," the mean, "protective" voice taunted. I didn't understand myself. Why wasn't I just gushing forward, running barefoot, buying roses and chocolate for everyone?

I'm one of those people who needs to talk things out, so I talked and talked with my partner, Paul, who eventually didn't really care if I chose to burn my book or eat it for breakfast, just as long as I'd stop talking about it.

Finally, the truth fell out of me. "I do want to be published by a New York publisher. I do want a big-league publisher," I said, and started crying with the bald-truth admission. Then I surprised both of us, saying, "Just not right now." That was the truth. It hung there like a bare lightbulb. It was a truth that absolutely baffled me, still it felt like I had taken a feeling-blob, a black mass in the littered cosmos, and distilled it into words.

Listening to the truth of the moment, not judging or adjusting it, I realized that I didn't feel one hundred percent available or galvanized by the possibility being offered. I wanted to feel ready to do this high dive, but I didn't. In my journal, my wise voice said, "It will do no good to force or push anything. You cannot be where you think you should be, only where you are, and where you are is the threshold of the right path for you."

I told the author that I really appreciated her offer, but it didn't feel right and that was that. I turned around and went back to the rather daunting business of having a newly self-published book to launch into the world. Yet for some reason I felt excited and pure and whole. I had listened to myself. It was bold and crazy, but I felt honored and protected, even if I didn't fully understand my own remarkable leanings.

Then, maybe just three weeks or so later, I read an e-mail in my office. "Your Fairy Godmother has arrived," it began. You already know the story. It was a woman who had been in the publishing industry and had worked for Random House and who had read my book. She gushed on and on about how much she loved the book. And then she volunteered to help me get it published by a major New York house. I printed the e-mail and took it into my meditation room.

I don't know how many times I read that e-mail, but no doubt enough times to have recited it by memory in pig Latin, should the need arise. Something felt right about it all, as though this were a dream unfolding, as though I'd been here before, as though I knew it would always happen just like this and she was the one, she was the one, she was the one. There was no holding back this time.

"I want to do this," I told Paul later that day. He stared at me in disbelief as I had been storming back and forth in the kitchen just weeks ago, jackhammering away as to why it wasn't right for me to do traditional publishing just yet. "No, I'm not hormonal," I said, just in case the thought had crossed his mind, "or bipolar," shooting him "the look" that may have suggested homicidal. I know I must have seemed like I'd reversed absolutely everything I'd said about "just not now," everything I'd adamantly said just days before. But I'd said that truth in another lifetime. Some new consciousness had sprung to life like bluebells on the hill.

That's the thing about this crazy adventure in co-creation. Timing will turn on a dime. You are always evolving. You are always growing, getting in touch with new information and perspectives. With the right opportunity, you feel the energy to say yes. Readiness comes of itself. You can't force it, fake it, or bribe the bouncer at the door. You grow your first baby tooth, you say your first words, and you finally feel ready to show your gifts to the world, or to hire an assistant and put together a team. One day, at the right time, everything changes, and not a second before. Every moment has its own original arc and harvest.

"It's not an opportunity if it doesn't feel like an opportunity." I wrote and underlined this message in my journal many years ago. I'd had a nervous, thin man take one of my classes and tell me he might be able to publish my writing. Back then, if you even mentioned the word "publishing," it was like instant opium or a tractor beam to me. George had a small publishing company, now that I think of it, probably just a photocopy machine in his closet, no more commercial than an Easy-Bake toy oven, and it probably smelled of his awful hair gel. I hated the smell of that hair gel and how he spoke really fast and loudly as though volume could make up for lack of substance. Still, one part of myself kept threatening in a husky whisper, "You better not miss this opportunity." Here's what it meant: "You're a loser. This person thinks you have some mysterious merit. You better jump on it before he comes to his senses. God knows when something like this will come along again." For the record, this part of myself, the desperate beggar who would eat way too much at the salad bar, does not make good decisions, at all, ever.

I met Mr. Icky Slick at a coffeehouse and he never once looked at my writing. He spent the entire time blazing on about himself, doing some kind of elaborate sales pitch, probably with the fantastical notion of scoring a future date. It took all the restraint I had not to slap myself in the face in front of him. I'd known the truth inside myself and I just hadn't listened. Besides, hair gel never lies.

That night I wrote in my journal a reminder to myself for all time. "It's not an opportunity—if it doesn't feel like an opportunity." "If it feels like a 'should,' it's not your turn and it's not your taxi." Now, just to be clear, I have accepted other opportunities that felt big, scary, and hairy to me. But they always felt like the time to take this step. I always had the sense that I was supposed to do this, supposed to grow in this way, and that this was a sturdy, true vehicle that would serve me well. I may still have felt a thousand butterflies inside, but I didn't feel a bowling ball in the pit of my stomach.

Readiness is by invitation only. Trust each moment to take you where you need to go. You won't always have the same feelings or thoughts or perspectives. One day you wake up and things are different. New opportunities now become available. I think of our opportunities as a carousel ride with colorful horses that sail around and around and around. When it's your time, you'll see your horse. You'll jump and fly through the air like a natural. You're always a natural in the right time.

INSPIRED SUCCESSISMS

Perfect timing is about two sides of the same coin,
the faith to act, and the faith to wait.

What if you knew you were on the right train, right on track?
What if you knew you would be given everything
you need at your ideal time to receive it?

I would have saved a lot more time if I had less fear.
I'd have paid attention to the moment in front of me,
as though it offered me a once-in-a-lifetime
opportunity or training course.

I want only the gold that comes delivered to my door.
Finally, I know my opportunities have my name on them
and I don't have to shake the tree to get them.

Timing is natural and instantaneous.
When it's time to expand, my instincts nudge me,
and a next wind current comes.
I am meant to fly in my own bright time.

Timing will turn on a dime. You are always evolving.

It's not an opportunity—if it doesn't feel like an opportunity.
If it feels like a "should," it's not your turn and it's not your taxi.

Readiness is by invitation only. . . . You won't always
have the same feelings or thoughts or perspectives.
One day you wake up and things are different.

WHAT HAPPENED BEFORE IS NO MORE

For the first time I considered how, despite my resistance to external authority, I often allow the authority of my experience—that which has come before—to shape what I see in this moment. . . .

ORIAH MOUNTAIN DREAMER, WHAT WE ACHE FOR

To shrink one's sense of potential based solely on past experience— what could possibly be more arrogant? It's a way of playing God, of damning the entire future before it ever has a chance to arrive.

RAPHAEL CUSHNIR, SETTING YOUR HEART ON FIRE

Many of us who do work we love sometimes feel this sense of having been sent to the back of the line or looked over by the Great Prize Giver in the Sky. We try to stay positive and believing, keeping our energy up, but deep down inside we're blowing out the candles and mourning in the dark. The background theme song plays something like this: "It should have happened by now." Or "I guess I'm never going to get that big break."

It's easy to allow the passage of time to become some kind of indictment against you. You know, if you were a real genius and all, you'd have a record label by now, have boatloads of income, and probably your own reality television show just so we could see you breathe. Let's face it, our media-crazed culture shoves it in your face. I know I'd watch pop stars on television, young, sparkling, thin, and insanely wealthy. I'd read about start-up companies in *People* or *Fast Company* magazine or authors who took the world by storm on their way to turning twenty. Meanwhile, I felt like I was aging, accumulating chin hair and lines instead of wealth, and nowhere near my garden spot on the mountaintop. Why wasn't I further along?

"Well, how do you know where you are?" said a quicksilver elfin voice in my journal one day. It's obvious, I thought. I calculated the years I'd already put in. It was clear I was riding a donkey to success on the back roads of the slow track. "That perception is your problem," said the voice in my journal. "What happened to being on an adventure of unforeseeable possibilities? Now you're on some kind of named-and-known, set-in-stone road. When you define the territory, you're no longer in divine territory."

It was true. I'd lost my sense of innocence. And if you lose your innocence, you've lost your perspective and your way.

Timing isn't about a trajectory. It's about innocence. It's about opening up to the moment in a naked way and crossing over a new threshold every single time. I once had a Buddhist friend tell me that enlightenment isn't about how much time or effort you put into meditation. Enlightenment is a quality of mind. It comes as a result of a total letting-go of the limited self. The one who sits down in the moonlight for the first true time is the one who wakes up.

My journal entry reminded me of a story I'd once heard about Merlin and the great king Arthur. Arthur says to Merlin, "I will never forget you." The impish Merlin replies, "Well, I do hope to forget you." Arthur looks crestfallen. "Why would you want to forget me?" he whimpers. Merlin, wizard of enchantment, looks at him with pure, magic love, and says, "Why, so that I could meet you again."

And this is how we do inspired work in the world. We intentionally let go of limiting "past experience." Otherwise, we will never experience the unrepeatable combination of available atoms, impulsive magic, or opportunity before us. We will enter the memory of the river instead of the river. Yes, it's a tall order to approach the present without the past. But that's just something we tell ourselves, too.

Contemporary spiritual teacher Eckhart Tolle, Mr. Now, as he's known around my house, says, "Present-moment awareness creates a gap not only in the stream of mind but also in the past-future continuum. Nothing truly new and creative can come into this world except through that gap, that clear space of infinite possibility." So there you have it. You can have infinite possibility—or none.

This is a rigorous and courageous path of staying humble, unsullied, and open to the truth. We are on soul time. We are partnering with a wild, divine, unlimited partner. Anything can happen at any time.

The world teaches us to learn from our experience, but that kind of "learning" often denies the sequence, capacities, and dimensions of the nonlinear. In the Zen Buddhist tradition, students are introduced to the phenomenon of beginner's mind. Beginner's mind is an expansive intelligence. It's available mind. Anything else is a small box that constrains our natural abundance and infinite chances. Zen master Shunryu Suzuki explains, "In the beginner's mind there are many possibilities, in the expert's mind there are few."

Where are you starting to define your future based on your past experience? Whenever you lose heart, know that you have entered the gulag of linear time, an illusion of a painful certainty. You will need to break free and remember the mysterious energies with which you work. Inspired work is never impacted by how things have proceeded before. This kind of abundance flows from an eternal, outside-of-time source.

The world doesn't inflict scarcity or take away our chances. We do. I remember when I wanted to throw in the towel after an incident with my publishing house. My publisher generously decided to relaunch my book *This Time I Dance!* with a new cover, a new foreword, and a new publicity and marketing push. I saw it as a second chance to make up for all the things we didn't do the first time. Getting ready to meet with the team in New York and go over things, I could hardly contain myself. I felt like gardens were blooming everywhere, even though it was only March. I fussed with my hair and straightened my black jacket for the thirtieth time. I wanted to look sharp, think sharp, say earth-shatteringly brilliant things, and be worthy of this surprise and unusual opportunity.

But when I got into the office, the gardens dried up and left dust on my fine black jacket. The meeting was fast and abrupt. The publicist and marketing person didn't make it. Then I found out, they didn't *have* a publicist, and would be training a new interim one when they could, say in about a century from now, or at the very least, way too late for *my* book. I smiled a great big unruffled plastic smile and swallowed the panic and incredulity for later. Finally, I was informed that the chain bookstores would most likely not carry my book because it hadn't sold enough copies in the first forty-five days of the first launch. I felt like there was this huge bowling ball coming down the lane, fast and furious, knocking down each and every one of my shiny pins. Now, I had nothing to pin my hopes on.

There would be no second chance, as I'd imagined. "Everything is going the same way it went the first time," I wrote in my journal that night. I felt betrayed by God. Why did you set me up for this? Why was I given this opportunity if it was only going to be a savage repeat of disappointment? Something in me broke. It all felt like a dream, as though I'd been given a glass elevator ride up to a great height, only to have the cables cut. I couldn't stop falling inside.

Now that I "knew what was going on," I felt my blood go black. I completely lost confidence. Of course, my assumptions were the problem: *I thought I knew what was going on*. I didn't know what was going on. I couldn't know. I'd vowed to work with an Inspired Essence that had no fear, limits, or lack of crazy power, magnetism, and bandwidth up its shimmering sleeve. How could I know what was going to happen?

I still had a second chance and a third and a fourth and a billionth. Yes, the circumstances changed. Then I'd allowed my attitude to change. And that was the pitfall. I'd stopped trusting in the miraculous strength of my True Self that had taken me every step of the way so far, including a spontaneous relaunch of a book, which never happens in the "real" world. I'd made up a drama about how nothing was working out now. I allowed that story to narrow, blur, and diminish my reality.

The day I let go of that story was the day I stepped into my second chance.

Step beyond your negative story. New opportunities always await you. A fresh world just came into being while you read that sentence. Deepak Chopra describes a spiritual "Law of Pure Potentiality." He says, "We are in our essential state, pure consciousness. Pure consciousness is pure potentiality; it is the field of all possibilities and infinite creativity." Your limited story applies only to your limited self.

I've experienced pure potentiality, even when I didn't have those words. I once wrote an article and sent it in to a large national magazine. The magazine didn't respond. "You're not worth a rejection slip," contributed my inner defeatist. "This is just like when you tried to freelance before," it whined. "Same old thing. Work for hours and it ends up in the void and no one reads it." Yet for some reason, I believed in the importance of this piece for this particular magazine. I knew the gate had already slammed shut, but I decided to approach the magazine again. It seemed wacky and obstinate, but also intuitive. I submitted the article as though there had never been a past. A day later, I got an e-mail from the managing editor of the magazine. They loved and bought the article. They even chose to use it for one of their featured books. I have no idea what happened at that magazine. Yet this I know: I stepped into magic present time, which has no story line.

The moment that timing is weighing on your heart, know that it is not timing. It's an interpretation. You're choosing to believe something that does not set you free. The great Irish rock band U2 sings, "You got stuck in a moment in time." That's what happens to many of us. Something happens and we give up our spirit. We give up our love of adventure. In that moment, we become tourists just reading the brochures that others have left behind. We are no longer encountering the terrain. We're living in our assumptions. Empty your mind. Trade history in for mystery. Be willing to be innocent and step into a new field of opportunity every amazing time.

INSPIRED SUCCESSISMS

When you define the territory, you're no longer in divine territory.

Timing isn't about a trajectory. It's about innocence.
It's about opening up to the moment in a naked way and
crossing over a new threshold every single time.

You can have infinite possibility—or none.

Where are you starting to define your future based
on your past experience?
Whenever you lose heart, know that you have entered the gulag
of linear time, an illusion of a painful certainty.

We are partnering with a wild, divine, unlimited partner.
Anything can happen at any time.

Inspired work is never impacted by how things have proceeded before.
This kind of abundance flows from an eternal, outside-of-time source.

Your limited story applies only to your limited self.

Trade history in for mystery.
Be willing to be innocent and step into a new field of
opportunity every amazing time.

6.

YOU'RE A POWERHOUSE, NOT A RENTAL

I don't believe in blasphemy, but if I did, I think it's when we invalidate our gifts, work small, or mumble about what we have to offer. If the heavens were less heavenly, I'm certain they would spit. But maybe that's just me.

Oh, you hate marketing or promoting yourself, and would rather it all just go away, only, whoops, your business goes away instead. Honey, your gifts are inspired, given to you by Brilliance, not chopped liver. Honor the light that comes through you—by honoring the work you do.

Respect your power, know your power, walk your power—and do not let a crabby accountant in your head degrade your progress based on skin-deep balance sheets. In my book, true value has nothing to do with numbers. And, hey, this is my book.

PROMOTION IS DEVOTION

*Many entrepreneurs make the mistake of thinking that their price is
too high when, in reality, the value communicated is too low.*

SETH GODIN, *THE BOOTSTRAPPER'S BIBLE*

*I'm not against good works, but I am opposed to starvation. After all,
even missionaries are paid a salary, and martyrs are in it for a longer-
term payback.*

ALAN WEISS, *MONEY TALKS*

For years I've thought it's unfair that we visionary, spiritual, help-the-world types have to promote ourselves. Marketing should be someone else's job, someone who loves it, loves "elevator speeches," pitches, slogans, and speaking to the consumer in a way that makes them consume like savages. Unfortunately, not all of us can afford a Madison Avenue marketing team. We're not making that much money. Hey, maybe it's because we don't know how to market. Go figure.

But you know, there's some wisdom in making those who hate to market, market. It's not about hyping, showboating, conning, or groveling. It's about *owning* our brilliance. We have been given sacred gifts from the Sacred Gift Department and it is our responsibility to polish these jewels and use our lives like prongs to hold them up to the light. It's our healing to actively value the love that comes though us and to us.

Forget therapy, baby, selling what you love is where it's at. If you want to unearth all the places where you feel wounded, unlovable, inadequate, a cross between your mortified junior high self and dreams where you stand before the FBI in your underwear, try self-promotion. Seriously, I'd say it's right up there with primal scream therapy.

Salespeople will tell you that the first sale you ever make is to yourself. The rest is just good communication. I always remember a woman I met years ago who said, "I can help clients start their own business, and I'm the best one out there." She said this easily, breezily, and not as though she'd have to run out of the room and throw up into a brown paper bag afterward. "How do you know that?" I asked. She answered, plain as rice, "If you don't know it, you shouldn't be out there." Right then and there I practically fell to my knees and prayed, Please, God, give me this woman's brain chemistry for a *day*, a dram of her confidence, or at least a sneak peek into her medicine cabinet.

I'm not saying you have to be her, but I've watched too many individuals who do the work they love, actively diminish their own value. They charge less than they should, and talk about their work as though they're actually trying to convince you, *no really*, that it's not that great or important. They feel squishy about charging for miracles they perform with ease. Here's the deal. Just because it's second nature to you doesn't mean it's second class. I'm thrilled my physician finds his work easy. I don't mind one bit that he loves it and can bring me back to health without struggle. In fact, we call those kinds of people virtuosos, specialists, or rock stars—and pay them more.

Nikki is a psychotherapist who transforms her clients' lives. Still, she says she hates selling. She's a self-proclaimed touchy-feely type and doesn't want to invade people's privacy, push, or sound desperate, which of course she is. So she "hides her light beneath a bushel," and soon she will need to live there, because only a trickle of people know about her skills. "I just don't like talking about myself," she says. "So, don't," I say to her, and you. Part of valuing what you do is getting yourself out of the picture. You're not selling *you*. You're selling a solution, a hope, an experience, a doorway, or a tool or tincture of the divine. Just provide information with clarity and dignity. Spell out the benefits people can receive, or what you can help make possible. You're not smarmy because you're direct. You're not selling anything. You're offering some people an end to their search.

Tell us why *you* love this work, not why *we* should love it. This isn't about spin. It's about telling the truth, the deepest truth about your excitement and fascination. It's always healing and authentic to share your love. Have you ever seen a singer tell you the story behind a song? It's like being invited to a party, welcomed in through the front door. As an audience member, I love "being in on" the journey of the song. It makes my heart plump up into a soft, warm apple turnover with every chorus. Hey, it's my song, too, now. Use your love to educate us, not obligate us to buy your premium package. If you simply share your love, you're not susceptible to rejection because you're not looking for anything. You're just telling us there's a party going on.

Sometimes you have to work hard at seeing the value you offer. You have to unzip your duck suit, that waterproof layer that insulates you from allowing in praise and recognition. Let it in, baby, or you won't ever let your powerhouse self out. The people who admire you have been given this special task in life to help you see yourself. In *A Course in Miracles*, it says that you will learn your value by seeing the gratitude in your brother's eyes. Often your clients or customers teach you your value. They glow with recognition or behold what's outstanding about you. They have received the gift. They do not discount this power.

Think about the person you love (or would love) working with or performing for most. How do they see you? How do they view what you enable them to experience? Start seeing yourself that way, and more of those kinds of customers or clients will hire you. If you want to make more money, you've got to swallow your honey. Everybody pays you what you think of yourself.

I talked to a bestselling author once and grilled him on how he got to the point of supporting himself effortlessly with workshops. He said, "One day I heard all this great feedback about my seminar, and I took that in. I really listened to what people said, and I thought, If I'm really that guy, and I'm helping people to do those things, then that has major value." After that, business just came his way. "I finally got my ego out of the way and allowed the good," he says.

Of course for many of us, religion may have put shame and valuing ourselves in the same gift bag. I see a hunchbacked old woman in a black gunnysack dress. She spits when you praise a child. She spits when you think you did well at a meeting. What is all that saliva about anyway, and, come on, really, does the presence of drool ever light a fire? I've heard it's about protecting against the evil eye, but I'm thinking it *is* the evil eye. Then there's the philosophy that sees us as less than earthworms, born unworthy, broken, filthy, hopeless, and evil, and, man, doesn't that just give you a nice warm boost and a place to start? Here's the truth: You are a steward of an amazing ability. There is nothing divine about deprecating your gifts and talents or diminishing their worth in any way. Shining is sharing an abundance with us all.

Of course, there's the whole "money is evil" thing, too, and its frocked medieval cousin, "it's more enlightened to be poor." Years ago, I taught classes on a donation basis at a spiritual center, passing around a basket like a panhandler at a train station. People would throw in a few dollars, while they left to spend gobs more money on beers and chicken wings, for God's sake. I felt frustrated. I saw life-changing value in these classes. Still, many other spiritual teachers counseled me that "it wasn't spiritual" to charge much money. Apparently, I learned later, it *was* spiritual to resent your students for not donating funds to the center, and downright holy to judge "gas-guzzling" SUVs.

One night I wrote in my journal: "If I practiced law, you'd pay me $350 an hour to sue someone. If I taught you how to forgive, heal, or fulfill your mission on this earth, you'd only drop a dollar in a basket. There's something wrong with that." I was fine with offering help or discounts for those who really couldn't pay, but I wasn't fine with teaching others that a latte, a plate of nachos, or a nose ring had more value than this work. With initial trepidation, I decided to offer classes that charged a set fee, an honorable fee, and required an eight-week commitment. My new classes soared in popularity. It turns out, students put more energy into the classes they paid more for and they got better results. When I valued the work, so did they.

Sometimes it's hard for us to know how to charge people, how to value our work. Years ago, I was struggling with pricing because, again, for those who worked with any kind of holistic focus, it was customary to charge trifling "spiritual" fees. It also seemed customary to drive beat-up old cars with brake problems and bumper stickers that proclaimed, "The Universe Is Abundant." One day, Don, an in-your-face older businessman, talked me into a different context. "How much would you charge as an attorney?" he asked. "This is different," I said. "No it's not," he said. "People are paying to be with an honors graduate from Harvard Law School, to have that kind of mind delve into their lives with them." I suddenly got what he meant. They were paying to be with *me*, and I had to look at this one-of-a-kind experience, not just the going rate.

Now, maybe you don't have an Ivy League education. But you do have incomparable credentials. You bring everything you are to this work. Your life experience provides your training and exclusive attributes. I once worked with a client who had permanently cured himself of a major health condition with a particular meditation. He wanted to help others heal, too. "I don't have any credentials," he said. He meant he didn't have a Ph.D. in his closet (though you can buy one on the Internet these days) or an ancestral lineage in Buddhism. I looked at him blankly, like maybe he didn't have credentials—or brain cells. "Results, experience, and love are the best credentials on the planet," I said. People want help more than they want paper. Besides, when you have real, true, passionate experience with something, at least as far as I'm concerned, you do have a Ph.D.: Personal Healing Dharma.

Recently, I saw an artist at an art festival selling canvases and prints. She charged higher prices than other nearby painters. I read the description of her work and noticed she said these pieces contained *curandera* vibrational healing energy and would radiate a frequency. Good for you, I thought to myself. She owned her contribution and narrated a value in a neutral, this-is-so way. She wasn't bragging. She wasn't padding. She was serving her public with information.

We are here to shine our light. We are here to own our value, love what we love, and croon it from the rooftops because we can't help it, not because we're trying to sell something. Finally, in the end, I don't know who needs to buy my material, and it's not even my concern. But I know that *I* need to buy it with all my heart. That's what all of this is about.

INSPIRED SUCCESSISMS

It's not about hyping, showboating, conning, or groveling.
It's about *owning* our brilliance.

Just because it's second nature to you doesn't mean it's second class.

Part of valuing what you do is getting yourself out of the picture.
You're not selling *you*. You're selling a solution, a hope,
an experience, a doorway, or a tool or tincture of the divine.

You're not smarmy because you're direct. You're not selling anything.
You're offering some people an end to their search.

Use your love to educate us, not obligate us
to buy your premium package.
If you simply share your love, you're not susceptible to rejection.

If you want to make more money, you've got to swallow your honey.
Everybody pays you what you think of yourself.

You are a steward of an amazing ability.
There is nothing divine about deprecating your gifts
and talents or diminishing their worth in any way.

I don't know who needs to buy my material, and it's not even my concern.
But I know that *I* need to buy it with all my heart.
That's what this is all about.

YOU'LL HAVE BIGGER FISH TO FRY WHEN YOU'RE NOT FRIED

Have you ever noticed the term "cash flow"? There's flow in cash flow. More cash brings flow. But more flow brings cash.

A JOURNAL ENTRY

When I consistently take things just to make money, I turn what I love into a job. I lose my spark. The magic slippers turn back into work boots. Eventually, I become bored and stale and lose the business anyway.

A JOURNAL ENTRY

Maybe you're great at what you do, you're an overachiever and you can get any job done and done well. It's one of the secrets to your success. And, unchecked, it can also be the secret to your poverty. Because real abundance comes from *growing*—staying true to your heat-seeking, light-gobbling self, and the glimmer that ignites you now.

Here's a good example. Dianna designed unique silver jewelry for a living. Her talents took off. She sold to private clients and to exclusive retailers and had back orders, front orders, and sideways orders. "I got so busy tending orders, I didn't have as much time to come up with new designs or marketing materials. I became a factory," she says, a crack in her voice. And then her real admission, "Being this busy tires me. I am doing better financially, but I think it keeps me small."

She's right and she has the brown bags under her eyes to prove it. It was time for her to hire people, raise her prices, steal time away, take an organic cooking class or hike in the Andes, create a new line, leverage her popularity, or all of the above. Abundance always comes from growing your soul or vision, then growing your work, and then *growing your vision again*. Because when your work becomes all about putting out fires, you just can't be stirring one up.

This is one of the laws in creative work. We keep growing. We instinctively seek our newest expression, our next peak or gravitational pull. There will come times when the success of one level is now the shame or failure of another. It's time to grow. Your soul gets bored—been there, done that, want to express a new frequency. Evolution is part of the divine equation. That means letting go of your identity again and again. Personally, I hate this part, and if you took one look at my closet, assuming you could fight your way in there, you'd see what I mean. Just to give you a hint, feng shui people I know have stopped giving me their business cards and, I suspect, tuck a clove of garlic in their pockets when they see me. Still, abundance requires surrender, letting go of control somewhere or somehow, and running with your heart wide open into the feral loving arms of the unknown.

One year in my business I came up with this theory for myself of catching bass instead of minnows. I realized I was spending so much time catching minnows, small tiny fish, and needing tons of them, that I couldn't possibly catch a bass. I was busy all the time, but not *active*, actively growing the next iteration of my work. At the time, I'd met this high-powered woman with great business connections and I hadn't had the emotional resources to follow up with her in a serious way. I was tired and busy and angry and it seemed like an awful lot for this woman to waltz into my life right now and expect me to appreciate the opportunity. Of course, it was an opportunity, but when you're in the war zone, everyone starts looking like shrapnel. She swam by. I realized then that I was burning out instead of burning bright. I had to let some minnows go, to make room for bigger fish.

That summer, I decided to take a step back and try my "big fish" theory out. I wanted work that felt bigger to me, work that felt like it used more of what I genuinely had to offer. I also wanted to be paid more, to be more respected for my experience, now that I actually had some. I decided I would say yes only to things that felt alive to me. I was going to turn down speaking engagements that didn't feel right up my alley, and no longer coach clients who instead of hitting the emotional tennis ball back over to my side of the net, lay down on the court and ordered room service. This felt scary, since I still had to make a living. But I put a border around this intuitive madness, deciding to experiment for three months in the summer. Of course, like an immediate simulated test case from the Universe, the phone rang the next day. It was a demanding person wanting me to speak to an organization that paid very little and attracted people who were not my ideal audience, not *anybody's* ideal audience, really.

Still, they wanted me, oh how nice. And they paid a little something, say enough to buy a jar of applesauce. Well, and I *did* have an itch for cash, and the fresh gaping chasm in my schedule. My ego began its usual wheedle, "What could it hurt? It's only a few hours. You never know what could come from it." But I did know what could come from it. I could take hours out of my day to drive to this place and feel as though I'd put on a lead suit, the heavy drape you wear at the dentist's office to shield you from radiation. That, or I could, metaphorically speaking, put on pants two sizes too small, and a shirt that used to look great on me, maybe like when I'd lost my mind and thought that a peasant blouse was actually attractive—expressions that no longer (if ever) fit my true self. I could swallow boredom, and the tiniest tinge of rage, and then I could begin to hate those people for not seeing who I really was, not valuing my big, true, radiant self. Of course, I'd come home, all tired and sour, totally uninspired to do any new work, and even more convinced that I couldn't make it in the big leagues because here I was, still in the small time. Then, I'd really have no choice in the matter, I'd just have to eat the raisin bagels and ice cream in the fridge on my way down the self-destructive sliding pond. Now, tell me, who could resist an offer like that?

So I made myself honor my new deal, become the exhilarating variable in my own private experiment. I said no to the speaking engagement, the temptation into stagnation, and deliberately stared into the void instead. It was like playing a game of cosmic entrepreneurial Chicken; but I didn't give in, didn't blink first or change my stance. I raised my rates for speaking and for coaching. And I swear it's just like the higher powers said, Okay, she's ready, she means it now, because she's given up speaking at the networking meeting from hell, even with that free gift certificate to Olive Garden.

Because that summer, out of nowhere, I landed one of the best working situations ever. One of my all-time favorite clients started her own company and brought me in to train her employees at my new hourly rate. She loved my material, and urged me to run with it. I taught weekly business and spirituality classes through her company and helped create a company culture of love, power, and dynamic sales and service. Then she even sent her employees to me for coaching. The whole thing felt like high tide had just rolled in. I had stepped into a new era of my career. It wasn't just that I was making a good deal more money than ever before. It was that I was making great money doing something I wanted to do more than anything else.

Wild success comes only when we keep chasing the work we really desire. It's how we turn surviving into thriving. Jamie built her own travel agency from scratch. When I met her she seemed a bit like a small rodent scratching from the inside of a glass cage. Let's just say, I wouldn't have wanted her booking *my* dream vacation. She'd built her business on hands-on customer service and commitment to details, but now it was running her life. She says, "I was working with people who didn't appreciate me and who always demanded more." Finally, with a little help from a doctor who said something coaxing like "I don't want to see you on a stretcher," she agreed to cut back temporarily and take time to reflect. That's when she realized she wanted to build custom trips to Asia. She wanted to offer fewer trips overall and focus only on the exclusive trips where she felt she could really step into her expertise. You guessed it. She found her energy, her mojo, and her market.

Marla, a fund-raiser for a nonprofit organization, had a similar shift when, she told me, she decided to focus more of her efforts on larger donors, instead of all her donors. "I work harder to get two thousand dollars than I do to get a hundred thousand," she says. "The big cats deal with you differently. I work my butt off for the smaller guys. They feel a lot of limitations and they bring those limits into our work." Initially, it was hard to trust her new focus. Now, she says, her militant selectivity creates new productivity. "I love taking the time to really nurture key relationships and devote more quality time to them. I couldn't do that while working with too many clients."

I know that some of us could imagine cutting off our ears before we could imagine cutting back on customers or projects. Well, nature, that powerhouse industry, offers us a time-tested business development strategy. Watch a master gardener prune a rosebush. They lop off any straggling growth. They send the growth energy back into the foundation. That's where all abundance comes from. If you nurture your core creative strength, everything will grow strong. But if you keep pouring strength into all the outgrowths, you steal energy away from your vitality. You also have another problem. You want to kill people.

One of my business coaching clients, Don, talks about "opportunity costs." He asks himself, "What am I not doing because I'm doing this activity?" He gave me a choice example. "I want exposure for my work, so I accept the speaking gig with thirty people. Well, if I really want exposure, maybe I could stay home and write an article for a name magazine that reaches thousands or millions." *Oh, hello.* "Great point," I gasped, because I wanted to hang up the phone, and change my whole life.

In Alcoholics Anonymous there's the concept of "taking a fearless moral inventory." It's where you look at where you have resentments, and where your energy is stuck in the past. Well, I suggest you do a "fearless energy inventory." Where do you leak energy? Which clients or tasks make you feel like you're treading water or like you've outgrown this work? One of my good friends periodically goes through her dresser, hunting down her "low-self-esteem underwear." She tosses out the faded and the frayed. Where are your stretched-out activities? What's no longer elastic? What message do you give yourself again and again when you work in these circumstances? Letting go is letting in. Abundance doesn't come from being busy, tired, and stretched out. It comes from pulling back, rejuvenating, and expanding into the next inspired expression.

INSPIRED SUCCESSISMS

Real abundance comes from *growing*—
staying true to your heat-seeking, light-gobbling self,
and the glimmer that ignites you now.

When your work becomes all about putting out fires,
you just can't be stirring one up.

There will come times when the success of one level
is now the shame or failure of another.
It's time to grow. . . . That means letting go
of your identity again and again.

Abundance requires surrender, letting go of control
somewhere or somehow,
and running with your heart wide open into the
feral loving arms of the unknown.

Wild success comes only when we keep chasing the work we really desire.

Watch master gardeners prune a rosebush.
They lop off any straggling growth.
They send the growth energy back into the foundation.

If you nurture your core creative strength, everything will grow strong.
But if you keep pouring strength into all the outgrowths,
you steal energy away from your vitality.

Letting go is letting in.

THE BOTTOM LINE IS
A FLAT LINE

Okay, my classmates were analytically brilliant and precise. But precise in the name of what? Of figuring out the unit cost of widgets? . . . I became increasingly mistrustful of their sterile precision. I started suspecting that their obsession with detail was a way of masking cluelessness about the bigger picture . . . My classmates could analyze, but I, thank God, could rhapsodize. In business as in life, that's a far more precious thing.

PETER BARTON, WHO BECAME A CENTRAL FIGURE IN THE CABLE
INDUSTRY, ON HIS EXPERIENCE IN THE HARVARD BUSINESS SCHOOL
(QUOTED FROM *NOT FADE AWAY*)

Infinity cannot be understood by merely counting up its separate parts.

A COURSE IN MIRACLES

O ne of the most persistent concerns I hear from clients who are doing something they love is "but it's not making money." Which means it's not making *enough* money. Or, the real deal, it's not making enough money, *yet*. That yet is the difference between inspired life or death, giving up or taking off. That *yet* is the gateway.

We give numbers a ridiculous amount of respect. We treat them like mountain lions and go all stiff and drained in their presence. Hey, have you ever noticed how the word "number" has the word "numb" in it? I have journals filled with scribbled numbers in the margins. I know those were times when I felt fear and pain. I'd start adding up what I needed to earn, what expenses I had to pay, and just how many Starbucks or pairs of earrings I might reasonably or unreasonably need in my lifetime. I jotted numbers like an autistic child rocks back and forth. It was a barbaric attempt to assuage uncertainty, like somehow I could do this one great equation with my life, and make it all add up on paper. But it didn't. For me, it always came back down to trusting what I knew in my gut, in the creative oven of my dreams, in the place where I wasn't numb.

Don't do the math.

The bottom line is a flat line. It's static and inactive, not breathing and alive. It's the snake's skin, shed and ditched, while the snake slid on. It's a ghost of former conditions. And I'll tell you what, I'll listen to my spirit more than to ghosts any day of the week.

There have been times when a part of me felt as though it was starting to make true progress and then my "voice of realism," citing numbers, pushed me back down, face-first, in the cold, hard snow. Despite my intuition that something was baking in the kiln, taking shape, "realism"—that is, my old definition of realism—said, "Who cares? You're failing. Potential means nothing. It's a pile of dirty snow in the blazing sun."

I have often felt as though I am going through internal court proceedings in my head, perhaps tortured flashbacks from a past in law. My soul is on trial. The Advocate for the Inner Way within me flashes a serene smile at the judge. It nods to progress, increased speaking possibilities, developing confidence, unstoppable exuberance, the light shooting out of the top of my head, for instance, and a sense that I'm finally finding my way.

"Your Honor," interrupts the Relentless Bully representing the World's Expectations, "I'd like to present to you Exhibit A." Exhibit A is the quarterly report from my literary agent reporting the number of books sold. It's a bad number, a sad little trickle of cash. Silence falls in the courtroom. It seems my continued faith isn't justified. The evidence is beyond clear and consequential. It's all over, just like that. "But it's the wrong evidence," shrieks my heart. "It's the evidence of the past. It's what has been."

At this point, I want to quote every spiritual teacher and the emerging wizards of quantum physics, who all reiterate "the power of now" and that the future extends from the pulse of the present, not the bones of the past. See, but the Relentless Bully goes wild whenever I mention spiritual *any-thing* or even progressive science. It launches into questions of my sanity, my choices to trust unorthodox sources, the fact that I no longer own even one gray business suit, and then, of course, the time I dated someone—for an extended period of time, mind you—who wore beads and *chanted*. So it goes, the arguments in my head.

Still, let me tell you more. When I began my business nationally, I put myself on the road periodically to lecture and offer workshops. The expenses were daunting: airfare, hotels, rental cars, food, pet-sitting, and more. On some trips I lost money, and on the successful ones I made bus fare for all, or broke even. Yet something miraculous was happening and I knew it. Each trip reinforced me. Each new group or city fed me some kind of soul peyote that helped me see the essence of what was really going on. I was deepening in my confidence, my abilities, and my vision. The audiences loved me, and while they were small audiences in these beginning trips, their love was huge medicine to me. They reminded me that I had a true eagle feather, a gift, and that there were those who needed my message and presence and would receive it.

I remember one speaking engagement in particular, because I made myself write about it, while in the fever of my truth. I had spoken to a women's business networking group and these women lifted me up on some kind of bier and carted me through the streets, proclaiming my light. Well, maybe it just felt that way. They were no longer ordinary women. In just an hour, they had become business moguls, high priestesses, industry leaders, change agents, and visionaries. Responding to my talk, they remembered their electric power, and as they did, they helped me remember mine. It was an experience I was beginning to have often, and I needed to write about it, before the clock struck twelve, the pumpkin carriage disappeared, the fire turned to ashes, and I woke up a loser.

"I know this is right," I wrote in my journal, afterward. "This kind of response means everything. This is gold." I drank in the sense of big raw power, energy, and sweeping momentum. I felt the throbbing of a life to come. Yes, that actual speaking engagement made only a dent in bringing my checkbook into fiscal steadiness. But it hit the jackpot in my consciousness. I knew in that moment that I had something of staggering value to offer—and that value would translate into money.

And it did. Over the years, I've continued to see streams of money come in from those trips. People recommended my retreats and events to their friends. Some became coaching clients. Many ordered my book or CDs or online programs, even years after I'd met them. Some brought me into their organizations or conferences to speak. Some started their own businesses and we collaborated in new financial arrangements. Some of those trips created links to my website and increased visibility on Google, visibility that would cost a tidy sum to buy, as though I'd ever thought of that. It just goes on and on. I am so grateful that I didn't let numbers stand in the way of reality.

If the numbers don't add up for you yet, then focus on the *value* you're receiving. I realized I wasn't being paid a salary, but I was hauling in benefits that would have cost a fortune. My trips were laser-focused, results-oriented market research. I got to test my material out on students and co-create it with them. More than that, I felt like every presentation was an immersion experience spent with a black-belted shaman, the shaman of discovering my own authority in the world. They were healing, intimate, cell-rearranging tutorials that I got for the steal of the century. I wisely paid the tuition and did my "course work" in the world. In their book *Success Built to Last*, success experts Jerry Porras, Stewart Emery, and Mark Thompson confirm, "If you should be greedy about anything, it should be about acquiring 'intellectual capital' for your dream."

Lila, a fiber artist, looks at her financial outlays as long-term investments that may not show profit immediately. She tells a story about how she scraped up every penny she had, and even some she didn't have, but that nice big generous Citibank did, to be in a particular trade show. "I just knew I had to give myself the chance to get exposure and orders for my work." At the show, she met a woman who loved her unusual scarves and hats and her story. The woman was a television producer and Lila ended up on PBS and eleven other syndicated shows. She didn't make much money at that trade show, but she brought in a whale of a miracle, a commercial value she could not have bought.

So when do you pay attention to numbers? It's a personal equation. Me, I'll always be a card-carrying mystic and do the work for the integrity of the work. That said, I also love making money for the work I do, and I need to eat, and eat out. So I do consider the numbers. I just don't give them the only authority. They don't get to wear the crown. They're just one ingredient in my pie. Sometimes, a workshop of mine won't make that much money, and I'll use that as an indicator not to offer it again. It's not just because it didn't make money. It's because, all things considered, it's not that important to me, or my magic is now romping down another street, dropping feathers and sequins to trace the way. If something is consistently not generating that much money, I might use that as a "check engine light," run a few diagnostics on it, see where I could add more quality, cut costs, or promote with more accuracy.

In other words, the bottom line can be a useful tool or a destructive weapon. It's a measurement, not a prophecy. It's a number, not a magistrate. In any evaluation, choose with your strength and not your weakness. Only you can do that math.

INSPIRED SUCCESSISMS

I jotted numbers like an autistic child rocks back and forth.
It was a barbaric attempt to assuage uncertainty,
like somehow I could do this one great equation with my life,
and make it all add up on paper.

Don't do the math. The bottom line is a flat line.

Yes, that actual speaking engagement made only a dent
in bringing my checkbook into fiscal steadiness.
But it hit the jackpot in my consciousness.

I am so grateful that I didn't let numbers stand in the way of reality.

If the numbers don't add up for you yet,
then focus on the *value* you're receiving.

I realized I wasn't being paid a salary,
but I was hauling in benefits that would have cost a fortune.

I do consider the numbers. I just don't give them the only authority.
They don't get to wear the crown. They're just one ingredient in my pie.

The bottom line can be a useful tool or a destructive weapon.
It's a measurement, not a prophecy. It's a number, not a magistrate.
In any evaluation, choose with your strength and not your weakness.

IF YOU CALCULATE YOUR WEALTH IN DOLLARS ONLY, YOU'RE POOR

The price of anything is the amount of life you exchange for it.

HENRY DAVID THOREAU

I don't just want money. I want what money buys: time, freedom, and experience.

A JOURNAL ENTRY

This is what's amazing to me. Most of us decided to create work we love because we wanted the experience of living a life that had soul impact—and perhaps did not involve control-top panty hose. We rejected the idea of selling the hours of our life for a fantasy of order and security. We abandoned that country and established our own. Yet when it comes to our net worth, we prowl over the border and steal treacherous glances. We sing the old pledge to the old allegiance, money and appearances. We actually question our life's value because we don't own a five-bedroom home or a flat-screen TV. But maybe it's time to question our thinking instead.

Because if I could splash some ice water in your face, or tickle you, I just might. I want you to emerge from this fever of conditioning right now. Put down that archaic measuring stick, because Wall Street standards are like saying the earth is flat. Financial calculations have no way of measuring true net worth: the astonishing wingspan of the fat, happy dove in your heart, the electromagnetic current around your head, or the way you inspire your children. Wild success isn't about your portfolio or possessions. It's about the feeling that you are doing the right thing with your time on earth.

Let me tell you about brilliant abundance. Recently, I felt overwhelmed with work, fearful, and as though I was looking for the G-spot of my peace of mind, somewhere in the Bermuda Triangle where instruments turn into demented objects and radio communications end up on Mars. So I took a few days off and drove to New Mexico. I rented an inexpensive cabin outside of Taos, surrounded by mountains, sage, wind, sun, and not much else. I wanted to get back in touch with my sanity, the vortex of my creativity, and the grounding of my soul. I took my journals, my art supplies, and my faith that somehow I'd come back to my equilibrium. It worked. It didn't take long in that rustic gentle space with its adobe walls and kiva fireplace, surrounded by a quiet as loud as thunder, before I was reverberating with contentment.

During that time, having sipped tea, written, and watched a blue-winged bird land on the silver green sage, I wrote in my journal: "This is a moment worth living for." Some moments are like that, just an answer to absolutely everything, in and of themselves. Moments like that give you courage. They are little vials of faith. They are medicine in which the illness you didn't even know you had begins to clear up. It's those times that mean more to me than any amount of money. It's also about being able to organize my life so that I can have these kinds of experiences. Oh, and by the way, I didn't need much in the way of finances to get away. I did need time and I needed to be in the right life. I had both, by choice. That's my abundance.

Lissa is a painter, a musician, and a mosaic of other expressions. She says she started feeling rich when she looked beyond the dollars to what in her life made her feel grounded and secure. "I realized I needed to value my creativity," she says. "It feeds my life force more than anything else in my life. It's what I'm here to do, and I know it."

Another one of my clients has started her own online retail business and loves the spacious feeling of freedom it brings her. "I watch everyone leaving the beach on Sunday, having to go home and get ready for work," says Susan. "I feel their Sunday dread, having to think about the week and what they'll do and what they'll wear." With relief and gratitude, she practically chirps, "I can come back to the beach on Monday or Tuesday. I'm a free agent. And I never have that old, thousand-pound sadness about everything."

Rob, a chiropractor in private practice, tells me about a three-week vacation to Italy he's planning to take with his family. "The thought of, as a fully grown-up adult, having to ask if I can have time off just seems ridiculous to me now." He has faced great uncertainty in his business at times. But owning his own life is one of his rewards.

I once talked to a woman who sold uniquely designed fabrics in a boutique and at art festivals. She lived modestly doing her unusual work. "Money isn't my definition of success," she said. It felt refreshing to hear someone, living in my country, the United States of *Bling*, say this. "I homeschool my son and he has special needs," she continued. "Doing what I do gives me the flexibility to take care of him in these precious years." We'd found what I call the abundance spot, the bull's-eye in your third eye. This woman's wealth won't show up on a tax return, but it will show up in her bloodstream. And I'm thinking she can and will take that serenity with her when she leaves this world. Now, that's security.

This is what I want you to know. On the path of doing inspired work, success often does translate into money, so you can take a deep breath now, but more important, it always guarantees abundance. Of course, you may have to identify the abundance, to recognize and appreciate all the exponential, intangible, and incomparable benefits that come from doing the work you love. For example, studies show that people who do the work they love tend to resist disease and physical discomfort and live longer in general, and they have better relationships—and wild, intrepid sex. Okay, I really don't know about the sex thing, but I bet it's true, and if it's not, you might have time and energy to take a class in it.

How much is it worth to you not to sell your spirit? How much is it worth not to have chronic fatigue, fibromyalgia, heart disease, or ulcers because while you may have stress, it won't be the unholy sickening stress of betraying your own soul? Or how much is it worth to be able to walk your dog in the middle of that first spring day and not feel as though you're walking around in striped convict clothing, having to race back to your desk before your boss starts speaking in tongues? How much is sunlight worth over fluorescent lights? If you're self-employed or a free agent at your company, discretionary time is part of your benefits package, baby. Do the math. It adds up fast.

Here's another kind of abundance to add to your bottom line. Sometimes the lack of finances opens us up to more connection and creativity in our lives. When I first put myself on the road to promote my book, I couldn't afford to stay at a Hilton or a Marriott. Heck, sometimes Budget Desperate Motel felt sumptuous and over-the-top for me, even with thin sheets and sad coffee. In a rare moment of swallowing my pride, I called a woman I'd met at a conference and asked if I might stay with her while in her city. I felt awkward; she felt touched. She lit up and opened her heart and her home.

She put me up in a guest room with sage green walls and antique lace curtains and a soft, plump bed. She set aside thick purple towels on a chair for me. She offered me peppermint herbal tea, homemade granola bars, and all the alone time I needed. Yet, instead, I stayed up with her enjoying deep conversation and felt ease, joy, and overwhelming gratitude. Her partner gave me directions, maps, cell and office numbers, and drove me to the train station in the morning. I felt like I had instant family, instant loving family in this unfamiliar city. I realized as I lay in that cushiony bed and listened to the birds outside the window that if I had all the money in the world, I wouldn't have wanted a different experience. My spare budget forced me to have an intimate, bonding, magical, spontaneous experience of sitting at someone's kitchen table, being in their world, and, as I am prone to sweeping flourishes, and an Aquarius, feeling community with all of humanity. Suddenly, I felt sorry for famous authors in hotel suites with room service, HBO, *white* towels, and tiny little soaps.

Let me give you another example. When my first book relaunched, I couldn't justify spending thousands of dollars to hire a publicist or a marketing person. I had been stuck in my head for months, frustrated that others could probably fund an entire team of promotional people and market drool and sawdust if they wanted, and possibly did, gauging from some of the top stuff out there. I was so busy obsessing over the fact that I couldn't hire certain resources that I missed other resources, quite literally in my own backyard. Then one evening, I bought some pizzas and sodas and invited some of my local students over to sit at my new patio set on a July night lit by candlelight. The crickets sang the gospel.

These were not individuals trained in marketing or publicity. But they were smart people (and consumers) who cared about me and cared about my work. We discussed my situation, set an intention together, and called on the ancestors (preferably the successful ones), the angels, the highest love within us, the Great Publicist and Marketing Genius in the Sky, or pretty much anyone taking calls that night. Then we brainstormed into the evening. I couldn't believe the approaches and strategy we produced, not to mention the energy, laughter, and gossip. I could have spent tens of thousands of dollars and wouldn't have yielded this kind of support and customer-based suggestions. This quality came from people who loved me. It didn't come from people I could buy.

Where are you shortchanging yourself with an inappropriate focus? It's raining twenty-four-karat gold in your life and you may have only one bucket out. Get out every bucket, tub, drawer, or Dixie cup you can. Lie down on the sidewalk, spit out your gum, and open your mouth and your hands. Tally up and value all the joy, love, freedom, integrity, and peace of mind in your life. Baby, these things don't come cheap—and you won't find them on eBay or even Rodeo Drive. Why would you fixate only on numbers, and miss such enviable wealth? A bold new life requires bold new standards. Really, I don't care how much money you make. If you calculate your wealth in dollars only, you're poor.

INSPIRED SUCCESSISMS

Wall Street standards are like saying the earth is flat.
Financial calculations have no way of measuring true net worth.

Wild success isn't about your portfolio or possessions.
It's about the feeling that you are doing the
right thing with your time on earth.

On the path of doing inspired work, success often
does translate into money . . .
but more important, it always guarantees abundance.

You may have to identify the abundance, to recognize and appreciate
all the exponential, intangible, and incomparable benefits.

How much is it worth to you not to sell your spirit?
How much is it worth not to have chronic fatigue,
fibromyalgia, heart disease, or ulcers?

If you're self-employed or a free agent at your company,
discretionary time is part of your benefits package, baby.

Tally up and value all the joy, love, freedom, integrity,
and peace of mind in your life. Baby, these things don't come cheap.

A bold new life requires bold new standards.
Really, I don't care how much money you make.
If you calculate your wealth in dollars only, you're poor.

SUPERSTARS KNOW
WHO THEY ARE

When you emerge, I want you to stand forth knowing that you walk another way and rely on power not of this world. This is what I need for you. Right now, you are still childish and give your power to "important" people, channels, and things. You find your greatness in them instead of remembering that your greatness attracts them to you.

A JOURNAL ENTRY

I'm often not recognized by the established powers. But I can establish myself. Oprah didn't get on Oprah. *She became Oprah.*

A JOURNAL ENTRY

Valuing yourself means working consistently with people who treat you well. No one has more weight than you—when you commit to living your calling. You may feel like the new kid on the block, all squeaky and shy, but remember the source and power of your talent. Let's put it this way: There are no fat cats when you work with the Cat's Meow. You're cosmic royalty in a skin suit, baby. You move with a thousand bells ringing your name and secret dimensions reverberating within, and everyone needs and wants what you have. The catch is, *you* have to remember what you have.

If you consistently feel as though someone isn't treating you with respect, then they don't recognize your worth. Someone who doesn't recognize your worth can never be "a great connection" for you and your work. Beggars can't be choosers, but you're no beggar. You're a big, fat answer to someone's prayer. When you walk into the rooms where you belong, you walk in broadcasting easy invincibility and competency. You glow with an inspired vibe and a power station behind you. There will be people who recognize your power and promise. Only the people who "get you" should get you. They deserve your time and energy.

Years ago, I was in a very painful dilemma. I had just self-published *This Time I Dance!* and, as I shared with you in the earlier chapters, a well-connected woman in the publishing industry, aka my "fairy god-mother," found it on Amazon, loved it, and offered to help me put together a package to send to the president of the big New York publishing company of my dreams. She knew him well, that would be the president, had shared cocktails and laughs with him. I was a giddy Cinderella who had just met a ticket out of invisibility.

But then over the next few weeks, things began to feel anxious and weird. Phyllis didn't return some phone calls. But she was a busy woman and I, an insecure and desperate one, wagged my tail against the odds. Then there were missed deadlines, stories, dramas, and weeks passing by. Finally, she began disappearing altogether, even from cyberspace. I felt as though I was skidding on black ice, still trying to get somewhere. I desperately wanted things to work. I couldn't bear the idea of going back to my life alone, without this hookup to the Emerald City, or, in this case, midtown Gotham.

"Sounds like you're an emotional hostage," said Nancy, my life coach at the time. Sometimes it seems insane to me that I actually *pay* people to tell me things I really don't want to hear. I continued to justify sticking with the situation. "She's really good at what she does," I'd say, kind of like a child pleading to play with automatic weapons, for just a few more hours. I'd defend her. Maybe she didn't mean that exact day when she said she'd get back to me by that exact day, I'd wheedle. Maybe I had to learn to adjust my expectations of people, flow like water, melt like snow. The Dalai Lama had forgiven the Chinese for invading an entire country, for God's sake.

Really, I was dealing with only a missed phone appointment or two or three, ten at the most. Finally, Nancy snorted like a horse on the other end of the phone, a horse that smelled a barn full of crap. Then she said softly, "This is the beginning of a pivotal career relationship. Do you want to start your dream journey like this?" Just at that moment, every part of me wanted to scream, Please don't shine the light there. But it was done.

That night, weeks of agony receded and I knew what I had to do, come what may. I had to speak my truth, and risk my one thin bridge to having my book published by a big publisher. I felt surrendered and strangely calm. "Spirit got me here and will carry me all the way," I said to myself as willingness, fear, exhilaration, and faith warmed my veins like apricot brandy. Suddenly I was willing to believe that a loving universe might have more than just one rickety way for me to accomplish my dreams.

Yes, Phyllis may have held the keys to the kingdom, but I could never be locked out. I could let go of the leaking lifeboat, knowing a cruise ship would come along, or a dinghy or a dolphin, because I would always be delivered to the dock of my right life. The next day I told Phyllis I would prefer not to work together, even though I would be forever grateful for her reaching out to me. It was one of the hardest things I've ever done in my life. Phyllis bowed out, and, after that, generously sent the package to the publisher for me anyway. Then, later, with the representation of a literary agent, I walked through the door to my dreams, on solid freaking ground.

After that experience, I thought about the Bible story of Abraham being asked to sacrifice Isaac, his one son and love of his life. I'm not much of a Bible person, and on top of that, I *hate* giving things up. But suddenly I got it. Getting my book published was my Isaac, the desire that had become so much of a need, that I was willing to trade anything for it, including my self-love, self-respect, sanity, and connection to my destiny. Yet just like in that story, when I risked "sacrificing" my good, there was no tragedy required. Instead, I was liberated from pain—the pain of making someone else more important than listening to my own inner voice. I had been in love with the illusion of good, not the reality. I finally got it: if I wanted my wildest dreams to come true, I had to remain wildly true to myself.

But in case I didn't get the lesson, I had another dose of it right after this experience. Just so you know, I prefer to think of myself as a "thorough" learner rather than a remedial one. After Phyllis, I found a literary agent who was willing to represent me, now that the package had gone to the publisher. After we met for coffee, she sent me an offer. I e-mailed back asking if we might talk over just a few other things. She responded by bluntly withdrawing her contractual offer. I knew she must have misinterpreted my e-mail, had a small brain burp, or maybe had an alien or poltergeist take over her body and throw a little party. I knew I could finesse everything back into place with a conversation. I am nothing if not finesse girl. Yet some stray thought kept interrupting with unusual discernment. It said, "I shouldn't have to beg someone to date me."

Now don't get me wrong, begging is *definitely* in my repertoire. Tiny me wanted to run to the phone, apologize immediately, and offer to wash her car, repaint her house, feed her grapes, and sing and dance my way back into the nest. Still, the wise part of me, sound as stone, repeated with annoying finality, "I shouldn't have to beg someone to date me."

This much was clear: She didn't see me as a superstar. Or if she did, and could dismiss a relationship that quickly without further comment, she wasn't someone *I* could work with long term. I decided to not answer her e-mail right away and instead, riding on a strange cocktail of panic and indignant self-worth, I solicited three big-league agents, the ones I hadn't dared to try before. I knew if they said no, I could patch up the situation with Ms. Quick Draw. To my amazement, every one of them called me back within a day. I am still stunned, years later. If I hadn't dared to own my own worth in that moment, I wouldn't have signed with one of the biggest agents in the industry. I wouldn't have gotten such an awesome contract. And I may have been busy doing yard work for a woman with multiple personalities.

Yes, it's easy to imagine that other people have more power than you do. But remember, you come bearing an essence that has never been here before. Avoid focusing on the power that others can give to you. Start focusing on the love, individuality, and excellence that you can bring to any situation right now. Otherwise, you will cheat yourself and the individuals who need your talent.

I learned this the hard way in an early media interview. It was an in-studio radio interview with Mr. Beautiful, Warm, Relaxed Voice. Mr. Voice spoke into his microphone and asked me a very deep and thoughtful question. Then as I began answering him, he ignored me, buried his head in his papers, and damn near cleaned his fingernails while I spoke. It was clear we weren't having a real conversation, but an on-air conversation; he couldn't care less about the topic. At the time, I hadn't done many interviews, and his chilly behavior threw me. I faltered as I spoke because Mr. Voice was clearly preoccupied, editing his will or reading a letter from his porn-star girlfriend. When I left the studio, I felt sick inside knowing that I'd missed an important opportunity to captivate my listeners, the ones who needed to hear me that day. I realized that I had cheapened my gifts by focusing on the host's interest level, instead of my own. These days, I'm not focused on how someone responds to me. I'm not looking for permission or praise. I bring my gifts to the table and offer them to the hungry; I share the love I am meant to share.

After years of dedicated people-pleasing, I've finally realized that there is no one on this earth who can give me power or value. Besides, I am steeped in light if I'm willing to own it. It's up to me to listen closely to my heart's ongoing counsel, as I represent this unrepeatable galvanizing presence in the world. I will walk away, figuratively or literally, from any situation that doesn't feel true to my soul. I will not be walking away *from* power or opportunity. I will be walking away *with* power and opportunity. My truth is my power. So is yours. It's where the magic lives.

INSPIRED SUCCESSISMS

Oprah didn't get on *Oprah*. She became Oprah.

Someone who doesn't recognize your worth
can never be "a great connection" for you and your work.

Beggars can't be choosers, but you're not a beggar.

You're a big, fat answer to someone's prayer.

There will be people who recognize your power and promise.
Only the people who "get you" should get you.

I finally got it: if I wanted my wildest dreams to come true,
I had to remain wildly true to myself.

Avoid focusing on the power that others can give to you.
Start focusing on the love, individuality, and excellence
that you can bring to any situation right now.

There is no one on this earth who can offer me power or value.
Besides, I am steeped in light if I'm willing to own it.

I will walk away, figuratively or literally, from any
situation that doesn't feel true to my soul.
I will not be walking away *from* power or opportunity.
I will be walking away *with* power and opportunity.

7.

THE BAPTISM OF WILD SUCCESS

You may have noticed, because you're clever, that it's hard to succeed when some part of you views your life like so much rotting melon in the alley—I'm just saying. A broken you never succeeds. There is no "big time" without big you.

Here's where it all begins. It's the day you acknowledge yourself so much you allow the Universe to shower you with wild abandon. It's always been your destiny to thrive. But you've been groping for gold stars, while you had the galaxy in your pocket.

That's the big karmic joke of chasing success. You can always arrive. After all, you didn't come here to get gold from the world. You came here to give it.

TAKE IT IN OR
YOU CAN'T WIN

I have arrived and I'm arriving still. It's an ongoing state of develop-
ment. I'll always be hungering for more because I'll always have new
things to express. But I choose now to see my hunger as the precursor
of my realization—not as a lack of accomplishment. If I'm creatively
alive, it's always going to be a mixed bag of arriving and still having
further to go.

A JOURNAL ENTRY

When I was anorexic, I'd look in the mirror, and while I was a tiny slip
of a thing, I'd see a huge woman, a woman who had blown up over-
night because she'd had five french fries. When it comes to success, I
have reverse anorexia. I look at substantial accomplishments and see
thin, flimsy achievements, sure to vanish if you blink.

A JOURNAL ENTRY

We live in a society that flushes like a teenage girl over tabloid success, those who hit the piñata in life, big time. The media is crazy for instant flash and cash. We don't hear anything about those of us who are tak-ing the consistent steps it takes, about eight billion of them, and some of them uphill with bunions and blisters, not that I'm complaining or any-thing, on the way to realizing our life's work. Nobody praises the intrepid dedication it takes to be in the middle of the journey. Nobody, that is, but us—we who are committed to taking this all the way. Because we know that it's in the middle of it all, if not the burning desert itself, that we need to bear witness to the success we have already achieved.

Wild success is not a path of quiet desperation clinched by a big bang. It's a path of honoring yourself every step of the way. You may already be great at this, but me, I had some remedial work cut out for me, something like writing ten thousand times on the blackboard of life, "I will not be mean to Tama anymore. Tama is a good person who is trying her best." See, I was forever auditioning for a part in my own movie, instead of embracing the leading role. I was waiting to "make it," instead of making it every step of the way. I saw most of my achievements as nondescript motel rooms on the road to somewhere "big." I was so busy studying the map, I never gazed in the mirror and said, "Way to go," to the one who didn't always know which way to go, or how to show up in one piece, but was showing up anyway.

Admit it, you know I'm not alone in this. Many of us burn for validation, string the moon up in the sky to get it, yet treat our own triumphs like used paper plates after the picnic. Of course we tell ourselves that once we get "there," we'll really take it all in. But "there" is a moving target. We're so busy yearning, striving, and groping, we pass through holy lands and power spots and never arrive. So here's what I want you to know. Success comes in the middle or not at all.

One part of you is crazily grinding away like a weed attempting to crack through the cement in the middle of midtown Manhattan. It's your job to nurture those attempts and cheer them on as though your life depended on it. Your creative life does depend on it. Your inspired life needs constant love and support. No one else can bless you in the same way, and no one else will. It's an indispensable practice, on the order of breathing or talking to God, I'd say, to witness to your own strides, stellar, moderate, and very, very small.

Because let me tell you, the anti-cheerleader of success is alive and well within you. Its sarcasm and acid can leave you believing you're a loser even when you win. Here's the voice I mean. *Oh, I got lucky. I couldn't make that happen again. It's not really a success because . . .* fill in the blank, and *It's not that big a deal. Besides, it's just a drop in the ocean to where I have to go.* You may think it's no big deal, but only because you've allowed yourself to think you're no big deal. It's murder by diminishment. Critical self-talk stirs broken glass into your sugar bowl; you cut yourself whenever sweetness comes. You may not even consciously hear this voice, but it's a "realistic point of view," a "concern" that suddenly arises, or a subtle suggestion that changes shining cherries into sour grapes and leaves you feeling bruised.

Believe me, I know about the seething dark power of that voice. I've seen it eat away the confidence of my clients and students, people who had everything going for them except themselves. I've been one of those people, too. Like you really need an example—but I'll share one anyway. I used to keep a photo album in which I saved and displayed the articles I'd published. The album had filled during the years with multiple by-lines, though I hadn't yet written for any newsstand magazines like *People, Ladies' Home Journal,* or *The New Yorker.*

One day, setting the latest article under the cellophane page, I noticed that I felt down, like maybe I'd accidentally killed someone and forgot about it until now, or maybe I'd been told I was going to die real soon, and I'd never see my dog, a plate of pad thai, or a Starbucks coffee again. I felt sad and unsure of myself and as though my ribs and bones and eyelids hurt with the weight of this very wrong thing that had no name. Finally, I overheard the source of the pain.

"Pathetic," hissed my own voice within me. "These are all no-count magazines. You're actually collecting these two-bit treasures as though they mean something. No real writer would delight in this drivel." I was stunned. Then I flashed back on feeling like a proud peacock, being an excited little girl, scoring a 98 on a spelling test and telling my family. "Did anybody get a one hundred?" my father asks. "Yes," I admit, feeling as though I am handing him a very loaded revolver. "How come *you* didn't get a one hundred?" he says, and his tone shames me into the floorboards forevermore. And that's that—my 98 is now a torn butterfly or broken vase, something that fails to perform. I didn't learn to celebrate success. I learned to eviscerate it.

As I looked at my photo album again, I traveled back in time in my mind. There I stood five years before with a manila envelope sheathing a crisp manuscript, standing before a mailbox, yes, in the carriage and buggy days of "snail mail," kissing and blessing the package for luck. Believe me, I would have imported eye of newt, vials of holy water from Lourdes, or begged a shaman to shake rattles and spirits if I thought it would have helped my odds. At that moment, I had never ever received an acceptance letter, only form letter rejections. Every rejection was like a rock I had to swallow.

If I could have handed the photo album crammed with published articles to that self of five years ago, she would have cried with gratitude that the dreams she cherished had come true. She would have flung the mail she carried like confetti, streamers, or winning chips from Vegas. She may have fallen to her knees and sung to the skies with yellow butterflies soaring from her mouth, "I did it, I did it! I did it!" Yet just a few years down the road, this album was filled with castaway success, because I *did* do it. No big deal.

Later in my career, I had another pivotal moment like that. I was offering my first five-day retreat at the famous Canyon Ranch six-star spa. Though I was surrounded by sumptuous white towels and gleaming organic fruit, blackflies swarmed in my mind. Secretly I felt bad that I had only the minimum number of women sign up to make this retreat possible. One head fewer and we would have had to cancel the whole thing. "Obviously, you're never going to make it nationally," said the dark voice, wrapping it up, reporting my grim failing future as factually as a CNN news clip. "Face it. You'll always be a *sort of* success but never the real package of money, popularity, and ease." I stumble around in fear and private shame, right there in the middle of paradise, believing that I won't have my time in the big tent, that I won't ever be able to get my work and message out into the world.

One night during the retreat, we sit in a circle sharing our experiences and reflections. I tend to be pretty honest with my groups, not one to miss some great free therapy, and that night I decide to share what's on my mind. "I really want to have my career go national," I say. "I want to be wildly successful at doing the things I love." Rita sits there like a small bird in her purple cotton tank top and light blue sweats, her blond hair wet from the sauna. She smells of lavender oil. She is in the middle of a broken life, a life hanging by strands, strands that are beginning to collect pearls on this retreat. She has struggled with alcohol and men and self-esteem, and has never ever dared her dreams or even named any of her desires, much less accomplished them. She speaks in a fragile voice that changes my world. "I don't understand, Tama. I'd give anything to be where you are." The sincerity in her voice breaks my heart, and makes me gasp inside.

When Rita speaks, my illusion of myself is shattered. In her eyes, I am whole and free and accomplished. I know what I want. I have taken steps to get there. And I've even gotten huge amounts of it already. And she's right. The other women nod and smile in agreement. And right then and there, I see that it's time to let myself into the club and celebrate. I have the key and I've been withholding it from myself all along. Yes, there are milestones up ahead. Yet there are milestones behind me, too. Success is not a pinnacle, but a perspective. Years later, I heard the fiery Marianne Williamson say something similar about measuring ongoing spiritual progress. She said, "I'm not depressed anymore by the gap between me and someone like Jesus, but I'm impressed by the gap between me and who I used to be."

These days, I still have wild ambition. But I'm not as desperate, because I'm receiving my own recognition all along the way. I am replacing the discounting voice with the one that makes things count, makes them real, and makes them last. I am telling the sweet frightened part of myself a fable, the tale of the success of Tama. It's a bedtime story she needs to hear day and night, so that lesser stories have no room to take root. I tell her about her courageous feats of spirit, allegiance to higher forces, brave choices, and stubborn stamina. I am on my side now. I want to see every one of my own successes because I know seeing them will beckon even more. I want to acknowledge all the good and adorn the broad shelf of my heart with quiet trophies, some that I alone will see in this lifetime. I want to shine the metal of my medals, not to brag to others, but to salute my trusting self and let her know how grateful I am for all her efforts and clarity. She is the one who believes before anyone else in the world ever sees a thing. She deserves to be seen.

Become a witness of your own success, if you want to have any, that is. Celebrate being in the middle of things, on your way, and having arrived already, so many times and in so many ways. Practice basking in what you have and who you are. List all of your progress, count all of your ribbons, inner and outer, and I'd even say go buy yourself a token of appreciation at this very juncture, say the French chateau your soul deserves, or maybe the postcard of one, a symbolic treasure or totem of support. Kneel before the power and counsel of your rearview mirror. Things are closer than they may appear. See yourself five years ago. What have you learned since then? What have you accomplished? Remember the moments of emotional healing and inner shifts, too. Wherever you are, hold yourself in appreciation, commemoration, and infinite gratitude. I guarantee you there is someone who would love to be where you are.

If you continue to take your success for granted, nothing will ever change for *you*, even if everything changes. If you don't take your good in, you can't ever really win.

INSPIRED SUCCESSISMS

I choose now to see my hunger as the precursor of my realization—
not as a lack of accomplishment.

It's in the middle of it all, if not the burning desert itself,
that we want to bear witness to the success we have already achieved.

Wild success is not a path of quiet desperation clinched by a big bang.
It's a path of honoring yourself every step of the way.

"There" is a moving target.
We're so busy yearning, striving, and groping,
we pass through holy lands and power spots and never arrive.

Success comes in the middle or not at all.

Yes, there are milestones up ahead.
Yet there are milestones behind me, too.
Success is not a pinnacle, but a perspective.

I want to see every one of my own successes
because I know seeing them will beckon even more.

Wherever you are,
hold yourself in appreciation, commemoration, and infinite gratitude.
I guarantee you there is someone who would love to be where you are.

STOP BECOMING SUCCESSFUL AND START BEING IT

In the past I've worked myself to death and then when I succeeded, I was too tired to care. Now I know that if I deny my feelings on the way to success, I will deny my ability to feel my success—even if it comes around. The means and the ends are the same. The quality of the journey is the quality of your life. No moment can justify deprivation. No trophy can help ease the rage and sadness of a soul denied. Real success is being true to yourself and cherishing the race as much as the ribbon.

A JOURNAL ENTRY

I have a friend who is a kung fu master at the art of savoring her life. She puts garden-fresh mint in her tea and delights at the stray holly-hock leaning against the garage wall. I have never been good at this. I have a feeling it's the shadow side of being ambitious. I am too busy drinking in the good of other people's lives and what I don't have.

A JOURNAL ENTRY

f you really want to experience wild success, I have one thing for you to start practicing immediately. Stop focusing on *becoming* successful and start focusing on *being* successful. I'm not talking about semantics. I'm talking about the difference between night and day.

I once had a spiritual healer tell me that success is not about moving up in the world, but about moving down into the deepest realms of your feelings and feeling grateful for your deep powerful Self and all the love and energy and connection that you already have. That was supposed to clear things up for me, but at the time, I was lodged in my reptilian fear brain, and I wanted to know how to catch flies. Abstract thought sailed over my scaly little head. I was pretty crazy for success, hey, maybe that's why I was consulting a healer in the first place, and I wanted a foolproof formula. I didn't get, or really want to get, the cosmic recipe of "as within, so without." But all these many years later, I've come to understand that joy is a prerequisite of real success and not a result of it. That's right. The juiciness comes first, and then you get a swimming pool or a book deal.

Enjoying the ride creates the ride. If you hold your breath, waiting to succeed, you won't ever make it up this mountain. You can't wait until you reach the pinnacle, the mythical zenith, to feed yourself, reward yourself, and lean into the satin pillows of self-love and gratitude. There's no party, profit, or award that will make constant self-abandonment worthwhile. This is one sweet holographic journey and not a deprive-yourself-and-get-to-heaven kind of trip. If you travel yearning and empty, you will arrive yearning and empty. The view from the penthouse won't make the void any better.

I've spent most of my adult life waiting to succeed. I was aching to cross some red velvet finish line with the orchestra playing as I fell to my knees, because now everything made sense. Over there I would have a fit body, a loving relationship, and I would finally become one of those organized people and be able to find a book on my shelf within minutes instead of months. I'd practice yoga, hike in the backcountry, get a dog, travel, and take a thousand art classes just for fun. Over there it would all be different. *I would be different.*

In *A Course in Miracles*, it says that this is the ego's favorite hoax, the old when conditions are just right, then I'll start fully living my life. The exact quote is this: "If this were different, I would be saved." It's the get-out-of-jail-free card, only it makes our lives a jail because we don't see that we are already free. Waiting for something to change puts all the power and possibility beyond our control. But we, the consciously alive, creative, and visionary, don't wait for circumstances to change us. We change circumstances. We do it by embracing and igniting the lives we're in.

I've found that the moment I decide to stand in reverence for my current life, I stand on holy ground. I bless my life and then it blesses me. It deepens, expands, and grows fresh cherry blossoms even on branches I thought had died.

Many years ago, I ached to move out of a small apartment, but I couldn't afford to move. Daily, I watched the once elegant wallpaper peeling in the halls of the building. I listened to the new neighbors jabbering, stomping, and, it seemed to me, consorting with live mariachi bands in their ridiculously dramatic lives. I'd look morosely at my tiny nest, and the evil voice in my head assured me that every one of my Harvard Law School alums had toolsheds and *guest* bathrooms bigger than this spiderweb I lived in.

Then, one day I heard a story about a Zen master who moved into a Zen center for just six months. He started tending the overgrown gardens. He stripped and painted the forlorn walls. He repaired the floors and even bought an expensive silk wall hanging. One of his students soon spoke up with concern. "Master," he said, "you're only going to be here for six months. Why are you working so hard on this transitional place?" The Master answered that everything is temporary, and more pointedly, "because I intend to *be here* for six months."

That story struck me between the eyes. I looked around at my studio apartment and saw how I had been sort of just existing there, aching to get on to the next destination, and not giving this egg any of my warmth. So I decided to treat my apartment like a beloved bonsai garden or like a poem, to make every element sing with true energy. I had an uneven area in the ceiling replastered and scrubbed the large architectural windows that were the apartment's most stunning feature. I let go of books, papers, and keepsakes that felt more like baby fat than treasures. Soon the space became alive for me. It wasn't suddenly ideal, but it felt honorable and precious in its own way. I felt more connected to myself and my life, and I wore my new alignment like the scent of lavender, clean, bold, and free. In a few months, my business started making more money and the man I was seeing wanted to live with me and create new lives together. We found a larger place and moved. When I left, I left with love in my heart and memories of beauty from that time and space.

Where are you putting off things in your life? Where are you waiting to succeed? May I suggest wading into your life, instead of waiting? What would you do if you knew success would hit like a tropical storm? Do you need to get things in order? How would you be spending today if you were already successful? Bring on the joy now.

If you ever hope to arrive in your life, you have to arrive in this moment. I have been an ambitious overachiever all my life, and I'm consistently amazed to find that it's loving the life I have that makes me feel successful. I have had big things happen in my career, things that shot my excitement and adrenaline through the roof, but nothing pierced me in the same way as *savoring* my life.

I want to share a journal entry with you from a summer day in which I began to allow myself to *feel* successful, to take in my experience instead of racing on to create the mirage of more. "I am not as caught up in the effort and task of becoming successful. Dismantling from the obligation of it is like letting go of a thousand-pound weight that I didn't even know I was lugging around. I am simply enjoying my life, not bearing the load of ravaging ambition on my shoulders, wearing desires to get ahead lightly, like a summer shawl in moonlight. I never imagined that success would look like cutting carrots in my kitchen, but as I take in this exact time of my life, I realize no one else can give me this kind of delight. They can pay me and applaud me. But no one else can give me the experience of gratitude for it all.

"I love speaking, coaching, and connecting with a growing following and being on the road. But I am also taking the time to love being home, unwinding, wearing sweatpants, looking like the last person on the block you'd think would be inspiring. I love that my neighbors know very little about my work and more about my lawn.

"Recently, I returned from a trip back East where I visited my family and the family of huge green trees, vines, lakes, and humidity. I feel so healed as I walk into new territory with my family. Because I am happy about my life, I can be generous with them, not needing their validation or acceptance as I once did. Now I just want to connect. And that is the essence of it all these days. I find joy in connecting to my present life, singing its praises, focusing on what's working and filling with the most simple and inscrutable pleasures in this extraordinary life. I am consciously slowing down my awareness and deciding to live in my days. I thought success would be about money and recognition, but for me it's about this new ability to feel grateful beyond measure."

How grateful do you feel for your life? There is always more to achieve or more to experience or own. You can always "chase cheese," as a friend of mine likes to say. Still, I suggest you sit down and make a meal of it every now and then. Shine in your own good life. Shine so bright and you may just pull a few stars down from the sky.

INSPIRED SUCCESSISMS

Stop focusing on *becoming* successful
and start focusing on *being* successful.

Success is not about moving up in the world,
but about moving down into the deepest realms
of your feelings and feeling grateful.

Joy is a prerequisite of real success and not a result of it. That's right.
The juiciness comes first, and then you get a swimming pool
or a book deal.

Enjoying the ride creates the ride. If you hold your breath,
waiting to succeed, you won't ever make it up this mountain.

If you travel yearning and empty, you will arrive yearning and empty.
The view from the penthouse won't make the void any better.

We, the consciously alive, creative, and visionary,
don't wait for circumstances to change us. We change circumstances.

If you ever hope to arrive in your life, you have to arrive in this moment.

I am consciously slowing down my awareness
and deciding to live in my days.
I thought success would be about money and recognition,
but for me it's about this new ability to feel grateful beyond measure.

THE BAPTISM OF
WILD SUCCESS

Dancing costs you your identity. Dancing costs you your self-consciousness. Dancing costs you your lack and your hatred and your anger and your caution. Dancing costs you your limits. Dancing costs you your past.

A JOURNAL ENTRY

I dreamed I was in the basement of my family's house. The bathroom downstairs was dirty and reeked of urine. I think this is what I felt inside when I thought of my past. In the dream, I started cleaning the bathroom up. I painted the walls a nice bright lilac color. The room started looking safer, more like a spring day with hyacinths blooming. I felt like I was releasing the shame of my childhood, the fear and sense of scarcity. I was reclaiming my interior being, making things bright, safe, present-oriented and mine. I could now imagine allowing more good into my life.

A JOURNAL ENTRY

Many of my clients believe in wild success, but also secretly and subconsciously whisk it off their doorstep. They believe in struggle, limits, failures, intense competition, "reality," and most of all, a secret shame inside that gains momentum and validation with every passing year. Wild success will demand wild liberation. It means stepping outside your worldview, your childhood, your neighborhood, the way things have been going, and receiving what the Universe wants to give you. Wild success often asks you to die to your past. It's a conversion experience. Because only a new person gets new results.

I remember having a meeting with two other authors one day, discussing ambitions and plans for our books. Linda, a tall, sinewy blonde, who, I'd say, had big fat advantages right there, said she planned to sell a million copies. She was already making more money, just on her weekends, and effortlessly so, than I was making in months of time. She trilled on about her success plans, gargantuan desires that she would probably realize by Tuesday. She wasn't just a dreamer type, but someone who could somehow hypnotize the stars to cooperate and line up like chorus girls just for her, and then she'd claim it was nothing, nothing at all. I could feel my lunch grow heavier in my stomach as she talked, and the old desperation returned, the desperation to be her, or someone like her, or just someone who wasn't me, lame and unsure and still putting it all together. I felt myself wilt, sour, decay, and disappear altogether, while smiling at all the appropriate times.

Then came the ancient self-attack fest on my way home. If only my family hadn't been as disordered, emotionally violent, and damaging, I wouldn't have had to spend years just trying to stand up straight in this life, believe in myself, and recover from a seemingly endless uncertainty. If only my mother would have believed that her choices mattered in some way, then maybe I would have learned some self-respect and power. The ugly litany of damnation continued, trampling over years of therapy and spiritual exploration. It was the immediate default program: I am screwed up and defective and will pay the consequences all my life.

Finally, I stopped near this trail on my way home to take a power walk meant to exercise, or exorcize, my emotions. I grabbed my notebook and my water bottle. I asked the heavens for help, prayed silently, maybe just a tiny bit derisively, to regain some peace of mind, some ground to stand on. Maybe it was the pain or the exhaustion of having had this war with myself for so long, but something cracked open in me. Something buoyed up to the surface of my consciousness and demanded to be acknowledged. I sat down on the trail, leaned against a rock, and I wrote the powerful words I heard in my mind:

"I want to take back my power from all the myths that I've believed. I want to own what is true now and come clean. I am not a wounded daughter of a darkened family. I am not a broken spirit raised by the sorrowful or neglectful, the tormented and the frightened. I am a daughter of Light. I am a child of wonder and innocence. I am a rapturous song waiting to be sung. I no longer need to believe in limits of any kind. I no longer need to believe that I am small. I am not limited by my past. And I no longer have an identity in my past. I came in with a birthright. I came in with a mark upon my head, a fast star upon my shoulder, a light in my eyes, a flutter in my heart. I came in with a strength not of this world or time."

Yeah, take that, Linda. (Okay, I know, I know, it's not about Linda.)

That realization felt like a lightning bolt had singed and cut the cord of lineage, cause, tethers, and dim expectations. Suddenly I was free from the straight line of my past. On that straight line, I'd started too late. I didn't have enough resources going in and there were just too many layers of sadness, and it was just plain obvious that all the king's men couldn't put Humpty Dumpty back together again. I'd need a longer timeline than one person could have in a lifetime. But suddenly I was free. I was off the grid. I felt as though success was possible at any moment now, because I was part of a miraculous soup that stirred in every single direction and dimension.

True potential is not a matter of the genes that float in our bloodstream or the dominant atmosphere of our childhoods or of being tall and blond. It's not a matter of nature versus nurture. It's about being a force of nature, a cosmic extension of intelligence, will, drive, and a tsunami of light and genius. That generosity is always available.

So this is the work. Can you allow yourself to open to more peace and abundance than you have ever known? Can you leave your past in the past? Can you behold a new identity within you? Lord Buddha left his former life behind him. Jesus communed in the temple, then said to his mother something like, I no longer recognize you as my rule of thumb. He said that to a Jewish mother in Israel, mind you, which just tells you right there, he was either on acid or backed by divine immunity. He didn't trash his past or analyze its effect with a shrink putting three kids through medical school. He simply acknowledged his true identity, one that had always been there, the child of an Infinite Stream of Grace.

Real healing will always look the same. It's the coming back to wholeness and openness, no matter what's happened in your life. It doesn't matter how you get there, whether you believe in the love of Spirit, the redemption of the good red earth, or the work of a resourceful healer. It may take time, lots of it. But whenever you're ready, do open up to the goodness that surrounds you, tingles in your cells, and enhances your every breath. Do come back to your natural birthright, your own mysterious power. Do claim the identity of your essence more than the identity of your circumstance.

One Fourth of July, I decided to align with my new identity, and wrote myself "A True Declaration of Independence for the Free Soul": I was breaking away from the oppressive nation of my old woundedness. I invite you to join me in this declaration:

I want to break free from holding back my power. I no longer want to live with only my low beams on. I want to shine so unequivocally that others decide to abandon their own shadow choices. I want to break away from the undermining thinking of the "realistic" world—and choose some independent thinking, some firecracker, celebrating, birth-giving thoughts.

As of this very second, I allow myself to be blessed.

I allow myself to be uncorked, unabashed, and showered with delicious good in every facet of my life.

I don't need to fit in anymore in the world of struggling, suffering, complaining, belittling. I am going nova and that's okay. I am willing to have things be easeful and brimming with sheer wonder, and I am willing to deserve this. None of us deserve this. That's why it's grace. It's not about deserving. It's about allowing Spirit to love and give to us.

Spirit, I am willing to allow you to give to me now. My work here doesn't have to be oppressive. I don't have to plod uphill anymore, dimming my song, or accepting crumbs and crusts and bowing my head. I can keep my heart wide open and parade through wide-open doors in a welcoming world. I believe you want every golden circumstance for me. I believe you want me to experience more fun, jubilance, connection, generosity, nurturance, and synchronicity than ever before. I believe you want me to know your nature, and your nature is not one of limitation or punishment or lack of any kind. I believe there are doorways to your kindness that I haven't opened yet. There are oceans and skies I couldn't see because I subscribed to the map of the world. There is honey I've never tasted, bounty not of this realm. But I am willing now to let go of the familiar and invite your unimaginable love to heal me.

I am willing to let go of what I think is possible or right or worldly or to be expected—and I am willing to allow you to rampage through me, dance through me, breathe through me, grace through me, vibrate through me, burst through me, gleam through me, dream through me. I am willing to co-create with you, and I am now willing to no longer limit your power with strained, tired thoughts about my own. I am no longer willing to shape your destiny by crunching mine into a little ball of stunted possibilities.

Finally, I am willing to allow myself to be cherished and loved and nourished wherever I go and in whatever I do and it's not too much to ask for, it is barely enough, because there are so many dimensions of goodness and promise that I have yet to experience. The more I allow myself to receive—the more I can open up to receiving and giving my true love to this world as I have never given it before.

Remember, this takes practice. I've opened up to extraordinary possibilities because I wanted extraordinary results. It has felt awkward and naive and rosily impossible sometimes. Other times, it has felt clear, unsentimental, and obvious. As I let go of old self-images that no longer serve me, the truth is just there. Success is waiting to rush in.

What self-images do you cling to that block your way? Retire them with love, retire them with glee, and dip them in the river of reclamation and present time. Believe in your spirit more than your ghosts. A cracked vase won't ever hold water. Dare to see yourself as eternally whole and infinitely loved. Wild success comes to the wildly beloved.

INSPIRED SUCCESSISMS

Wild success will demand wild liberation.
It means stepping outside your worldview, your childhood, your
neighborhood, the way things have been going,
and receiving what the Universe wants to give you.

Wild success often asks you to die to your past.
It's a conversion experience. Because only a new person gets new results.

I am not limited by my past. And I no longer have an identity in my past.
I came in with a birthright. I came in with a mark upon my head,
a fast star upon my shoulder, a light in my eyes, a flutter in my heart.

Do come back to your natural birthright, your own mysterious power.
Do claim the identity of your essence more than the
identity of your circumstance.

I allow myself to be blessed.
I allow myself to be uncorked, unabashed, and showered
with delicious good in every facet of my life.

I am willing to co-create with you,
and I am now willing to no longer limit your power with silly,
tired thoughts about my own.

As I let go of old self-images that no longer serve me,
the truth is just there. Success is waiting to rush in.

Believe in your spirit more than your ghosts.
A cracked vase won't ever hold water.
Dare to see yourself as eternally whole and infinitely loved.
Wild success comes to the wildly beloved.

GETTING EVERYTHING
BY GIVING IT

I finally understand that others don't need me to fit into the club of the ordinary. They need me to fit into my own skin and ignite the radical possibilities in all of us. I've been so afraid of being different. But everyone else is different too. They have genius, love, and wild untapped potential within them. They may just not know it yet.

A JOURNAL ENTRY

Why should you not embody bold grace and abundance? Who does it serve to have you be stunted? Your grace can raise consciousness and awareness and the level of love on this planet. We need you to rise to the light that you contain so that others can rise as well. It is not yours to worry about whether you have more good than others. It is your assignment to use the circumstances given you.

A JOURNAL ENTRY

The world is not holding you back. You are holding the world back. You are holding back your strength, and your strength can make a difference at this time. You have a power in you that can move mountains and, better yet, people. But you're still allowing others to tell you what's possible or right. Maybe you're still chasing kudos to glue some sequined wings onto your hobbled back. But no amount of approval will ever set loose the inspired potential that you already possess. You have the power to shed your ordinary skin. You have the power to turn flesh into hope, disconnection into union, and this moment into a balm to some section of humanity. You are holding back the floodgates of your own wild ride.

Wild success is not about what the world can give to you, but what you can give to the world. It isn't about the desperate rat race to secure things that vanish overnight. It's a feeling of ease and authority. It's knowing you have something to give and that as you give it, you are given everything you could ever need. When you step into this realm, you know you don't have to grasp to make anything happen. You know you will be delivered. You know you will deliver. Your True Self takes a breath. Even your little self takes a breath. For me, this was entering the big time.

A Course in Miracles talks about grandeur versus grandiosity. Grandiosity is of the ego, the striving part of us that wants to feel better about ourselves by having big things happen, winning popularity contests, money, fame, and a few parking passes in the rock-star arena of life. Grandeur is simply the largesse of spirit we show up in. We may also still attract money, fame, crowds, and opportunities. But the circumstances don't validate or redeem us. The agents, talk shows, investors, and the like show up to accommodate the strength and light that we already possess, the wild kind, the kind that can never be taken away.

For years, I waited for the world to give me permission to shine. I wanted the world to carve out a path for me, reserve a beach cabana in my name, or roll out the red carpet. I didn't realize I was the magic carpet. I was the burning bush. I was someone who could make a difference in someone else's life. Finally, I began to practice showing up the way I would if a million people were validating my greatness and begging for my expression. I stopped bargaining with the world for approval, cash, compensations, and invitations. I started allowing myself to feel the exquisite authority of giving what I had to give. And here's the marvel I discovered: Unconditional love is unconditional power. When I started standing in my love, I didn't need the world to see my power. I saw it. I knew it. Everything else was just inevitable.

For so long, I wanted to write and speak and offer my creativity to mankind, if it would have me. I often said, "I want to live in a world that champions visionaries and creative and alternative abilities." I'd repeat it like a drunk at the bar, summoning grandness while laying my head down on the sticky counter and closing my eyes. I wanted that world to just appear. I assumed other people would invade the mainstream, stake a flag, and paint all the doors purple. But finally I realized that maybe our culture didn't need my idle wishes. Maybe it needed my contribution. Maybe it needed my sensitivities—and my sweat.

Yes, I know, many of us feel as though we're just stumbling through the fog, trying to find the front door to our own life, and that we don't have anything to offer humanity. We may feel like your average garden snake, or, sometimes, your average garden snake that needs just a bit more therapy than your average garden snake. Yet standing in our power isn't about how wonderful we are, as much as it's about how *willing* we are. We are willing to play for Team Light. We are willing to give what we have. We are willing to let our own sad opinions of ourselves grumble in the background, but not stop us from standing in the foreground or standing on the new ground of sharing our true selves.

Years ago, I gave a talk to a crowded room. Up until then, I'd always spoken from a riser, a small platform, not a stage. This room was crowded and did have a stage, an unusually high one. It was a freaking Himalayan mountain, if you ask me. There's no way I'm getting up there, I thought to myself. A friend rushed over and said, "You have to get on that stage." But I wanted to speak at the same level as the audience, just be one of the gang. "But they won't be able to see you," implored my friend. "No, the riser will be fine," I said, like a thin-skinned, blue-haired grandma from Mayberry, not one to unbutton her cardigan, much less stand on top of a mountain and implore people to live their soul's destiny. It was a tepid, unremarkable experience for the audience. For me, it was a turning point in my career. It was obvious to me that the Universe was teaching me that playing small wouldn't work anymore. I couldn't shine the light and hide myself at the same time. I had to make a choice. I had to step up onto the stage of my life.

You will have to make a choice, too. You will have to decide to play big, shine in your own way, and take a stand for your talent, message, or service. As a speaker, I've learned that if you're not willing to rock the boat, you'll never rock the house. Inspiration asks you to be a servant and sometimes you serve by leading. Can you imagine if Martin Luther King didn't want to be a "loud mouth" or a "big shot"? Or what if Jesus mumbled? There comes a time when you will have to stand up for the magnificent truth that trembles in your heart and bones. When you step out in this way, you are actually letting go of your ego, not letting it decide for you. You will stand out—and disappear into your gift at the same time.

I remember churning with the fear of alienating myself by owning my own strength and power. This had been a lifelong anxiety. Back in school, I sometimes lied about good, okay, killer, grades to make others feel better. I "played small" because I desperately wanted to be liked. Doing a session with a business success coach, I told him, "I'm afraid I'll lose people if I stand in my strength." He didn't miss a beat. "You will," he said. "You will lose weak people, spiteful people, people who want to keep you down," he said. "But you will attract other people, people who want to play with other people in their power. You will attract the people who love the light." He sold me, and I hope I'm selling you.

You are here to give what you came to give, not what others want you to give. You can be "nice" and take your cues from others who don't hear the same music, or you can sing the song that no one has heard, but some have waited an entire lifetime to hear. Ron, a student of mine, wanted to facilitate a men's support group. Some of his friends had different ideas about how the group should run. "I don't want to step on anybody's toes,"

Ron said. "But the idea for the gathering came to you," I said. "You are being asked to hold the tone." Ron chose to be polite and jovial instead, even though he felt bored and annoyed after every single meeting. He sat on his initial instincts. Rather, he made sure that everyone had a voice. But he lost his. And so did our world.

True power comes when we let go of the need for approval. We let the arrow fly from our heart and we don't know where it will hit, but we know it's our one true arrow and setting it free sets us free. And, of course, when it does hit, it rains diamonds and jelly beans—and there's not a doubt in your mind as to why you're here. Ralph, a man I met at a personal growth conference, told me he'd written a book about an experience of dying and coming back to life. He was afraid to share it. "It's kind of out there," he said to me while we gathered away from the crowds. "I guess I was afraid of what others would think," he continued. Then he gave part of the book to his neighbor, a woman grieving the death of her husband. The wisdom in his writing comforted her. "When I saw the look in her eyes after she read the manuscript," Ralph said, his brown eyes shining with freedom, "I knew I didn't care anymore about what some people thought. I had to get it out there to the people who needed it."

You are the steward of an unimaginable resource. Discover who you really are by giving and shining unconditionally. The world can't give you this power. The current culture often doesn't invite genius, because it doesn't know—what it doesn't know. Dare to experience your own grandeur, the feeling of giving everything you have and receiving everything you are, all in the same breath. As you do this, the quality, energy, and form of your expression has to expand. It's inevitable. Big love attracts big love.

INSPIRED SUCCESSISMS

The world is not holding you back. You are holding the world back. . . .
Your strength can make a difference at this time.

Wild success is not about what the world can give to you,
but what you can give to the world.

You have something to give and . . . as you give it,
you are given everything you could ever need.

Unconditional love is unconditional power.
When I started standing in my love,
I didn't need the world to see my power.

There comes a time when you will have to stand up for the magnificent
truth that trembles in your heart and bones. When you step out in this
way, you are actually letting go of your ego, not letting it decide for you.

You are here to give what you came to give,
not what others want you to give.

True power comes when we let go of the need for approval.
We let the arrow fly from our heart and we don't know where it will hit,
but we know it's our one true arrow and setting it free sets us free.

Dare to experience your own grandeur, the feeling of giving everything
you have and receiving everything you are, all in the same breath.

WILD SUCCESS IS EASIER

I don't think I'm afraid of big success. I think I'm afraid of abandon-ment, self-abandonment. I think I'm afraid I'll forget to take care of myself, tend the flames, and the magic will leave me. I'm afraid I'll lose my good and ease. But I give myself permission to walk through the door and see what awaits me on the other side. I trust myself to stay conscious, and if not, to scrape my way back to grace.

A JOURNAL ENTRY

I read today that a goldfish in a fish bowl grows a certain length. A goldfish in a natural pond can grow into the size of a small dog. Some-times, I think I can grow into a lion.

A JOURNAL ENTRY

Entrepreneurs and visionaries often stress about whether or not they can handle success. They're doing just fine handling mediocrity, mind you, or so they assume, though I do not. They talk about increased responsibility, deadlines and expectations, lions, tigers, and bears, oh my. They see wild success as going into a jungle and fighting for their lives. But I've come to see holding back your true power as living in that jungle and fighting for your life, only a degraded, outworn life that you don't even really want.

Success does look terrifying when we think of it as something different from the right use of our natural abilities. For years, I kept thinking of wild success as exciting and desirable, a date with an A-list movie star, but also outside of me and dangerous, like a hurricane that could pound my sweet, creative existence into wreckage. I'd set the intention to grow my business, and then pull the blinds, lock the doors, and crouch down by my computer.

Ultimately, I realized that I needed to stop looking at wild success as a bigger life and start looking at it as a *truer* life, an expression that would more accurately reflect who I really was. When I thought about "the big life," it made me feel small, sketchy, unequipped, and like somehow I would wear crummy shoes or spill my champagne on the way to being cool. But the truer life acknowledged the high vibration I already possessed. A truer life extended from the unalterable design of my soul's pedigree. This kind of success would help me feel *more* like myself, not less. "Big success" was no big deal. It was who I already was. I had the programming to swim in deeper seas. Thwacking around in the shallow end of a pool would always feel wrong and exasperating.

You will naturally fear and even block success if you imagine that it will interrupt your spirit, joy, and ease. I have a great example of this. It was years ago, when the large New York publishing house of my dreams, Tarcher/Penguin, became interested in my self-published book *This Time I Dance!* We exchanged friendly and positive e-mails. Then they stopped, dead cold. At the same time, I had the same exact thing happen with a big speaking engagement. "Maybe I have bad breath over e-mail," I told one of my friends. Then I heard myself say something odd to another friend. "Everything big that comes into my range bounces. It's like I have a force field around me." My friend, fresh from another workshop on how your beliefs affect your reality, jumped in with excitement. "You do. You do not want success," he said. "It's obvious because your life reflects your dominant beliefs." Yes, and I create the earthquakes, too, and the little green men that torture schizophrenics, I thought to myself. Still, I wanted to hear back from that publisher and desperate people do desperate things. I considered a new idea.

In the safety of my journal, I wondered if I was conflicted about my desires. Why would I defend against my biggest dream coming true? I decided to play a little game of emotional sleuth with myself. "Obviously, some part of me doesn't want to be published by a big New York publisher," I began. "If that's true, what fears or concerns does that part have?" Mind you, I was still smugly assured that no part of me would want to get in the way of this world-class dream. But when I began writing, smug hit the rug.

I wrote fast, deliberately exaggerating every fear and recording every hesitation, down to the fumes. There were just a few thousand more than I could have imagined. Here's a few I can remember: "I don't want a New York publisher because I'll be forced to bend over backwards and sign a bad contract. I don't want a New York publisher because I will lose control and be railroaded into situations I despise. I don't want a New York publisher because I don't know how to play in the real world and I'll make a bad deal and regret it for the rest of my life." After writing and reading these scenarios, I got it, that some part of me did not believe that signing a publishing deal would be natural and magical and just more of the yellow brick road I'd already enjoyed. The more I read, the more I realized that some part of me felt as though it was being asked to lose its power instead of gain it. Hello, force field.

Then, in a stroke of genius, I decided to reenvision what signing a publishing contract could offer, based on answering my fears. I wrote: "Could you say yes to a publishing contract if you knew you had a publishing team that was nurturing, compassionate, and wanted you to succeed? Could you sign a publishing contract if you knew that your cosmic success partner or own internal wisdom would help you get the best deal? Could you sign a publishing contract with a New York publisher if you somehow knew it was a spiritual experience, a garden, a coming home, rather than a cold, harsh, separate reality?" I kept going, creating more and more beautiful possibilities. The more I wrote, the more excited I became. Every part of me started coming to the table and joining hands and saying, YES, we could do that dream, yes, we could walk into that world, yes, we could learn to swim in that swimming pool, yes, yes, yes. The publisher got back to me later that week, and I signed a deal shortly afterward. The moment I saw success as an extension of my own good life and not some foreign, dangerous, soul-killing plague, the doors flung open. Yes, yes, yes.

Most of our success fears have to do with feeling out of control. I remember one of the first times I had multiple juicy opportunities come in all at once. I felt excited, but also buzzy and ungrounded, as though I'd breathed in too much oxygen at the top of a mountain. "Want to get a noodle bowl?" I said to Paul, my partner, code for can you talk, can you talk now, can you talk now, *please*? At one of our favorite Vietnamese restaurants, I barely let him order before I went off to the races and around the bend. "A lot of good is happening and I don't want to put the brakes on it this time," I began. "But I'm scared. What if it's overwhelming? What if I have to work all the time?" He sipped his tea, while I charged ahead into an engulfing future. "What if I burn myself out, snarf down all the crème brûlée of success, say yes to it all, climb higher, until I can't feel my life anymore and I burn out into a hollow crazy woman who hates the work she loves?" I was getting ready to ramp up again, but Paul finally looked at me with quiet kindness and said in his no-nonsense way, "This isn't your ride. It's God's ride." And that's it, my Gandhi man had spoken. He went back to his eggroll.

But I got it. I kept thinking I could pull the strings of my own success. Truth is, real success comes from co-creating with Spirit, at a moment's notice, moving with the rush of inspired spontaneous energy. I've never had much say in how it goes down, and later, I'm often humbled by the orchestration of it all. This is a wild ride, but it's not unsupervised. I am not walking into a dark, feral forest alone. Nor am I walking into the hub of commerce, the fray, new office space, or a tangle of contracts and responsibilities unattended. The robust grace that has taken me this far will take me all the way. I may feel hesitant, mortal, and even substandard, but I possess the kundalini power of ten thousand red stars going nova. It's not about what I think I can do. It's about what I am willing to open up to doing in any given moment.

There is an uncanny ease that takes place when you operate on full tilt. It's as though you're given your gifts when you go to your appointed place. You are graced where you belong and not before. You have coins, rabbits, inspiration, and business acumen up your sleeves and down your legs. Sometimes you have no idea how much you can handle and accomplish, as though you have never even been alive before this moment, until you are in the situation. The circumstances magnetize the power out of you. This has always been true in the practice and presence of anything creative. I'm often not in the mood to write when I first sit down. Yet when I show up, I can find myself carried out to sea for hours then tossed back on the shores like a woman who has seen a naked white whale, a burning bush, the rapture of a comma, and the meaning of life.

"Be good to yourself," coos a friend of mine, which really means don't do three talks in a row and then a television show. But balance and pursuing your joy is such a personal thing. For me, there are times when I do need to pull back because my joy is in being on a muddy trail with my filthy, happy dog. But other times, I love the flood of opportunities. Because when I'm in my zone, I'm not being taxed but energized. When I've had article assignments, speaking engagements, coaching clients, and books to write, I find I am more alive and free. I am engaged and inspired by the demand. They are not obligations but invitations to uncover deeper reservoirs of starch and gold, abilities, readiness, and light. When I'm truly in the zone, heaven on earth, baby, I hit a rhythm where the work moves through me; I'm not laboring or thinking, but being nourished and carried. I am amazed, and amazing, I will say. My cells click on all cylinders. I am laughing with gratitude. This is the full right use of my life.

The success we fear is the world's version of success where we are spinning out of control; we're doing things through fear and numbness, not *choosing*, and not staying faithful to our soul's incoming instructions. This is not the version of success we're after. Wild success demands joy. We can be joyful only if we remain on call to our electrifying spirit. Wild success doesn't come from effort but from effortlessness.

Let go of your ideas about the big life, the fast lane, and the glitterati. Remember, wild success is all about your stepping into the life in which you belong, the life in which you've always belonged, the life in which you can finally hit the note you came to sing and everything accommodates you. It's the life you were born for and the life that gives birth to you at the very same time. You are meant to succeed in the work you love.

INSPIRED SUCCESSISMS

I needed to stop looking at wild success as a bigger life
and start looking at it as a *truer* life,
an expression that would more accurately reflect who I really was.

A truer life extended from the unalterable design of my soul's pedigree.
This kind of success would help me feel *more* like myself, not less.

The moment I saw success as an extension of my own good life
and not some foreign, dangerous, soul-killing plague,
the doors flung open.

It's not about what I think I can do.
It's about what I am willing to open up to doing in any given moment.

There is an uncanny ease that takes place when you operate on full tilt.
It's as though you're given your gifts
when you go to your appointed place.

I am engaged and inspired by the demand.
They are not obligations but invitations to uncover
deeper reservoirs of starch and gold, abilities, readiness, and light.

Wild success demands joy.
We can be joyful only if we stay on call to our electrifying spirit.

Wild success is all about your stepping into the life in which you belong,
the life in which you've always belonged,
the life in which you can finally hit the note you came to sing
and everything accommodates you.

WHERE DO WE GO FROM HERE?

MEETING YOUR HIDDEN POWER

wanted to end this book neatly, letting the last chapter be a resounding final note. But the truth often defies fitting into perfect packages, so I'm going to let this sunflower bloom outside the picket fence. In other words, there's still one more thing I want to tell you.

So much of this path is about following what feels joyful and leads to strength and expansion. But I'm a full-disclosure kind of girl, and I need to tell you that some of my path has not been the melt-in-your-mouth crystal cotton candy kind of bliss. Maybe I didn't catch some course on how to hold your vibration right or belly laugh your way to abundance, but some of my resounding peace came from things that made me squirm. I want you to know that.

From over here, I'll tell you that those times led me to a deeper joy, a country of possibility that existed outside the parameters and horizons of my familiar identity. Still, at the time, I wondered if I was doing something wrong, or if maybe I just had poor reception or sketchy karma and would always have to wait a little longer in the rain.

More recently, I think of it as yoga, stretching fiercely tight muscles and releasing new expressions. You probably already know this. But just in case you don't: Yoga, that oh-so-relaxed practice, can sometimes make you want to scream for mercy. Maybe that's why they have you chant in Sanskrit in the beginning of a class. It's so that you remember that all that tension is surrounded by a thick molecular blanket of world peace and garbled grinning gurus, and that you actually *choose* to experience this initiation into hidden goodness.

In my career, I had to grow around the area of speaking. Part of me railed against this. "I'm a writer," it would scream, and hurl breakable porcelain objects across the room like the starlet in a black-and-white Hollywood film about a spoiled star. I've always had a gift for speaking. I've taught workshops and facilitated with ease, working the crowd like an orchestra, stirring the string section into moods and stories. I loved working spontaneously and coaching groups. But I had to grow into speaking to large audiences, lecturing, standing there with all eyeballs upon me, sometimes theater lights, jumbo projector screens, audio-visual issues, and no intimate group work to engage or distract the audience. I didn't want to do it.

I did want to do it, for the sake of my career, as it seemed that my path was pointing in that direction. I knew it would help me get my work out to more people. Loving friends and professionals in the industry promised it would help build name recognition, increase book and program sales, and blah, blah, blah. But I kept feeling as though I was being asked to stand naked in an air raid zone, while saying a little something inspirational. You couldn't convince me that I'd see more book sales than bullet wounds. I kept wondering how this could be bliss.

The first time someone asked me to speak, I lied and said I had another engagement. Well, I *did* have another engagement. I had to run to my room and journal like a madwoman so that my heart could slow down and I could start breathing again. Then another time, calling back an organization to talk about a speaking engagement, I hung up on the voice mail about eighty thousand times like an obsessive but shy stalker, a wasted teenager, or, really, like a terrified child-woman who couldn't even leave a neutral message *about* speaking. I tried to set my mind right through a thousand entries in my journal. Yet some things just won't resolve themselves on paper. Sometimes you have to step up to the microphone or into open fire.

So I accepted a speaking engagement. I did it with the idea that I would finally know if this was the pull of my spirit, or if this was yet another ploy of my overachieving self, to shove me onto some perceived fast track to validation and income-earning potential. I approached the situation as a personal experiment. I would be the lab rat, the researcher, and the unknown variable. Yes, kids, this is what you do when you have a "complex" personality.

The first time I ever straight lectured to a larger audience, I went to a city that I knew I never needed to step foot in again. Looking back, I think I was preparing to be on the *speaking lam* rather than the speaking circuit. I spent an entire day in the lobby of a Marriott, journaling by a faux fireplace, quietly praying, and negotiating inaudible deals with cosmic powers. Other travelers looked at me with concern, as though I couldn't quite figure out what sights to see and might never leave the lobby. Finally, I came to this brazen arrangement with the Big Speaker's Agent in the Sky. If I bomb, I will never do this again, and you will have to find another way to make my career grow. Furthermore, I'll be needing a big fat morphine drip, partial lobotomy, or immediate return to the mother ship, and all three together would be even better. If I succeed, I rigidly agreed, I'll take it as a sign you want me to continue on this path. I got three standing ovations the next day. So there you have it. The mother ship would wait.

I'm not going to go into all the psychological stuff about why speaking challenged me, who bungled up the programming code in my childhood, and how I healed and more. All I can say is that our work may draw us into arenas we may not have consciously picked. I have a client who was asked to teach teenagers, when she had never been a mother and had never planned on teaching stress reduction to anyone but adults. Another client unexpectedly found himself heading toward a television career, something he hadn't envisioned, and yet something that had his name all over it. I read somewhere that the same thing happened to Oprah, yes, Oprah, who had planned to be a teacher, not a mogul of media and a network rock star.

Sometimes a Divine Brilliance engages us to grow into mysterious aspects of ourselves, revealing capacities and dimensions we didn't know we had, or a desire, so shrouded in fear, we rejected the desire. Sometimes our yearnings expand as our strength and clarity does.

You won't be called where you don't belong. It's not like you're suddenly going to be asked to perform open-heart surgery or opera, unless the knife or the note is already in you. With speaking, deep down I knew I had the presence. But I felt removed from myself, as though I couldn't get to the power inside me. A jaguar guarded the door, a door sealed and encrusted with years of neglect and self-rejection. The room behind the door was at the end of a dark hallway. Still, I could feel the heat there. Eventually, you have to go where the jaguar lives. You have to meet your hidden power.

You will do this in your own right time. For a long time, I deferred to my fear. I chose big-girl helpings of self-acceptance and compassion, because it felt reasonable and even sacred to do, and it was for the time. I didn't push. I didn't take keynote speaking engagements and accepted only breakout workshop engagements, even though a part of me felt a little sad in my tiny shiny sandbox. Finally, when the sadness grew, I was no longer comfortable being comfortable. That's when I realized I wasn't honoring myself anymore. I was honoring my smallness. And just like that, it was time to grow again.

Why does it need to be so hard? Students and clients often ask me this, as though God takes my calls or follows me, and only me, on Twitter. I don't know the answer. Maybe we're all afraid of our deepest powers.

Maybe we keep falling in love with the tip of the iceberg, instead of allowing our whole shimmering and shocking identity to emerge. That's been my experience. I am learning that I am not who I think I am. I am not the small self. Even though a part of me thinks I will die if I have to go over there, I don't die. Instead, I am carried into a bigger room of expression. A strong wind blusters and I am suddenly reinforced and magnified—and challenges become tiny field mice skittering away. I am dying to my fears. I am dying to a life of control. And I am awakening to a bigger life, loving on every level, and breathing fire, grace, and majesty.

This is the tour of duty no one else can give you. This is what it means to live an inspired and unstoppable life. We are called to show up for ourselves and the relentlessly evolving grace within us. We shed one identity and skin, and discover yet another. We are endless and infinite. We are summoned to listen to the voice of the present, even when it changes shape, size, and direction. We are called to follow the trail of love wherever it leads. As long as we follow what is true, we will be all right. We'll be more than all right. We'll be amazing.

I used to think that wild success would be about arriving on top of a mountain and sitting down, at last, with the pile of coveted goodies. That's not the case for me. Wild success isn't a destination but an awakening, and the evolution continues, as far as I can see. But I can say that I feel more stable, powerfully abundant, and alive than I have ever felt in my life. Even as I know I will continue to face the unknown and unknowable, I feel more peaceful and grateful than ever before. I know this way will take me all the way. I'm already a satisfied customer in this lifetime. I've gotten what I came for.

If you choose to believe you're called to this life, you trust your inspired guidance, and you love with everything you have for as long as you have, you will be unstoppable. You will savor a soul-answering success, not of this world. Carlos Castaneda, who wrote a series of popular books on shamanism, called the trials of the path "a worthy opponent." The world is a worthy opponent. It will attempt to derail you a thousand times and then a thousand more. But it can't. It's the challenges that stoke your creative fire. It's the limits that pull you into your limitlessness. You are inevitable, inevitably successful. You have a power inside you that can change the nature of the world. You are not who you think you are. The jaguar paces within you. You are stronger and more gifted than you yet imagine. Still.

Journey well, my beautiful friend. I want to meet you out there on the frontiers of inspired living. I'd love to know you are giving this world every impeccable ounce of your strength, vision, and love, and that you're experiencing a fiber of joy you never imagined. My dearest success comes from knowing that you—my family of independent thinkers, visionaries, artists, entrepreneurs, healers, social architects, and business leaders—are walking this walk in your lifetime, adding to the reserves of all of humanity, and awakening to the dimensions of your own inspired power.

I am so grateful to you and proud of you for every step you take. I know what this life asks of you. Oh, but what it will lavish upon you . . .

Remember . . .

You are meant to succeed in the work you love.

Your desire will take you all the way.

I believe in you. I'm jumping up and down in the bleachers. And though you may not feel as though you know where this is going, I do. And I'm here to remind you.

I send you all my love and blessings.

THE PRACTICES:
PORTALS BACK TO
INSPIRED LIVING

A good mother knows that you can't just leave a gifted, dynamic, perhaps hyperactive child unattended. You must give it a puzzle, a Nintendo, or, maybe these days, a huge computer networking issue to solve. Otherwise it will explore dangerous places. It will put dust or coins in its mouth.

Our minds are like these children. It's best to give them activities and projects. I am going to offer you some helpful practices. They are meant to raise your vibration, shift your focus, and distill and activate your inspired power. Yet even if they didn't do any of those things, they may just keep your mind away from playing with matches.

I want you to notice something here. I'm calling these techniques practices, hey, maybe because I want you to *practice* them. That means forget about perfection. Aim to keep coming back to what works for you. Please don't let rigidity cost you sanity. "All or nothing" has no place on a path that works through osmosis, alchemy, and upon instant contact with the truth.

Daily life has a way of being daily life. It doesn't read self-help books, consult your schedule, or have its people call your people. I don't care how many self-help books you read, you will probably always encounter challenges, wounded individuals, your own bumpy thinking—and the occasional loss in cabin pressure. Practices help us stay consistent and devoted to an inspired strength and a love that has teeth.

With conscious practices, you feed yourself the good stuff. You build immunity to everyday fluctuations and seductively cynical or negative thinking. These practices will restore you and you will resist them, because that's what we do, we resist what's great for us. I don't know why. So the answer to resistance is always forgiveness. Don't beat yourself up for what you didn't do yesterday or for the past three weeks or twenty-seven years. Don't get lost in analyzing, rhapsodizing, or building monuments to your failure. Start now. Choose now. Enter the wondrous healing space of the only moment there is, this present moment. And use one of these tools, one of these practices, one of these portals back into the place you want to be.

The Win List

A list of actions I have taken to support my dreams and myself.
Things that went well.

When you are putting your dreams into the world you may feel like you are not doing enough. That's why I want you to do a daily Win List: It will remind you of what you are doing right and how you are showing up and how things are moving in the right direction. It will train your mind to pay attention to the right things. What you focus on grows, and this is an exercise in focus. It's like gold panning. You're only looking for the gold. I tell students, "If you want to magnetize more good into your life, create Magnet Eyes."

Let's face it. You may have a deep-rooted, self-protective suspicious bias. A part of you may be reluctant to believe you can be happy, catch the wave, and win the big Lotto of living your mission and not living on cat food. So as you dare your dreams, this part hunts for trouble and discouragement, and prepares for disappointment. With this uncorrected focus, you will start believing that you are not supported. You will miss ongoing examples of personal growth and inspired progress. You will never see the evidence of what you're not looking for.

Besides, I'm no friend to this one within you that waits for an inevitable "showdown," and the chance to be right about a life you do not want. I'm interested in you showing up—no matter what—for the rest of your life. If you do this, you will inevitably see movement, breakthroughs, and success. So here's a vital practice that can help you show up and witness for yourself how you are continually moving in the right direction.

Keep a Win List every day. I suggest you list ten items, because that will stretch you some days. This isn't a "to do" list, or a dry "what I got done today" list. It's a bit more flavorful, generous, and accurate than all that. I want you to write about shifts, movements, and miracles. I want you to write about inner and outer actions, and synchronicities, support, abundance, and all the blessings that have opened up for you and through you. I want you to write about the times you showed up, and the times Life showed up on your behalf.

Please include the tiniest inner shift: I got out of bed today ten minutes late, instead of twelve minutes late. I wrote my Win List. I wrote in my journal when I felt scared. I spoke my truth in a conversation. (You may have backed down a minute later, but I want you to acknowledge the time you did it right. Every step in the right direction counts.) I wrote today for an hour. (I don't care if you think it "sucked" or nothing came out of it. I care that you showed up and I want you to care that you showed up.) I got a new client today. Hey, and don't be afraid to milk the success of each event. Here's an example: I got a new client today. I got a new client today who paid in full up front. I got a new client today who works for a big organization and may recommend me to speak there. I got a new client today who is bright and fun and I immediately loved working with him.

Inspired Self-Dialogues

Taking your fear, doubt, or frustration to the Loving, Intelligent Presence within you and having a conversation.

The most generous and useful thing you can do for yourself is "talk" to your Inspired Self. Challenges will arise. Moods will flag. But you don't have to let a funky energy move in, unpack its bags, and rearrange your furniture. Fear can color everything you think and do. It's so important to diffuse the energy. You do not need to walk through anything alone or unguided. Please don't let depression or anger have the last word on any given day.

Write to your Inner Teacher, the Wise One, the Advocate, your Beloved, your Success Coach Extraordinaire, God, Spirit, a cool figment of your imagination, a way better "figment" than your fear. I don't care what you call it. I care that you call on it. And I care what it calls you and it will call you Little One, Buddy, Beloved, or something kind and true, if it's the right voice. It will call you to your genius. Personally, I love dialoguing with this voice. It has saved my life. I have scribbled these dialogues so many times that now I can even do them in my mind.

I want you to write your fears or concerns to your Inspired Self and write back to yourself *as that voice* and answer those concerns. Your Inspired Self is the most loving and powerful and on-your-side voice you can possibly imagine. Some of you may have religious beliefs or a spiritual path to draw on here. Your Inspired Self or Loving Voice may be the voice of God, Jesus, Krishna, the Shekinah, or the Grandmother Spirits. For some of you, this voice may be the voice of a nurturing parent, brother, college professor, friend, or lover. For years, I've called my voice Inner Teacher, then shortened it to Teacher. Sometimes the best way to access this voice is to think of what you'd say to a best friend or your child, someone you want the best for in life. When you start, you may feel as though you are making this up. It may feel awkward. I don't care. Do it anyway. The more you do this practice, the more this voice will become real to you. The more you listen to this voice in any way, you will begin to hear it in other ways as well. It's a beautiful thing. And the worst thing that can happen is that you write a few cool, kind, encouraging things to yourself.

Here's an example from one of my journals:

Me (M): I'm afraid I am writing a book that won't sell that much.

Inner Teacher, Teacher for short *(T):* Dear One, you have always doubted your own path, and you have always walked it with grace. I am with you. I am not guiding you into dangerous or useless territory. I am calling you to where you will thrive. You desire what you deserve. You desire what you are. You know this inside, which is why you have come this far.

   (I could have stopped there, but if I didn't feel peace or didn't trust the advice, I'd continue the dialoguing until I felt peace.) Like so . . .

M: How do I know that I'm not just telling myself what I want to hear?

T: You know by how it feels. You know what feels like truth and what feels like wishful thinking. One feels solid. The other does not. You also know because you have the energy to go forward. That means something is calling you forward. Also, you may think that you are telling yourself positive things because that's what you want to hear. But I ask you to consider that you may tell yourself frightening and dark things because they are what you want to hear. It is not always comfortable to hear positive things. I ask you to go forward, precious one, because you can never lose by following your truth. You will always benefit by experiencing the fruits of your truth. You can never benefit by deciding to put your truth aside. It will always haunt you. You will always wonder. Follow your truth and you will know the truth.

M: Thank you.

Everyone's inner voice will sound different. Yours doesn't have to be poetic or say catchy, savvy things. I only want it to be a voice you trust. One of my clients had an inner voice that called him "Asshole." At first, I wondered about that voice. But when I heard his tone, the warm, jovial, playful nature, I knew he was listening to a True Friend within him. It wouldn't have been appropriate for him to talk to a voice that called him Beloved. But when he said, "Hey, Asshole," there was delight and communion. Make sure your voice is Your Voice.

Also, don't be afraid to write your ugliest fears or to "talk back" to your Inspired Self. This isn't a place to be polite or "stay positive." This is a place to admit your darkness, frustration, sadness, or confusion, and to let your Inspired Self offer you the powerful perspective you need. It's meant to be a cathartically honest and healing conversation.

Mojo Mantras

Taking one inspiring phrase and repeating it throughout the week.

I'd like you to reflect on one Inspired Successism each week. (Feel free to take another line from the chapter you're working with that touched you, made you think, or even one that baffled you and made you curious.) Make that line your mantra this week, a saying you repeat often to yourself, your affirmation, "the guru" of the week.

Digest this saying every day like a soul vitamin. Journal about it. Rewrite it in your own language if you'd like. Discuss it. Visualize it. Write it out a hundred times on the blackboard in your mind. The thing about creative truths is that they often take you down the rabbit hole where you can discover more truths. They unlock other secrets, resources, and insights. There is a vibration in each sentence that may unconsciously prompt you. It can steer you toward memories, objections, deeper amplifications and applications. Notice how you feel while under the influence of these truths.

Offerings

A weekly check-in with myself—naming my next acts of devotion.

Once a week, I'd like you to make an offering to yourself. I'd like you to brainstorm and write some next steps you want to take toward your dream. I call these offerings because they are actions of love you will place upon the altar of your life.

First, before you write these, disengage your busy mind. As much as possible, I want you to write these from your soul and not your mind. You may want to meditate, say a prayer, take a walk or a hot shower. Then think about what would feel GREAT to do toward your dream or to reignite your relationship with yourself. What steps would help you move forward? Even if you feel like you don't know what steps to take, what are some tiny steps you do know? You might ask, "What would help me most right now, and what is the tiniest step or the most exciting one that I could take to move forward?" Do not overcommit to yourself. Building trust with yourself is far more important than a showy, short-lived spurt.

This isn't a list of what you "should" get done. This is a list of what would feel great to see yourself do this week. (You may also need to back up and think about what you most want to achieve or experience with your work. There are the obvious demands and deadlines. But what are the deeper demands of your soul right now?) You know what you need to do. Just the act of naming these steps makes them stronger. They become focal points for you, a way to consciously take action in the world. I'd like you to look at these actions not as things to get done or outcomes to achieve. Think of them as acts of service and devotion, simply a deeper listening to your Inspired Self. Remember, if you are listening to an inspired inner voice and not taking action on what you hear, you are not really listening. Yes, dear one, that was supposed to sting.

Once you have your weekly list of very small steps and offerings, you may want to do a ritual to ask your Inspired Self for help with doing these steps this week. Review the past week when you approach your next conscious offerings time. When you haven't taken action on your past offerings, check in with yourself. Did you do something more positive instead? Even if you haven't taken those exact steps, have you made progress? Did this offering no longer seem as important? Did you choose not to do it because of fear? Can you choose again? Forgive yourself for whatever you did or did not do. Explore what you need to do in order to go forward. Apologize to a part of yourself if appropriate. And begin again. Always begin again.

* * *

I do want to stress that this is not a "goal-setting and accountability" exercise. Instead it's a clarifying of intentions. And if you didn't do what was on your list, I want you to pay attention to other progress in your life. I've often seen clients make huge changes and progress in their lives, even though they didn't literally take the steps they thought they would. I don't care that you didn't get it done. I care that you moved forward.

THE EXERCISES:
WHY WE NEED TO PRACTICE
THE NATURAL AND INSPIRED

Most success strategies and common wisdom appeal to the left brain. You'd think the left brain had a monopoly on success, but you'd be wrong. There is another way, but it really *is* another way. Inspired success runs on a different track, kind of like solar power uses a distinct way to heat your house other than oil, coal, or, say, burning your ex-husband's clothes and furniture. It has different rules and properties, and the principles of one sovereign realm have no sway in the other.

This is why I suggest you devote time to these practices and exercises. Every day, you are inundated with information, media, and common assumptions that do not support the living of an inspired life. It's in the water. It's what's for dinner. Without conscious attention, it's exacting to trust and flourish on this alternatively powered track. And I want you to fly with everything you have. I want you to remember that you have your own way to succeed. I want you to trust an inspired source to lead you to an inspired outcome.

When you change the way you succeed, you'll change how much you succeed.

This is a path that calls you to new mental strengths. The way you look at your situation will determine everything about your situation. With that said, I want to give you an overview I hope will set you free.

Your trials are *the* trials of a path of inspired strength, a journey to true self-expression, inevitable success, and unconditional freedom.

The difficulties are supposed to arise. Challenges position you to evolve into more than you ever thought possible. These lessons, puzzles, and dharma opportunities are *how* you practice—activate your brightest powers, and elevate your perspective, stamina, and dexterity. It's easy to be inspired when everything seems to go the way you want. It's *inspired* to be inspired when things have not yet revealed their gift.

Choose the Exercises That Choose You

I encourage you to do these exercises at different times during your journey. They are meant to help you pierce your experience *now* and now is always new. With any luck, you will be on this path for the rest of your life. Inspired principles and insights repeat themselves, spiral in and out, pirouette, wink, rejuvenate themselves in the cool showers of Mount Olympus, and intensify with application. So don't be afraid to do these exercises more than once.

For each chapter, I'm offering a list of suggestions. Please don't feel the need to do everything. This isn't a marathon or a contest. It's not necessarily a rule of thumb that if you "do" more, you'll get further. As with everything else, always, listen to your Inspired Self.

Think of these exercises as a buffet. Take what you hunger for. You can come back at any time for another selection. Let the exercise that speaks to you, speak to you. Take your time with each of them. Different exercises will arrive and shine for you at different times. If you're meeting in a weekly group, you might focus on only one of the questions. Meanwhile, the full spread is here for you to explore.

CHAPTER 1. OWNING YOUR INSPIRED POWER

Some Focus Points

You crave the life you belong in. Your craving is your calling. You have your dreams for a reason. Sometimes you must *choose to believe* you're called, as a practice, before you *feel* called and begin to see the evidence. Your perspective about "reality" influences every action you take or don't take. This is a path of unwavering good. It's a way of living from your Inspired Self, a boundless love that calls you to the most expanded and miraculous expression of yourself. You are learning to trust your inner voice to help you create the life you were meant to live.

Going Deeper

1. Experiment with being willing to believe that you have an inspired source of help. Write or discuss: What makes me believe that something greater is at work here? What experiences in my present life, or from the past, help me to see that I can trust my instincts and that my instincts may be messengers of uncanny intelligence or divine creativity? Recount a story (or several) about how the inspired transpired before in your life, something you could never have "made" happen alone. These are your inspired touchstones. The power that was real once is still real and is, even now, still available.

2. Write an *Agreement of Conscious Co-Creation*. You've just been offered the job of your lifetime, the chance to co-create your destiny. Write to

your Inspired Self, God, Spirit, or your Creative Muse and accept the invitation. Commit to live as though you have been "called" to do this astounding task and live your most powerful expression in this lifetime. Write about your intention to create this life by *co-creating* it, partnering with an Inspired Source. How will you be receptive to help? What attitudes or old postures or assumptions might you want to let go of? Are there ways you dismiss your guidance, your instincts, or your knowing sense? For example, when things snap into place, do you often say, "Yes, but," or focus on things that haven't worked yet, giving them more weight than the ones that did?

Here's an example of the beginning of a letter . . .

I am willing to accept that I am being called by You, my Inspired Self, to become what I am meant to become. I am willing to remember that I am not alone on this path. I am willing to remember that an Inspired Presence may have options, plans, suggestions, timing, and resources that are different from what my limited and uninspired self can imagine. I am willing to believe that my desires are arrows, cues, and intimations from Love to become what I am meant to become.

I commit to the Path of Unwavering Good. I will focus on the feeling and the evidence of something extraordinary at work. My focus on this energy will expand this energy. I am now more concerned with listening to my Inspired Self or inner voice than I am with how I appear to others. I put aside my skepticism and open to new possibilities and capacities. I believe there is a reason I feel inspired to do this work, project, or vision. I believe that I am meant to do this work because . . . (Keep going and keep returning to "I am willing to believe . . .").

You might write several versions of this letter and combine the parts that have the most heat for you.

3. If "the inspired life you imagine is real," describe the most joy-filled life you can imagine right now. What is your highest vision? What would feel good, right, precious, and true for you? Drip details onto paper. Desire builds energy. Do not worry about setting this down in stone or how it could ever happen. Get honest about what you really desire, whatever wisps you know in this moment. Allow it to seem "off track," "unrealistic," or "lazy." Allow this vision or picture to begin to breathe and change as you go forward. How would you feel and act if this vision were real? How would you do today differently? What beliefs get in the way of you thinking you can have this? What would your Inspired Self/Inner Success Coach say about these beliefs?

CHAPTER 2. YOU HAVE YOUR OWN WAY TO SUCCEED

Some Focus Points

You have your own inspired way to succeed. "The right way" may be getting in the way of *your* way. Why would you listen to an "expert" when you can listen to a genius? Pay attention to what lights you up, not what you're "supposed" to do. Jump into the stream and get started. Experience is your guru and your navigator. Experience helps to unlock your enthusiasm, intelligence, desire, and development. Give yourself permission to "fail" in order to learn and grow.

Going Deeper

1. What words of "black magic" do you need to banish? Who are you listening to other than yourself? (List the books, teachers, experts, family members, coworkers, etc.) Where are you telling yourself that "you have to" do certain things to succeed? What if the worship of the "right" way keeps you from *your* way? What if you knew that your own

instincts were matchless instruction or divine assistance? Remember, your Inspired Self may also ask you to seek out help, education, feedback, and advice. It will guide you to the right avenue at the right time.

2. What three things give you energy when you do them? What comes easy for you? What comes really easy for you? Where do you get the most positive response for your work? What activities drain you, or feel forced, or come from obligation instead of inspiration? Practice doing more of what's natural and fun, *without judgment or fear*, and pay attention to the data of your experience. What qualities or actions have helped you succeed at other times in your life?

3. Where are you holding back from doing things because you have to be perfect to do it? (Or something else has to be perfect?) Start now! Start now! Start now! Write a "Freedom to Freaking Fly" list: What would I do right now, how would I share my love—if I were willing to just wing it, ignore "image," and do it imperfectly? Where are you focusing on "not failing" more than focusing on daring, receiving, and developing? Stand in your courage and wisdom and write an honest "permission to dare" statement. (See page 91 for my "permission to dare" statement.)

Chapter 3. Mojo Mastery: Working the Inspired Way

Some Focus Points

The secret of "mojo" is staying present, open to the powerful co-creation currently and consistently taking place in your life. Something amazing is always present. But *you're* not always present. Your judgment, demands, and expectations block your experience of the extraordinary and instrumental. Go where things open up for you. Follow the flow. Be the presence of love for everyone you meet, and stir inspired connections. If you feel disconnected, stop working and do something nourishing for yourself. Feeling good makes you available to recognize and receive more joy, direction, and opportunity.

Going Deeper

1. Where are you not being present and electric in your current life? Write a list of hopes and pictures in your mind that may have now become *expectations* and *demands*. Remember, the Universe already has something amazing in place. Return to being open-hearted, acknowledging that you do not know how your best life will unfold. Can you write about a time when you thought you knew how something was supposed to go, and it turned out differently and better? Where are you dulling your excellence by trying to "fit in"? Do a spontaneous writing on this that begins: "Here's where I'm staying too close to the middle..." or "Here's what I keep thinking I 'should be' to make money or get results..." If you knew that "you would have your people," how would you be showing up?

2. When you work, where are you coming from fear? Where are you coming from love? Practice being present with people—showing up without judgment or an agenda. How can you focus more on connecting with your customers, potential customers, and, while we're at it, humanity in general? The more you come from love with your work, the more exuberant and innocent you will feel. This week, go on a "Love Campaign." Practice loving and serving everyone in your midst, without trying to "get" anything from them. For example, you might go to a networking meeting and simply hold the thought "How can I be the

presence of support for someone here?" Or "I don't know who I'm sup-posed to meet. Let me be led by energy. Let me accept and encourage everyone I meet."

3. Remember, work breaks restore you to passion and inspiration. What kind of fuel stops can you build into your life? Brainstorm a list of quickie rejuvenations: walking the dog, two Ashtanga yoga postures, listening to a guitar riff on a CD, journaling for three pages. Where can you turn up your joy, fun, or sense of being supported and loved? In-crease your commitment to being *available* to more creative juice and productivity by treating yourself piercingly well. Create a fun list, a restorative list, a nurturing list, a friend list, a book list, a "Mojo Make-over Strategy."

CHAPTER 4. THERE ARE NO OBSTACLES

Some Focus Points

Circumstances will fluctuate. Your experiences of ease and faith do not need to fluctuate with them. There will be loss, disappointment, and slow times on this path. But nothing is being "taken away." An Abundant Intel-ligence is always contributing to your joy and growth. Slow or strenuous times prepare you for growth spurts. They strengthen your inward clarity and commitment. Take your focus off "the story" and turn an automatic "victim reaction" into an instrumental, loving possibility. Nothing hinges on your circumstances.

Going Deeper

1. Where are you wasting your time, energy, and resources taking an event or condition and turning it into a big scary story about what will happen? Write after me . . . "I am willing to see the true possibility

in the circumstances before me, no matter what. I am willing to stop seeing and telling the story of what I'm losing." Wipe the slate clean and look at this moment with new eyes. Ask, "What opportunity am I being given in this moment?" Something is being "taken away" so that something else might be experienced. What is that precious new something? Write three possible gifts, lessons, or opportunities, even if they feel "fake." Go wild and write three new stories about "And this is how this time kick-started me to strengthen and grow into the next level."

2. Is there a place where you need to have some compassion for yourself right now? Real compassion leads to strength, not weakness. What emotion have you been pushing away? Can you create a sacred space just to feel the emotion? Write about it, scream it, draw it, just feel it without asking it to change. When you have expressed this emotion without judgment, what clarity, perspective, or feeling comes up for you underneath this emotion?

3. Doing your right work can be medicine. Brainstorm a list of ten steps you can take toward your dream now. If you don't have "paying work," offer your gifts to someone who needs them. Remember, you need to do this work, as much as someone else needs to receive it. Using your gifts will help you activate inspired strength and direction.

Chapter 5. Timing Will Turn on a Dime

Some Focus Points

Rushing yourself hurts, delays, and impoverishes your experience. Commit to the long haul and commit to the miraculous moment—and you will instantaneously enter a state of being that offers you everything you want from your dream. The timing isn't off. Your perceptions are off. There is alive, impeccable, and fluid timing occurring all the time. The "past" is in a passed moment. If you're on an inspired adventure, this moment has no limits and everything can happen right now, no matter what.

Going Deeper

1. Consider marrying your dream, committing to it for life. What would it feel like to know that no one time frame or event or situation means that much because you're in this for the long haul? Marry your dream. I mean it. Can you create a ritual around this? Write a certificate of commitment? And post this on your wall: "Time Is Love." Focus more on devotion than on "having a quickie," a rushed and hustled outcome. Feel the peace of knowing you are in this for good—and that every effort is adding to your good—and that you'll be there to receive that good.

2. If your timelines are making you feel small, bad, or incompetent, shred your timeline. Practice entering timelessness instead of time self-consciousness. Break up a project by creating a list of bite-size—for an ant—shifts or movements. Take one of those tasks and make it your present meditation, the one and only thing that matters. Where are you rushing yourself? What feeling(s) are you hungering for underneath the rush? How can you start to have that feeling now? What if this moment were the highest pinnacle in your career? How would you look at the work before you then?

3. Where are you starting to define your future based on your past experience? Ask yourself, "Where have I lost my innocence, constructed barriers to my present experience, dimmed my heart, and assumed I know how things are going?" Get out Merlin's wand, a stick of sage, a passage from the Bible or the Tao, and come back to present magic

time. *A Course in Miracles* teaches: "I don't know what anything is for." How would you feel and act right now if you had no past experience holding you back—if absolutely anything could still happen?

Chapter 6. You're a Powerhouse, Not a Rental

Some Focus Points

When you start to value yourself, the world will, too. You may have to let go of work that doesn't represent you anymore. You may have to jettison "important" people who don't see you as important. No one knows what you truly have to offer—until you do. It's time to respect your gifts, passion, and vision and determine just exactly why you love it. It's time to value your inspired work more than your bank balance, your comfort level, and any bankrupting ideas about modesty and self-promotion. And it's time to celebrate all the abundance in your life.

Going Deeper

1. Take a "fearless energy inventory." Where do you leak energy? Where are you working, putting time into something that makes you feel small? Maybe you've needed to raise your rates with a particular client or maybe you're still doing one aspect of your business that you *used* to enjoy? If this were a closet, which activities or people feel like outfits that don't fit the emerging you? What does your audacious, expansive soul want you to let go of right now? Write a list of any beliefs you have about money that might keep you from charging more money. Do you believe it's more "spiritual" to charge less money? If you knew your worth as a steward of uncommon talents and resources, what would you charge? Ask your Inspired Self to help you see, write, and experience some new ways to value the work you do, or to see charging money, or even money itself, differently.

2. Promotion is devotion. This is a path of owning the value of your natural and exceptional gifts. Think about how what you love can benefit someone else. What possibility do you represent for others? Remember, you're not selling you. You're offering a solution, an experience, a benefit, a hope, or an opportunity. Describe what you can offer someone. Tell the story of *why you love this work* and why you believe in it and why you're the vehicle for this. If a Higher Intelligence handpicked you for this mission (and it did!), why would infinite wisdom have chosen *you*? How do your "weaknesses" serve you in this? Try telling this story to a partner or group. Tell it again and again until you feel it, and until they feel it. Tell the true story and the true story will tell itself.

3. Get out the buckets and Dixie cups. Make a list of all the abundance and opportunities in your current life: the time, relationships, creativity, freedom, integrity, health, and peace of mind. Where are you telling yourself that because you haven't made a certain amount of money yet (or any other achievement), you haven't made it? *How would you feel if you didn't have this story?* Where are you making numbers more important than reality? What is the reality to you? What experiences, opportunities, and value are you receiving that you would pay to receive? How might a momentary lack of money contribute to creative opportunities and deeper connections with people?

CHAPTER 7. THE BAPTISM OF WILD SUCCESS

Some Focus Points

You will never feel successful if you consistently discount the success you've already achieved. Honor your progress and the courageous, precious one within who has always done his/her best. Start *being* successful instead of *becoming* successful, cherishing your current reality, your gold, and your ability to stand in your authority right now. Real success is about giving to the world instead of getting something from the world. There may be a part of you that does not want to wildly succeed, thinking success will feel isolating or out of control. "Wild success" isn't about what you think you can do. It's about what you were born to do and allowing that power to come through you.

Going Deeper

1. Where are you now compared to where you were five years ago? Get out that rearview mirror. Write a list. Can you buy yourself a totem of support, plant a tree, throw a fiesta, or do a ritual around where you have already arrived? If you are not where you want to be yet, how can you attend to or redeem your current situation? What would you do if you knew success would hit like a tropical storm? Do you need to get things in order? How would you be spending today if you were already successful? What are you waiting for? Complete this sentence in oodles of detail if you can. "If I were to slow down and start *being* successful instead of becoming successful, I would . . ."

2. What image or story from the past do you need to bless, forgive, or let go of in order to step into the new life? Write your own "Declaration of Independence," breaking free from the country of old beliefs, sad images, assumed but mistaken limitations. If you were anchored in your essence more than your circumstance, could you imagine a life of no limits? What would it look like? If you knew you would feel more of your true authority by giving unconditionally, what would you like to give?

3. When you think of "wildly succeeding," where do you feel hesitant, nervous, or uncomfortable? Where might you put the brakes on?

Write this: "If I were defending against my wildest dreams coming true or if some part of me didn't want this to happen, here are the gory, embellished details of its fears . . ." Now, turning those fears around, write about an ideal kind of success you could say a wholehearted YES to right now. Tell the fun, easy story of a juicy new kind of success. Also, write out "A Comfort and Sanity Strategy": eight ways I can stay true to myself or commitments I can make to follow my Inspired Self in the thick of wherever life takes me.

STARTING YOUR OWN "INSPIRED SUCCESS CIRCLE" (OH, DO IT! DO IT! DO IT!)

I f you would like to form an Inspired Success Circle and work the principles of *Inspired & Unstoppable*, I am thrilled to have you share this work. I would be THRILLED. In sharing it, you will strengthen it for yourself—and you will meet some of the most amazing visionaries, creative entrepreneurs, soul-searchers, freedom-seekers, and business colleagues you could ever hope to meet. Doing this practice with like-minded companions can lend your dreams more strength, direction, and assistance. You do not need "to know what you are doing." So few of us do in life, and if you try, you're ahead of the game. Please register your name with us at **TamaKieves.com** and when folks in your area ask about groups, we will send them your way. We also have pre-designed flyers you can download, banners for your website, and suggestions for how to get the word out about your group.

The Way the Group Works— and Thrives

I am always open to your creativity, so if you would like to add some of your own flair to your group—go ahead and dare it. I'm more interested in you following your Inspired Self than in you strictly following me. That said, if you are calling this an Inspired Success Circle, please use the material in this book. I am not as concerned about the exact form of the group or flourishes, but I am devoted to the content.

SUGGESTED FORMAT

I'd suggest meeting for eight weeks and then cycling through again, as desired. You can have the first week be an introduction week, and then cover one chapter per week afterward.

Each week, please set the inspired tone of your group with the opening invocation and meditation. The first part of the group is a check-in with how the practices are going. Share successes and shifts with the group. You can share with the whole group, or break up into clusters of two or more. In your cluster, you may also bring up a concern and ask for support.

The second part of the group explores New Mojo. The group leader reads a section from the chapter, or a few lines, and the group discusses and brainstorms. Then do one exercise or five minutes of free associative writing about how the theme speaks to you. Share with a partner in the group or the whole group.

Each week, please pick a partner (or threesome) and do the "Inspired Life You Imagine Is Real" exercise. Each person speaks for five minutes about what he desires right now, his wildest dreams. The listener listens with unconditional positive regard and encouragement and does not "fix" the speaker. Help the speaker stay on the topic of talking about what they desire. Do not let your partner digress into fears, difficulties, or past limitations. This is a *practice* of voicing only desire, love, and excitement—and in building the strength of undiluted attraction.

Join in closing meditation.

Between Group Meetings

Between group meetings, participants are encouraged to use the practices of Inspired Self Dialogues, Mojo Mantras, and Offerings and to do another exercise from the chapter. But all participants are welcome and encouraged to come to the group whether or not they've done the "homework." This group never evaluates the commitment level of those in the group, especially since this is an inspired process and there would be no way to gauge what is appropriate at any given time. This group is meant to strengthen and encourage everyone, every time, at every level. Just coming to the group will be a major forward movement. There is power in gathering together.

Opening Invocation

Welcome everyone! Our purpose is to create a safe and inspired space together. We are not here to fix each other or direct each other in any way. We are here to remind each other of the genius, love, and success strategies of our own Inspired Self. We strengthen our commitment and clarity by sharing this space together. We are here to be compassionate listeners to each other's challenges, yet to always believe more in each other's evolving strength than in the perception of a "problem."

Opening Meditation

I am meant to succeed in the work I love. My desires take me all the way. As I follow my desires, I unlock and activate all the resources within me. I am willing to begin again in this moment. I let go of everything from the past. I invite my Inspired Self to guide me, to help me receive whatever I need to receive from this time, and to give whatever I need to give. I ask to open my heart and my mind, and open to the hearts and minds of the amazing souls in this room. I ask to unconditionally begin again. I am willing to become inspired and unstoppable. I am so grateful to be here. I am so grateful to be here. I am so grateful to be here. Download a free copy of Tama guiding this meditation at **www.TamaKieves.com/IS/free downloads.**

Closing Ritual

At the end of every meeting, please close with two minutes of silence, preceded by this message read out loud together by the group.

I rededicate myself this week to trusting in the power of my Inspired Self. I devote myself to listening to my desires, instincts, joy, and knowing sense. I am meant to succeed. My desire is taking me all the way. I take the actions I am guided to take. I take this moment to begin again, to open to knowing that my Inspired Self is with me now and always. Anything can happen this week. I am letting go of everything that has come before and making myself available to this new and inspired strength and time in my life. I pay attention to, receive, and allow even more wild success into my life. Download a free copy of Tama reading this Closing Message at **www.TamaKieves.com/IS/freedownloads.**

A WILDLY POSITIVE
RAPTUROUS ENDNOTE
OR A TRUE BEGINNING

I want to thank each of you for the courageous choices you are making. As you learn to live and work in a new way, you strengthen that possibility for the collective. You are part of what will move humanity into a sweeter use of all its wondrous powers. Many of us have had to struggle to find our way. But as we succeed, we demonstrate new abilities, and soon all the monkeys know what "the hundredth monkey" discovered. The collective is changing. The world is changing, moving from the Age of Information into the Age of Inspiration. I wanted to dream with you about how we might foster a world that supported all people in discovering and living their calling. You know me. I believe everything starts with a dream.

I dream of a day when you can ask a seven-year-old what she wants to be when she grows up and if she says a lawyer or doctor, everyone lights up. And listeners light up just as much if she says she wants to design tattoos or study philosophy—because it's common knowledge that whatever the soul desires, the planet desires, and everyone will thrive.

I dream of a day when a teenage boy can say, "I want to write poetry," and no one will suggest he look into a trade. No one will ask him to turn away from his desire and plan another life.

I dream of a day when it's understood that what you love is a gateway into advanced consciousness and a source of prosperity for humanity.

I dream of a day when it isn't considered prudence to doubt your own dreams or desires. It's considered instability, aberration, or self-mutilation.

I dream of a day when individuals trust their inspiration more than their frustration, when love is presumed to be strength, sanity, and the technology of a higher order and not a trivial birdsong or pipe dream. I dream of a day when it's considered socially responsible, profitable, and magnanimous to feed the evolutionary promise within you.

I dream of a day when career counselors don't have lists of what you can be, but listen to the way your voice drops in holy reverence when you speak a desire that has no label and no limits.

I dream of a day when statistics don't matter in the measurement of the human potential.

I dream of a day when we watch the news we want to see in the world, the celebration of the achievements and causes we wish to recognize and strengthen. I dream of a day when the media devotes its energies and talents to the stories and events that help more of humanity flourish in some small or monumental way. I dream of the day when we recognize that what we focus on grows, and so we become more vigorously selective and intelligent about where we focus our attention, money, and time on earth.

I dream of a day when this book, and others like it, are taught in business schools or studied in corporate boardrooms because it's understood that "new fuel thinking" (replacing old-school thinking) and the strength of industry depends on inspired power, original resources, paradigm shifts, creative genius, and synergy.

I dream of a day when our education system does not focus on having us memorize facts and test answers, but feeds the natural hungers, strengths, and orientations of the mind. I dream of a day when public school is about learning what you love, and what gifts you have come to give the world. I dream of a day when everyone learns how to listen to their own inner knowing and comes to know they have a mechanism that never fails.

I dream of a day when the arts are put back in schools, when people realize that activities that strengthen any form of creativity strengthen *creative thinking*, and nonlinear capacities are recognized as productive and indispensable. I dream of a day when all forms of intelligence, emotional, creative, healing, and more are seen as relevant and necessary to the health of a flourishing world and are paid accordingly.

I dream of a day when faith is not seen as fragility but as the prerequisite to all unimaginable accomplishment. I dream of a day when we recognize connection to an Inspired Source as the highest form of strength and reason available to each of us, and we recognize that the power of our thoughts can break through any limitation we perceive. I dream of a day when we are trained to use our minds to serve us instead of hurt us.

I dream of a day when it's more prestigious to cherish humanity and respect our natural world than it is to own things we don't need.

I dream of a day when the world has finally lost its concern about finite resources because it has unlocked the infinite resources of the human potential.

I dream of a day when it's the status quo for every soul on earth to feel inspired, loved, secure, expressed, and viscerally free—and books like this one are unnecessary.

And by the way, I don't just dream of this day. I'm going to live every one of my days here on earth being part of what makes this happen. I hope you'll join me.

Let's create the new mainstream together. Let's create that day.

Join me at **www.TamaKieves.com**. Join your Tribe. We're waiting for you.

I WANT TO SUPPORT YOUR LIFE'S WORK . . .

I want to hear from you!

I LOVE feedback, stories, speaking engagements, invitations, powerful collaborations, spontaneous random acts of kindness (financial contributions, publicizing this work in any way, or volunteering blood, sweat, and genius, always welcome), media opportunities, and hearing about your creative success, ventures, and vision. You will inspire me as much as I inspire you. I know I can't do this work alone.

Join me at **www.TamaKieves.com** and join the Tribe! Let's share this revolution together. Download your FREE **Inspired Success Launch U Kit**—a video with personal instruction from Tama, an audio interview, and more goodies designed to set your mojo into motion right now at **www.TamaKieves.com/IS/freedownloads**.

My life's work is supporting you to take your life's work to the most astounding level possible. Stay inspired with monthly e-newsletters, invitations to special events, workshops, retreats, and free resources, the interactive blog, and daily vision, massive love, wild success tips, strategies, creative "rock the world" community, and unstoppable momentum on my Facebook fan page and Twitter.

Our website is an evolving world of support, synergy, and powerful connections—a portal to inspired living. Join us right now, dear one. Let's rock the world with our hearts on fire!

ACKNOWLEDGMENTS

I owe everyone on this planet an acknowledgment, because I believe we are all connected in some way, and somehow I got to be the one who said, "I'll write this book," and everyone agreed. Thanks, guys.

Again, I thank my students, clients, and fans, and those who have hired me to speak. It is such a privilege to do this work. It is a necessity for my soul. You have helped me become who I am meant to become.

I thank the spirit of my father, Sidney J. Kieves, for being an irreverent and mildly eccentric businessman, who always believed in taking chances, working in your pajamas, and not starting your work day before eleven a.m. He didn't have to drive a fancy car, even when he could afford one, and for that and so many other freedoms he modeled, I am grateful.

I thank Paul Kuhn, one of the most grace-fueled sources of quiet power you can meet in a lifetime. For his uncompromising love, unwavering commitment, and willingness to live really big or out of a cardboard box and be equally free. You believed me when I said I was an organization / "rock star" / author. And you never believed me when I said, "I don't think I can do this." Thank you for sharing this crazy, life-altering journey. I must have done something very right in many lifetimes to have attracted a royal partner such as you.

I thank Joel Fotinos for being a living, breathing example of being *inspired and unstoppable*, and for all his support, belief, counsel, and ability to make hours disappear into laughter, shiny ideas, and clarity. He is someone who walks in excellence yet never stops growing. I believe you are a soul brother.

I thank all the many organizations on this planet dedicated to serving and uplifting humanity. *You rock.* In particular, I thank the New Thought churches and the centers of consciousness that work tirelessly to help others use the power of their thoughts, faith, and choices to usher in new potential, joyous health, and true peace of mind. Among these are the Omega Institute, the Kripalu Center for Yoga and Health, Esalen, and Hollyhock.

I thank Grace Welker for the gift of last-second editing and for her startling talent, and even more her startling generosity.

I thank Oriah Mountain Dreamer for reaching out with tremendous kindness and for believing in the authenticity of my work, before I had become a "name."

And Liz Williams for seeing who I really was. Forever, I thank you.

And Ned Leavitt for saying "Yes."

And Susan Kennedy (aka SARK) for stepping out of her poster on my wall and becoming not only real but better in person. You treated me like a colleague, even when I felt like a feather.

I thank the people who supported *This Time I Dance!* in the very beginning and helped me "go national" by inviting me to speak or who organized a workshop for me. Seth Godin calls these people "the early adopters." I call them angels. Pat Cowan, Suzanne Eder, Elizabeth Kanna, Jan Janzen, Susan Lucci, Misha Parker, Karen Paolino, Dee Relyea, Marci Moore, Pam Williams, Ken Donaldson, Cherie Larkin, Felicia Searcy, Sue Borg, Barbara Stahura, Shanna McAleer, Pat Baccilli, Laney Wax, Jaya Deb Morrisey, Michelle Barbic, Judy Silva, and Noreen Kelty. There are many others, and also many who quietly made *everything* happen by buying books for friends, or recommending my work and becoming a link in destiny.

For inspiring me: Marianne Williamson, the Rev. Michael Bernard Beckwith, Esther and Jerry Hicks, Seth Godin, Anne Lamott, Julia Cameron, Rumi,

Hafiz, Pema Chödrön, Ralph Waldo Emerson, the *Sun* magazine, yoga, and *A Course in Miracles*. And for loving me: Lisa Spector, Ann Strong, Colleen Smith, Marci Moore, Pam Williams, and Janice Kieves. And my beloved fur friends, here and gone.

And I would like to acknowledge myself, almost most of all, for listening in my lifetime to my dreams, moving past my fears, trusting in a Voice of Love, and inching forward when a thousand winds blew and it felt as though I had but one small pink birthday candle to hold up my wish.

And with every fiber of every fiber of my being, I acknowledge my Beloved.